THROUGH
MIDDLE
EASTERN
EYES

About the Authors

Robert P. Pearson is a former professor of education at Swarthmore, Lafayette and Muhlenberg colleges. He holds a B.A. from Brown University, an M.A. from the University of Michigan, and a doctorate in international education from the University of Massachusetts. He has pursued research and writing in Middle East studies since 1962 when he first went to Afghanistan as a Peace Corps volunteer. He has also worked for the Peace Corps as a staff member and trainer in Washington, D.C., Libya, Morocco and Albania. Most recently he has served as an international educational consultant working in Croatia (with Bosnian Muslims), Ethiopia, Swaziland and Armenia.

Leon E. Clark, the author of *Through African Eyes* and a co-author of *Through Indian Eyes,* is the general editor of the CITE World Cultures Series. He received his B.A. and M.A. from Yale University and his doctorate in international education from the University of Massachusetts. For more than 30 years he has been involved in a variety of educational and international development activities worldwide, including assignments with the Ministry of Agriculture in Egypt and the Ministry of Education in Pakistan. He is now professor emeritus of sociology at American University, where he founded and directed the International Training and Education Program.

"Who are these Arabs, Iranians and Israelis? Why do they think and act as they do? How can we begin to understand them at all? Fortunately *Through Middle Eastern Eyes*, a new volume in a series of introductory cultural studies, is now available to help students and teachers answer these questions."

—*Communique Magazine* on the first edition

On this fourth revised edition:

"After September 11th there is so much misinformed opinion and ideas on Islam and its relations with the West. I congratulate Professors Leon Clark and Robert Pearson for having produced a volume that brings a sympathetic objectivity to the subject. Without this perspective the 21st century may well be seeing the the prophecy of those who believe that a clash of civilizations is inevitable. That is why I applaud Professors Clark and Pearson for helping us in the dialogue of civilizations".

—Prof. Akbar Ahmed
Ibn Khaldun Chair of Islamic Studies
American University

"...an innovative and unique source of documentary material offering [students] insights into Middle East life with which they probably would not otherwise have access. I recommend it to teachers as a text to stimulate and provoke lively discussion."

—Prof. Donald Peretz
Professor Emeritus of Political Science
State University of N.Y./Binghamton

THROUGH MIDDLE EASTERN EYES

Robert P. Pearson

Leon E. Clark

A CITE BOOK

New York • London

CITE Books are distributed by
The Apex Press, 777 United Nations Plaza, Suite 3C
New York, NY 10017 (800-316-2739 or 914-271-6500)

CITE (Center for International Training and Education)
is a program of the Council on International and Public
Affairs.
The Apex Press is an imprint of the Council.

Library of Congress Cataloging-in-Publication Data

Through Middle Eastern Eyes / Robert P. Pearson, Leon E.
Clark.
   Fourth rev. ed.
      p.   cm.
      "A CITE book."
      Includes bibliographical references and index.
      ISBN 0-938960-48-2
      1. Middle East.   I. Pearson, Robert P.   II. Clark,
Leon E.
DS42.4.T48 2002   92-44505
956—dc20   CIP

Cover design by Warren Hurley; photo by Rick Reinhard
Printed and typeset in the United States of America

Contents

Part Two: PAST GLORIES, FUTURE HOPES

Preface and Acknowledgments

As this book was going to press, four planes taken over by suicide hijackers on September 11, 2001 destroyed the twin towers of the World Trade Center in New York City and part of the Pentagon in Washington, killing a total of more than 3,000 people. This terrorist act, the most devastating in United States history, marked the first time since the War of 1812 that foreign "troops" had attacked the continental U.S.

The effect of 9/11, which this tragedy has come to be called, was instantaneous and profound, in both the U.S. and throughout much of the world. Commentators compared the attack to the Japanese bombing of Pearl Harbor on December 7, 1941, which drew America into World War II, and the Prime Minister of Spain, Jose Maria Aznar, claimed that 9/11 was even more important than the fall of the Berlin Wall in 1989, which marked the end of the Cold War. Some commentators went so far as to say the global battle against terrorism constituted World War III.

From the point of view of *Through Middle Eastern Eyes*, the events of 9/11 hold special significance because all of the hijackers were from the Middle East, 15 from Saudi Arabia, two from the United Arab Emirates, one from Egypt, and one from Lebanon. This raises a series of questions. Who were these hijackers? Why did they attack the U.S.? What is there about the Middle East, if anything, that would produce such terrorists? And what is there about Islam, if anything, that would lead these terrorists to believe

they were martyrs in a holy war and would be given a special place in heaven? This revised edition of *Through Middle
Eastern Eyes* answers these questions by presenting new
material collected as recently as December 2001. The last
five pieces in the book deal specifically with 9/11 and
the conditions that led up to it. The first, "Waging War
Against America," presents the *fatwa*, the religious decree,
declaring war on the United States and its allies, issued
by a group led by Osama bin Laden, the head of Al-Qaeda,
the terrorist network responsible for 9/11; the second,
"Terrorists on Tape," contains two videotape transcripts
of bin Laden and others, discussing their justifications
for 9/11 and their pleasure over its results; the third,
"Reactions to 9/11," offers a wide spectrum of opinion
about 9/11 from Middle East journalists, politicians, and
religious leaders, as well as American Muslims; the fourth,
"Fundamentalist Islam," explains the nature of Islamic fundamentalism by offering material on the Taliban in
Afghanistan and the theological struggle taking place in
Saudi Arabia today; and finally, the last selection, "Whither
Islam—and America?," discusses the response of Islamic
moderates to fundamentalism and the ways in which America can change its image in the Middle East.

Other selections in *Through Middle Eastern Eyes*—those
dealing with large and enduring issues—are equally relevant to 9/11, as well as being central to life in the Middle
East in general. Part I of the book, "Tradition and
Change," begins with a look at traditional life in Muslim
societies, showing, in selections such as "Learning To Be
a Man" and "Going to a Koranic School," how boys and
girls are taught traditional Muslim values at home and at
school. It has been said that people in more traditional
cultures are born into a set of answers, while those in
more modern societies are born into a set of questions.
This may help to explain why traditionalists in "Removing the Veil" and "The Grocer and the Chief" wish to
stick to the old ways despite the pressure to change. As
the selection "If God Wills It" shows, village life in the
Middle East is largely shaped by religion, producing

among villagers a feeling of dependence on God and a deep-seated respect for tradition and the past.

In the last section of Part I, we see that cultural change and the challenge of Western, secular values bring about an Islamic backlash in the Middle East. In the words of Ayatollah Khomeini, the religious leader who overthrew the Shah of Iran in 1979, "Westoxication is darkness," and those so intoxicated "have taken the West to be their direction of prayer." Here we see the Islamic fundamentalist theme of East versus West, with the East representing tradition and the light of truth, while the West represents the darkness of secular values. This is not a majority view in the Middle East, but it has come to dominate the news.

Part II of the book, "Past Glories, Future Hopes," explores the "golden age" of the Middle East and its subsequent loss of power to the Western world during the colonial period. After independence, Middle East states were left with three choices: (1) imitate their conquerors and become Westernized; (2) reject Westernization entirely and try to create a pure Islamic state; or (3) create something totally new, some form of integration of Western and Islamic values as envisioned, for example, by the late Gamal Abdel Nasser, President of Egypt, in "The Philosophy of the Revolution." To date, as illustrated in "Ataturk's Reforms," only Turkey has succeeded in integrating East and West.

The buildup to the events of 9/11 can be seen in the second half of Part II in such selections as "The Arab-Israeli Conflict," "The Intifada," and "The Persian Gulf War." From the Muslim point of view, the establishment of the State of Israel against the will of the Arab world was a colonialist venture, and the failure of the West to pressure Israel into a just peace for the Palestinians, coupled with the harsh sanctions placed on Iraq after the Gulf War, confirms the belief of many Middle Easterners that the West is still fighting the Crusades against Islam. Terrorists such as Osama bin Laden promote this belief, and for most extreme fundamentalists there are only two options: give in to Westernization or turn back the clock to traditional Islam. No amalgamation of East and West is acceptable. The last two selections in this book, "Fundamentalist Islam" and "Whither Islam—and America?", examine this debate between fundamentalists and moderates and offer at least a glimmer of hope.

* * * *

Leon Clark would like to thank a number of people who were helpful in tracking down material. They include Barry Beyer, Professor Emeritus, George Mason University; Sulayman Nyang, Professor of African Studies, Howard University; Zeina Seikaly, Director of Outreach, Center for Contemporary Arab Studies, Georgetown University; and Ambassador Edward Walker, President, the Middle East Institute. He would also like to thank his wife, Maria Donoso Clark, whose emotional support and intellectual companionship were indispensable for completing the revision of this book.

Robert Pearson would like to express his gratitude to his wife, Beeby Harold Pearson, for her unfailing support and good cheer during this and all previous revisions of *Through Middle Eastern Eyes*.

Leon E. Clark
Robert P. Pearson

Foreword

People—and nations—have a tendency to look at the outside world from their own perspectives. This is natural and perhaps necessary, for we are all prisoners of a particular space and time. But how limited and boring a single perspective can be! And how faulty and biased our information would be if we listened only to ourselves!

The goal of *Through Middle Eastern Eyes* is to broaden our perspective by presenting a Middle Eastern view of the Middle East and the world. Most of the material in this book has been written by Middle Easterners, and it comes from a variety of sources: autobiographies, fiction, poetry, newspaper and magazine articles, letters, diaries, anthropological studies, and historical documents.

Unlike most books about "other peoples," *Through Middle Eastern Eyes* does not settle for explaining the Middle East but also tries to show it; it does not rely solely on "expert" analysis by outside observers but also attempts to recreate the reality of everyday life as experienced by Middle Easterners themselves. Final interpretation is left to the reader. In effect, *Through Middle Eastern Eyes* has two objectives: to let Middle Easterners speak for themselves, and to let readers think for themselves.

This does not mean, however, that scholarship has been relegated to a secondary position. Basic concepts and insights from history and the social sciences have been applied throughout in the selection of material. And the "Introduction" preceding each reading places the reading in historical and cultural context, referring, where relevant, to academic attitudes and debates surrounding the issues at hand. In addition, "Postscript" commentaries and selections written especially for this book fill in gaps where they may exist between readings. But the overriding concern has been to *show* the Middle East rather than to *explain* it, to present the concreteness of experience rather than the abstractness of detached analysis.

In some ways, the Middle East may seem different from the United States, as indeed it is. But in many more ways, Middle Easterners as people are similar to people anywhere in the world. Human beings, no matter where they live, face the same basic needs: to eat, to work, to love, to play, to get along with others. Learning how Middle Easterners respond to these needs may teach us something useful for our own lives.

More important, getting to know Middle Easterners as people—sharing in their thoughts and feelings, their beliefs and aspirations—should help us to develop a sense of empathy, a feeling of identity, with human beings everywhere. In the end, we should know more about ourselves—indeed, we should have an expanded definition of who we are — because we will know more about the common humanity that all people share. Self-knowledge may be the ultimate justification for studying about others.

Leon E. Clark

Part One

Tradition and Change

Introduction

*One hand alone
cannot applaud.*
—Arab proverb

When most Americans think of the Middle East, they often think of such things as oil, the Arab-Israeli conflict, camels and the desert. We get these impressions from newspapers and television reports of events in the area that affect the United States as well as from travelers' descriptions of things that seem exotic or different. But events that affect America and things that seem exotic to us may be only minor elements in the life of Middle Easterners. Events that are of major importance to them may not be reported in American newspapers and may not even be noticed or understood by an American traveler. It can be very misleading to look at someone else's life only in terms of things that are familiar to us. *Through Middle Eastern Eyes* attempts to provide another perspective, that of Middle Easterners themselves.

The very term "Middle East" is an example of the way in which Americans and Europeans—in fact, all peoples— have traditionally defined foreign cultures in terms of their own. The "Middle East" or the "Near East" is contrasted to the "Far East." But what are these areas east of? What are they far from or near to? They are east of England and, of course, the "Far East" is farther from England than the

15

Middle East Map

From *Global Studies: The Middle East*, 4th Edition by William Spencer, pp. 2-3. Copyright © 1992, The Dushkin Publishing Grop, Inc., Guilford, CT. All rights reserved. Reprinted by permission.

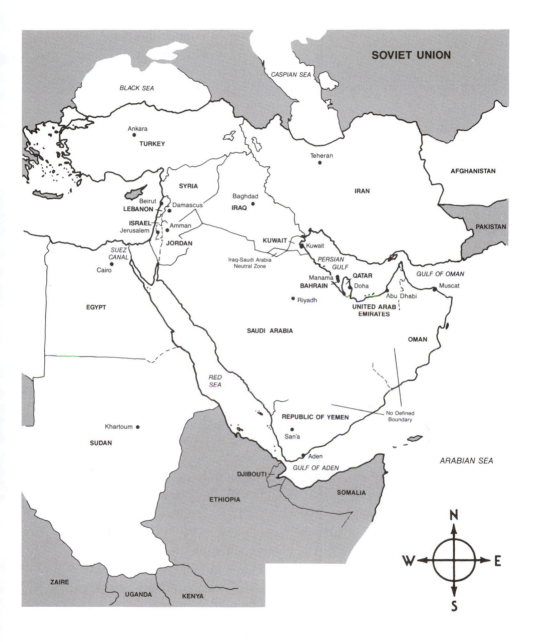

"Near East" or "Middle East." The term "Middle East" dates from the colonial period, when the location of various countries was stated in terms of their distance from Great Britain, the "mother country," which in effect became the center of the globe. Of course, from the point of view of Middle Easterners, Britain and the United States would be located in the "Near West," and in fact Morocco, Algeria and Tunisia, the westernmost parts of the Arab world, are known in Arabic as the "Maghreb," or "the West."

The map on pages 16-17 shows the Middle East as it is defined in this book. The area includes all of the pre-dominantly Moslem countries between Morocco and Afghanistan plus Israel. Afghanistan is included as part of the Middle East rather than Asia because many of its people are Persian-speaking and because, in culture and physical type as well as language, the people of Afghanistan are close to those of Iran. Similarly, the North African countries are included in the Middle East because they are predominant-ly Moslem and Arabic-speaking and because culturally they are closer to the Middle East than to Africa.

There is, of course, no single "Middle Eastern" culture, just as there is no single "European" culture. As is true of any generalized cultural group, the Middle East contains an enormous variety of subcultures, distinguished by par-ticular sets of values and ways of life.

One of the many characteristics that may distinguish a subculture is religion. The three main religious groups in the Middle East are Moslem, Christian and Jewish. Mos-lems pre-dominate in all countries except Israel, where Jews constitute 85 percent of the population, and Lebanon, where the Moslem-Christian ratio is about 60-40. But there are some Moslems, Christians and Jews in almost all Mid-dle Eastern countries.

Many lifestyles are also represented in the Middle East, including the desert-dwellers of the Sahara, the moun-taineer Berbers in North Africa, and the cosmopolitan resi-dents of Teheran, Istanbul, Tel Aviv and Cairo.

Subcultural groups are sometimes marked by different physical types. Although most Middle Easterners are Caucasoids of a Mediterranean type who resemble Italians, there are also Mongoloids, such as the Hazaras in the mountains of Afghanistan, and Negroids, such as the black Arabs who live in parts of North Africa.

The Middle East is thus an extremely diverse and complex region. Inhabited by more than 200 million people, it has a written history that goes back more than 5,000 years to the Sumerians of the Tigris-Euphrates river valley in Iraq. But, for all its antiquity, the Middle East is closely related to the West today. Home of the three major Western religions—Judaism, Christianity and Islam—it is the source of many other commonplace things in the life of the West, such as the Arabic numerals used in our arithmetic.

The goal of this book is not to "cover" all the diversity of the Middle East, but to spotlight certain values and patterns of life that are common to large numbers of people in the area and to bring them alive, where possible, in the words of Middle Easterners themselves. We have attempted to bring unity out of diversity by identifying themes shared by many peoples of the Middle East. What beliefs, religious and secular, link people from the different countries of the Middle East? In what ways are they similar in their world views, in their traditions, in the problems and changes they face? These are the kinds of questions we try to answer in *Through Middle Eastern Eyes*.

We shall begin in Part One by taking a look at traditions common throughout the Middle East, for if we are to understand how a culture is changing, we must understand what it is changing from. "Culture" here may be defined as the sum total of all the ways of believing and acting that characterize a particular group of people. It is essential to understand that a change in one part of a culture will bring about changes, sometimes unanticipated, in other parts of the culture, for a culture is an integrated whole, and everything in it is related to everything else. The introduction of technology, for example, in the form of bridges or trains brings about changes in the ways in which the people perceive time and work. If the bridges are metal, replacement parts must be ordered well in advance of breakage, for metal bridges cannot be repaired without parts produced in factories, as wooden bridges can. Thus the maintainer of the bridge must have a future time orientation; he must anticipate his needs. The train that brings him the replacement parts also brings other commodities to his town or village, such as food. Some of this food may be perishable. The train must therefore leave on time and arrive on time if the food is not to spoil. And this fact forces people to come to the station on time so as not to miss the train. They cannot set out whenever they feel like it, as some have done in the past; they must keep to a schedule. They may even be forced to buy watches to make sure they get to the station on time and to learn to read so that they can read the timetable. It is thus impossible for a country to absorb a new technology without other, seemingly unrelated, changes taking place.

This section starts with the birth of a baby and looks at the traditional family, especially at the way in which the family passes on traditional values to the young. When we think of the family, we generally think of what is called the "nuclear family"—mother, father and children. In America today, grandparents, uncles, aunts and cousins generally do not live in the same household as the nuclear family. When the children grow up and marry, the nuclear family is likely to get smaller rather than larger, for in our society grown children normally leave the household of their parents to set up their own nuclear families.

In the Middle East, however, the family is usually much larger, including grandparents, aunts, uncles and cousins, and the wives and children of the married sons, all living in the same household or in close proximity. In addition, Moslem men sometimes have more than one wife; therefore there may be more than one wife and set of children living together.

This larger family unit, called an "extended family," is an extremely important group in the Middle East. One is aware of his responsibilities to it. With so many "parents," "brothers" and "sisters," a person has a great many people to call upon in time of need. At the same time, he is expected to help others in his family. Thus his wishes must often be sacrificed to the welfare of the total group. For example, an older brother may have to forgo an education if there is no one else to run the family store.

The basic social and economic unit in the Middle East, then, is the extended family. However, extended families are parts of a larger whole—the tribe. Traditionally, the tribe and the extended families included in it demanded total allegiance of their members. Until recently, most Middle Easterners distrusted people outside their own family or tribe; they assumed that outsiders would look after their own family's or tribe's interests first. Now many Middle Easterners are beginning to think of themselves as members of a nation and thus are more willing to work for the benefit of someone they don't know.

After examining the family and the way in which it passes on the culture's traditions, we shall consider the Moslem religion, Islam, for it is impossible to separate the traditional values of the vast majority of Middle Easterners from the tenets of this religion. We shall approach Islam in the light of its effect on everyday life, to discover the ways in which religious beliefs traditionally have helped people to cope with their existence.

Today family life and traditional values are changing in the Middle East. Throughout Part One examples are given of these changes. We shall look at the establishment of secular schools, at the introduction of new technologies and their products, such as radios, at the developing generation gap between parents who have little formal education and their well-educated sons and daughters. Mothers who have always worn a veil in public places are confronted by daughters who not only refuse to cover their faces in the traditional way but insist on choosing their own husbands. For in the Middle East today the authority of the family is eroding, the way in which people learn is changing and a reordering of loyalties is taking place. Traditionally, for example, a Middle Eastern boy or girl would marry strengthen the ties between the two families. In the modern Middle East, however, increasing numbers of young people are marrying outside their extended families. As a result, their first loyalty may no longer be to the extended family but may shift to the new family. With the erosion of loyalty to the extended family comes the possibility of loyalty to a greater entity, that of the nation. As the nation provides individual services the family once performed—employment, health care and physical security—in return it expects loyalty to national goals. In this way, changes in one aspect of a culture, such as the education of the people, result in changes in institutions like the family and in the system of loyalties within the culture.

As one might expect, however, social change does not progress in a steady, regular fashion. Traditional values represent security to many people within a culture, and such people see change as unsettling.

If one could plot social change on a graph, change would be represented by stops and starts, and movements "backwards" as well as "forwards." Thus when cultures change, especially when the rate of cultural change is rapid, there is always resistance to the changes taking place. In some parts of the Middle East, there has been a backlash on the part of those who favor traditional Moslem values against the changes brought about by contact with the West. In Iran and Afghanistan, and to a lesser degree in Egypt and Lebanon, there has been a resurgence of loyalty to traditional Moslem values and ways of doing things which represent a reaction to Western customs and ideologies. How long lasting this resistance will be is hard to say, but it is clear there is a limit to how fast cultures can absorb change. On the other hand, it is equally valid to say that cultural change is inevitable and cannot be permanently reversed, for inventions cannot be disinvented and new ways of doing things soon become accepted as normal.

In the selections that follow, you will be introduced to some of the traditional institutions and beliefs in the Middle East as well as to changes occurring in these institutions.

The Importance of Children

*A house without a child in it
is like a room in darkness.*
—Arab proverb

❧INTRODUCTION: Although families differ a great deal in structure from country to country around the world, they all must serve the functions of caring for children and teaching them the values of the society into which they were born. Children are important in all cultures; they are especially valued in the Middle East. An American traveling in the Middle East notes at once how children are fondled and made to feel part of the family, although they are also disciplined firmly when necessary.

There are many reasons why children have come to be valued so highly. Until very recently in most parts of the Middle East, and even today in some, health conditions were very poor, and many children died before they reached the age of four. In the past, most people were farmers and large numbers of children, especially boys, were needed to labor on the farm. Because a couple could not be certain how many of their children would survive to adulthood to work the fields and ultimately support their parents in old age, large families were a form of insurance, not only preferred but necessary. It was believed that "each baby brought his own resources into the world with him"—that is, that the world would somehow accommodate all the children born into it. For these reasons, the birth of a child was and continues to be a very important event in the Middle East, and a woman's failure to bear children is grounds for divorce.

Among traditional families in the Moslem Middle East, it is

23

customary for cousins to marry and for the bride to move into the household of her husband's family. It is often said that the bride therefore needs children to replace the family she has left. The Egyptian short story that follows describes a married couple who are modern in that they live by themselves apart from their families, and yet also traditional, for the husband and wife are cousins and they wish to start a family as soon as possible after marriage.[1]

Badawi and Munira were no newlyweds: they had been married for seven long years without having either sons or daughters and during these years they had come to feel that their marriage was like a barren fruit tree.

Badawi was a farmer or, to put it more exactly, the owner of a market garden near the city of Cairo. On marrying he

Children in the Middle East feel the security of a large, closely knit extended family. This Libyan family adds a European chocolate bar to the traditional tea ceremony. (United Nations)

had left the market garden to his brother and had settled with his bride in one of the suburbs of the capital. Though Munira was his cousin, she had spent her life in the city. Quite possibly she herself would not have objected to living in the country, but Badawi, ever watchful for her comfort, had moved to a small modern home. His share of the work consisted of looking after the transportation of the produce and selling it by auction to the traders in the city markets; from time to time he also advised his brother about a certain crop so that it could be sold out of season at double the price. Badawi's spare-time hobby was reading papers, magazines, and an occasional book, for he had the opportunity of studying up to secondary-school level and had also learned how to wear a European-type suit. His brother's education, on the other hand, did not extend beyond the village school, and he continued to wear a *galabia* [a long robe traditionally worn by Egyptians].

One month of their marriage passed, then another. They wanted to have a baby. The earth had taught Badawi that he should wait, that he should allow time after sowing and watering for it to produce the first small, green shoots.

But after a while they began to be disturbed. Badawi did not wish to upset his bride, though he knew she was in fact already worried and that her mother . . . had also begun to share their concern. Their need for a child was an instinctive one, the need for the next step after marriage. Each began wondering: Is there something the matter that we can't have children? A year passed, a second year began.

It is not, however, in the make-up of a farmer to resign himself to the infertility of his land. The soil of the farm which Badawi and his brother now cultivated had been regarded as barren more than fifty years ago. His grandfather, buying it for next to nothing, had begun to till it, at first planting it with rice, then with beans. Then his father had taken over and had treated it with chemical fertilizers until he managed to make it yield a fine crop of vegetables both summer and winter.

When no children came Badawi and his wife came to

have experience of doctors as they went from clinic to clinic, from laboratory to laboratory, being examined and analyzed. They came to know other childless couples entering a world of doctors. At these clinics and laboratories they were told that they should be able to have children, yet somehow no plant grew. And so they gave up medicine, more uncertain than ever what the matter was.

Badawi wanted to have a son of his own, a small branch that would grow from his own branch; he wanted to enjoy seeing his own features coming to life in the growing child. He wanted him to be sturdy, intelligent, and full of energy, like his father. Badawi felt that he was like the branch of a tree and that he did not want this tree to be cut down; he wanted it to be handed on after his death in the same way as he had taken it over from those before him.

Two years passed, and his mother-in-law insisted more and more that medicine was nothing but humbug and robbery. Otherwise why did they not have children when neither of them was in any way to blame? Despite the fact that Badawi had studied up to secondary-school level, despite his reading of the magazine *The Doctor* and his being well aware that it was chemical fertilizers which gave life to the land, not charms or magic, in moments of despair he still fell back on a childhood filled with superstition. So he left the whole thing to his mother and mother-in-law. The two of them agreed that evil spirits must be the cause.

And so it was that their home was thoroughly cleaned, sprinkled with sand, and decorated with roses and other flowers; at the same time a bottle of rosewater and several pounds of sweets were thrown out on the ground. Incense was burned, drums were beaten, and no one was allowed inside. These rites were carried out for twenty-four hours. The old woman who had been called in to supervise also ordered that a sheep be slaughtered and that by dawn no single piece of it should be left; every scrap of meat had to be eaten before midnight and the bones buried before daybreak.

Badawi and his wife were told to wait for a month for the

results. The month passed, and there was indeed a pregnancy. The trouble was, though, that it wasn't Munira who
became pregnant but her mother, who was nearly forty-five
years old and whose youngest child was ten. It was said that
the spirits must have lost their way.

This disaster had a bad effect on Badawi and his wife.
Having previously tried scientific methods with scientific
calm, they now took to superstitious methods. As for
Munira, she felt real jealousy of her mother. It was as though
she faced one of Fate's puzzles: Why should it give something to someone who didn't want it while denying it to
someone who did?

An atmosphere of tragedy settled on the house. The hot
weather had ruined the tomato crop for which Badawi had
had high hopes. Though Munira was in no way responsible
for this, her husband became quick tempered and rude to
her. At her wit's end, she would burst into tears and say: "I
know the reason, it's because I haven't given you children.
You know it's not my fault, though!" to which he would
reply furiously: "Well, it certainly isn't mine." But before
long, little by little, his heart would relent and he would
wipe away her tears.

The previous summer Badawi's mother had died at the
farm. On the night of the funeral, after the flood of crying
had died down, Munira learned from the women who came
to pay their condolences that a strange Bedouin [nomad]
woman had arrived at the village three days earlier and
claimed to have the power of finding lost things, curing
the sick, and helping women to have children. Though
Munira's faith in such matters had lessened since she had
given gifts to the spirits, she was like a drowning person
grasping at any straw. On the following day, therefore, she
sent for the Bedouin woman and told her of the thing she
wanted. The woman asked for a piece of gold jewelry and
said she would return it at dawn the following morning.
She also gave Munira two small rolls of wool, telling her to
place one of them on her stomach till morning and promising that, with the help of God the One, she would become

pregnant.

In her hope Munira had given the Bedouin woman one of her gold bracelets—worth no less than twenty pounds[*]— and had then carried out her instructions to the letter. The next morning she had waited for the woman to return with her bracelet as promised. But the woman never came back, and on asking about her Munira was told that she had left the village the previous evening. Realizing that she had been cheated, Munira opened the two rolls of wool and found that one contained what looked like seeds together with some white powder, while in the other there was a piece of paper written on in such small and poor handwriting that she was only able to make out a few words, such as "At your service." Complaining about her bad luck more than the loss of the bracelet, Munira threw the lot away.

The days passed, and Munira returned to Cairo with her husband. On one of their nights together, outwardly laughing at her stupidity but with a sad heart, she told her husband of the story of the Bedouin woman. But despite this unfortunate experience, Munira believed she was pregnant. She waited a few days and then told her husband.

Badawi had toyed with the idea of divorce but had found it distasteful and had therefore rejected it. Munira was his cousin; he had grown accustomed to her and did not want to change. Besides, they loved one another, and just as the fault was not his, so, too, it was not hers. More than once he had been told that if he were to marry some other woman, children would be born to him. More than once his friends had urged him to take a second wife.[**] This, too, he knew was impossible, for it would hurt Munira to her very depths. Moreover this would be a new thing in his family, neither his father, grandfather, nor—he had heard—his great-grandfather ever having taken more than one wife.

Badawi did not allow such ideas to take root in his mind

---

[*]   One pound is worth about $1.60 (1992).
[**]   Under Moslem law a man is allowed four wives as long as he treats them equally.

but fought against them, putting them away from him in the belief shared by his wife—that everything is determined by fate.

When his wife told him she was pregnant, hope sprang up within him. Eventually Munira confirmed the good news, for she and her mother had gone to a doctor who told her that this time she really was pregnant—after six years and three months of marriage. Badawi danced with joy. Now the barren land had been fertilized, just as his grandfather before him had made his land fruitful. Now it was up to him to guard it and care for it until its fruit was born, alive, warm, and real.

Arrangements for welcoming the baby were begun, and the two of them gave much thought to the question of a good name. Would it be a boy or a girl? Munira started to make baby clothes, a small mattress, a small pillow, a small blanket.

Badawi could not help but wonder if the Bedouin woman had been successful. Perhaps those two rolls of wool, with that white powder in one of them, had been responsible? After all, he was not the only man to whom such a thing had happened. It had, for instance, occurred in the case of the former *omda* [mayor] of their village after ten years of marriage, and to Sheikh[*] Maihoub after no less than twelve years.

* * *

He remembered the first night of the funeral when all the people had left and Munira, in the living room, had exhausted herself with crying. Now here she was, nine months later, in labor. Because this was his first experience with such matters, it was quite impossible for him to reveal his fear and his feeling of helplessness. Six hours passed, and the roosters had begun to call like *muezzins*[**] from the

---

[*] A religious man who has memorized the Koran, the holy book of the Moslems.
[**] A man who calls the people to prayer from the tower of the mosque.

neighboring rooftops. He slipped into her room for a moment. The six years' struggle had become focused into these hours. He said a few tender words of encouragement before being ordered out by the doctor.

Badawi had the highest respect for the doctor, for his calmness, gentleness, and experience; he held in his hands the keys of life for Badawi's wife and child. Badawi was also struck by the doctor's great kindness, and the money he would be getting seemed to Badawi quite inadequate for being kept up so late and for the care and attention he was giving. Furthermore, the doctor's cheerful manner and smiling face helped Badawi to feel confident.

The doctor talked to Badawi about his own two children, a boy and a girl. The girl, though the younger of the two, was the cleverer and was in a higher class than her brother. Badawi talked to the doctor about his farm, methods of fertilization, the seasons for the various vegetables, and the way prices rise and fall. The doctor spoke about the government hospitals, their lack of equipment, and about the poor shape they were in. Badawi told him about his long struggle to produce a child, about the doctors he had met, and the facts he possessed about the pregnancy, as though wishing to make quite sure that it was genuine.

As a faint moon appeared in the east, they drank down a couple of cups of coffee. While the doctor reassured Badawi about his wife, the first light of dawn came, the first early morning breeze stirred. The doctor then went inside to see how things were progressing. A matter of minutes before sunrise Badawi heard the crying of his newborn child and was himself moved to silent tears.

Learning to Be a Man

INTRODUCTION: Badawi, in the last selection, is in some ways a modern man and in some ways a traditional man. He is in some respects a man of the future and in some a man of the past. His beliefs are in the process of change. Like most people, he is not always aware of why he believes as he does. Some things seem so right and "natural" to him that he does not think of questioning them; other things are confusing to him, and he is not sure what he thinks about them.

Traditionally in the Middle East, as is still true in many towns and villages there today, children and adults had fewer uncertainties about the world than Badawi does. They were born into a fairly closed society, in which almost everyone had the same basic values and was rarely exposed to different attitudes and beliefs. In such a society, people know exactly what they believe, and children are exposed to a consistent set of answers to their questions about life.

In the selection that follows, an American anthropologist describes how a Turkish boy, Mahmud, born in a traditional village, learns the answers to the daily problems of living that his village has come to accept. It is a great honor for Mahmud to sit with his father and the other men of the village, and as long as he does not interrupt the adult conversation, he is allowed to stay.[2]

The remainder of summer passed and Mahmud stayed indoors more and more, as the houses, though unheated, were warmer than the cool fall air. As the winter came and the snow fell over the countryside, most of the outdoor activities of the village ceased. The days grew shorter, the

31

*From the cradle, boys in the Middle East spend much time with their fathers,
learning the traditional male role.* (United Nations)

wind colder, and the snow piled high around the village.
On these cold nights it was the custom for all the men to
come together in the house of the Muhtar [the chief of the
village], and Mahmud looked forward to these evenings
with a great deal of pleasure.

Each day, after having finished the evening meal, the
old Muhtar's wife would put some small earthenware dishes
or copper trays filled with nuts or chick-peas about the
room, sometimes on small stands or sometimes on the floor,
and the old man would build a warm fire in the fireplace.
Soon after dark the men would begin to arrive by ones or
twos and take their accustomed places in the men's room.
This was the largest single room in the village and doubled
as a guest house for visitors who came at nightfall and
needed some place to sleep before going on their way the

next day. It had been a long time since the room had been used for this purpose, however, because the nearby growing city had hotels, and most of the modern travelers stayed there. However, the room still served as a clearing house for all the village business, as well as a place for the men to pass the cold winter evenings in warm comfort.

The room was perhaps 30 by 15 feet in size, and along one side a shelf nearly 15 inches above the floor extended about two feet from the wall and covered the full 30 feet of the room's length. The old Muhtar sat near the center of the shelf, waiting for his guests to arrive. As the men came in, the oldest in the village would seat themselves in order of age on this raised projection, while the younger ones would sit crosslegged on the floor. No women were ever allowed to come into this room when the men were there. The Muhtar's wife had prepared everything ahead of time, and when additional things were occasionally needed during the evening, one of the boys would be sent out to fetch it. Opposite the long bench was a fireplace, slightly larger than those in the kitchens of the other village homes, in which a fire burned brightly, spreading heat throughout the room. The single electric bulb lighted the space dimly and so the shadows caused by the firelight were not prevented from dancing about the walls.

Mahmud would have been happier if the electric bulb had not been there at all, the way it used to be when he had been a very small boy. Electricity had been introduced to the village only a year ago, and he remembered the days when only the glow of the fire lighted these meetings.

As the gathering grew in size, Mahmud heard many small groups of men talking idly about all sorts of personal problems, but when nearly all of the villagers had arrived, they began to quiet down.

The Hoca [a religious leader] posed the first question. "Muhtar Bey, when will next year's money for the mosque be taken up?"

"Hocam, the amount has not been set yet," was the Muhtar's reply.

"All right, let's do it now," the Hoca persisted.

"Let's do it now," the Muhtar agreed.

And Mahmud listened as the Hoca told about the things the mosque would need during the coming year. Then several of the older men told how they had given so much the year before that it had been hard on their families, and finally, the Muhtar talked interminably about the duty of each Moslem to support the Faith and ended by asking the head of each family for just a little more than he knew they could pay.

Following this request there were a series of discussions between the Muhtar and each family head, haggling over what the members of his family could afford to give. Finally, however, agreement was reached with each man, and the Hoca knew how much he could count on for the coming year. The Muhtar would see that the money was collected and turned over to the Hoca.

The business of the evening being out of the way, Mahmud became more interested, as he knew that he liked most what was to come now. He had learned that he was too young to speak at the meetings, because he had been taken out several times the year before by one of the older boys and told that he could not stay with the men unless he could be quiet, so he waited in silence for what would happen next. After a slight pause one of the braver of the teen-aged boys called to an old man.

"*Dedem*, tell us some stories about the olden times."

"Shall I tell about the wars?" the old man nearest the Muhtar asked.

"Yes, about the great war with the Russians," the youth answered.

"Well, I was but a boy then, but my father went with the army of the Sultan that summer, and he told me this story."

It was a great army, with the generals in front on horseback and all the men, thousands of men, walking behind. They left our village in the early spring, after the wheat had been planted, and marched against the Russians. With the Sultan leading them, the men walked unafraid as they met and defeated the Russians, killing twenty or even fifty of them for each Turk who died. The Russians became very much afraid and started to run. They ran far back into Russia, and the Sultan's army followed them. They ran without stopping all the way to the edge of the Caspian Sea, but even running is very slow across the mountains, and by this time it was beginning to get cold. In those days the army did not take food with it as it does today, but ate off the land. The Russians had already eaten most of what was there before the Sultan's army arrived, and when the Turks came after them, there was nothing left. Knowing that he had completely beaten the Russians, the Sultan ordered his men to turn back toward home, and shortly after it began to snow and the wind blew, and it got colder and colder.

As the Turkish army made its way over the cold barren wastes of Russia, there was no food at all, none. At night they slept on the cold ground, if they could sleep at all, and by day they suffered from hunger. The men had already eaten everything edible they carried. Finally, they were reduced to eating their shoes, belts, and other things that had any food value. When even this was gone, many starved to death. Of course a few had also been killed by the Russian soldiers. When they arrived back at our village, over half of the men were gone. My father said that he had walked the last few miles barefooted, because he had eaten his shoes along the way.

"Can one really eat his shoes, Grandfather?" one of the smaller boys asked.

"If you get hungry enough," the old man laughed.

"Tell us about the time Hoca borrowed the pans, Grandfather," one of the other young men asked.

"All right."

One day Nesreddin Hoca* wanted to make some *pilaf* [a rice dish] so he went to his neighbor and borrowed a pan. After making the *pilaf*, and waiting several days, he brought two pans back to the man.

Surprised to see an extra pan, the neighbor said, "Hoca Efendi, where did the second pan come from?"

* A comical religious leader about whom stories are told all over the Middle East.

"Efendi," replied the Hoca. "You are a lucky man, your pan had a baby."

The neighbor wondered about the Hoca, but since the old man was widely known for his foolishness, the man took the two pans and forgot the incident.

Some time later, Nesreddin Hoca came again to his neighbor's house, and this time he borrowed both pans at the same time. Many days passed, and when Hoca did not return the pans, the neighbor came to inquire about them.

"Hoca Efendi, where are my pans you borrowed some days ago?"

"Oh, my friend, I have sad news for you."

"Oh? What is that?" the neighbor asked, a little puzzled.

"I am so sorry, but your pans have died," responded the Hoca.

"Died?" asked the neighbor.

"Yes, died," repeated the Hoca.

"But how can a pan die? Pans aren't alive," the neighbor protested strongly.

"They just died. You made no complaint when I told you that your pan had a baby. A pan that can have a baby can surely die," the Hoca said quite simply and turned and walked away leaving his neighbor puzzling over what had just happened
. . . .

[Many more stories, most of them with a moral, were told until finally] one of the older boys came over to Mahmud, took him by the shoulder, and motioned for him to go out. They went into the kitchen together and prepared Turkish coffee. Whenever four or five cups of coffee were ready to go, Mahmud would take them on a tray and offer them first to the oldest man who had not been served, then, the next oldest, and so on, until finally all of the men had coffee. The rest of the evening was filled with friendly chatter, and the group broke up very late and went home, only to reassemble at the same time and place the following evening for another similar session, as these gatherings were nearly a nightly affair during the cold months of winter.

Traditional Girlhood

✽INTRODUCTION: As we saw in "Learning to Be a Man," boys learn what to believe and value by listening to their fathers and the other men of their village. Girls learn in similar ways. By listening to their mothers and by watching them and helping them, they learn the skills and values they will need when they get married and become mothers themselves.

The following selection demonstrates that young girls in the Middle East do a great deal of useful work around the house and in their village. Many Western psychologists feel that this kind of training is very good for young people, for it is important to feel useful and needed while one is growing up. Such children know who they are and what the world expects of them. In America, by contrast, many young children are never allowed to do anything truly useful and important until they reach adulthood.

This selection is based on a study conducted in Palestine (present-day Israel) by a Danish anthropologist and published in 1950. Alya and Sitt Louisa are Arab women who explain to the anthropologist how young girls are brought up in the village.[3]✽

FATME'S WORK

Alya [my Arab woman friend] tells [me] about the daughter of [one] of our neighbors who might be about nine years old and was already betrothed to a cousin somewhat older. Alya calls her: attendant on her mother.

When the macaroni is made the mother says: "Fatme, give me the board; get me the rolling-pin, the cloth for putting the macaroni on" . . . [the mother] then rolls out [the macaroni] and folds it up together; she cuts it and puts it on the straw tray. And . . . [when the water is] boiling— "Fatme, get the macaroni! Get the salt! Get the pan for oil and onions!"

A waitress for the mother. Fatme hands . . . [things] to her mother who says: "Give . . . [me] the spoons! Give . . . [me] the knife! Give me the ladle!" and . . . [Fatme] washes the spoons and the ladle and the wooden basin, etc.

[The mother says]: "Give . . . [me] the mattress, the cushions and the covering!" "Open the door and shut the door!"

Fatme carries her brother, puts him to sleep in his cradle. Then she airs the bedclothes, then she sweeps. If the mother is absent, she looks after and plays with her little brother. When her mother comes back from Bethlehem, she tells her mother: "Look after my brother! I want to go and gather dung" [to burn for fuel].

[Later Fatme] is told: "Go and gather the little stones for the [bottom of the] baking-oven! Go to Kusta, the shopkeeper, and get [oil]!" Another time: "Get matches!" etc. [Fatme] does not ask anything for herself.

She gathers all the small wood for burning. She gathers all the dry dung from the terrace and puts it ready for burning in the oven. If her little brother is sleeping, she fetches water and gives water and food to the chickens. In the evening she closes the chicken-house.

She gathers the eggs. In the evening she is asked: "How many eggs didst thou gather?" She answers: "I gathered three or two." Sometimes there are none. . . .

And I have seen other girls do similar things. I have also seen the girls go to collect wood, and in the spring to help to gather grass and wild vegetables and also seen them in the fields. In short the work of a growing girl is a grown-up woman's work in miniature. . . .

At home a girl is chiefly educated by her mother, although the father may do his share. Alya says of mother and daughter:

"If [the mother] cannot govern her, she tells the father about it. The father says to his daughter: 'If thou dost not obey thy mother, I shall whip thee. And if thou dost not listen to her, I shall whip thee very much!' Then the girl is frightened, for the breasts of men have no milk—the men have no mercy.

Further, a brother has all his life to answer for his sister's behavior, even if she is married. He must . . . punish her when it is necessary.

The *fellaheen* [peasants] consider that training should begin in earliest youth, best of all in childhood.

One of the advantages of child marriages is said to be . . . that the mother-in-law is able to train her daughter-in-law while she is still very docile and that it can only be good for everyone concerned that the young woman as early as possible becomes accustomed to the atmosphere, the habits, and the way of working prevailing in the husband's home where she is to remain.

It is said that a woman has two kinds of education. She is educated in her own home and then in her husband's home. The sooner the latter begins, the better it is.

The following proverb illustrates the belief that training to be effective and to have permanent value must begin with the child:

> Teaching the grown-up is like writing in sand.
> Teaching the youth is like engraving in stone.

TRAINING FOR WORK

We have already seen that a girl by helping her mother in little ways gradually grows into the housework; but it also happens that the mother gives her daughter direct instructions.

Thus, according to Alya, she says: "Come! I will teach thee to sew!"

Or the mother teaches her daughters to bake. I quote Alya:

"Sit near me when I knead and watch what I do! Just as I do thou shalt do!" She gives her the last of the dough, or

Learning by doing: this young Moroccan girl helps her mother and aunt with their sewing. (Leon Clark)

she cuts a piece from the dough and the daughter throws it into the oven: one or two pieces. The girl, by copying her mother, learns how to do it."

The girls must also be present and help when the baking-oven is attended to, especially by fetching dung for fuel and the small stones which are placed on the bottom of the oven and on which the bread lies. The oven calls for much labor and great attention.

People say: "The oven is a lady and needs a slave." In accordance with this it is said that the oven orders her slave, the woman. . . .

The women themselves are interested in learning their work and doing it well. It spurs them on, too, when they know that they will be scolded if they are incompetent, and on the other hand that they will be praised if they are industrious and competent. They know the whole village hears about it.

People of the West [point to] the heavy burdens the women of the East must bear. It is true that the women in many cases do and must overstrain themselves. But think of the pressure and competition which prevail in the West! Think of the achievements in sports which require the exertion of every last bit of power, physical and mental. Then think of the women who come in from the wilderness carrying great bundles of wood on their heads knowing they are watched by all the people. What a triumph it is for them! The greater their burden, the greater the attention and praise they receive. The women are proud of being able to carry heavy burdens. They train themselves to be strong and competent. It makes them respected personally. They are conscious that everybody is watching them and expressing their opinions.

Strength is not the only thing necessary. They must also show that they have staying power. She who springs from one thing to another is blamed. She who sticks to her work until it is done is praised. For example: In the spring the women go out into the wilderness to gather green plants for food. As they always go together they watch each other, give each other advice and afterwards speak about it. . . .

As regards the young girls there is a special practical reason to watch and value their work, and the young girls themselves are eager to show what they can do.

Sitt Louisa: "People like to choose one who sticks to her work. These young girls, they are watched. Before people take a bride, they observe."

When considering a girl as a bride, industry and skill are highly valued. The proverb says with a certain humor:

> The one who picks the wheat
> and the one who picks out the lice
> and the sewing one,
> take her, even if ye have your eyes shut!

The Bard

&INTRODUCTION: Another source of learning in the traditional Middle East was wandering minstrels, bards and other entertainers, who served the same function that radio and television do today. They brought news from distant lands, told entertaining stories, and put on plays, wrestling matches, magic shows and dances. Some of these performances and stories had a moral to them; others were just for fun. Although these traveling minstrels did not have a national audience as radio and television performers do today, they were able to bring news from one area to another and to emphasize the values of the culture by means of moralistic tales of national heroes.

Royal proclamations were read, tales told and plays acted in the town square or in local inns or cafés. The bards and minstrels were skilled professionals in the art of disseminating news or the history of a people. This function was especially important at a time when the vast majority of the people were illiterate and had no other way of gaining information, and the stories of the bards provided an important link and sense of continuity with the past. The oral tradition remains important in the Middle East today. Men often gather around the radio or television at night and discuss the news. Poetry is much admired, and men sometimes sit at their homes or in the cafés reciting classical poetry or trying a hand at making up their own verses.

In the selection that follows from an Egyptian novel, we see how the oral tradition is carried on in a new form. An old bard goes to a café where he has been reciting for many years. He is the last of his kind in Cairo.[4]&

A senile old man is now approaching the café. He is so

A bard in Afghanistan sings the glories of the past. The oral tradition is dying out in the Middle East and is being replaced by radio and television. (Louis Dupree in *Afghanistan,* © 1973 by Princeton University Press. Reprinted by permission of publisher.)

old that the passing of time has left him with not a single sound limb. A boy leads him by his left hand and under his right arm he carries a two-stringed fiddle and a book. The old man greets all those present and makes his way to the couch in the middle of the room. He climbs up with the help of the boy, who sits beside him. He places the instrument and the book between them and looks hard into the faces of the men present, as though searching for their reaction to his coming there. His dull and inflamed eyes, filled with expectation and apprehension, settle on the café's young waiter, Sanker. Having sat patiently waiting for some time and having observed the youth's studied disregard for himself, he breaks his silence, saying thickly:

"Coffee, Sanker."

The youth faces slightly towards him and after a slight hesitation turns back on him again without saying a word, completely disregarding the request. The old man realizes the youth will go on ignoring him, and, indeed, he expects nothing more. Just then help comes, as though from the heavens, with the entry of someone who heard the old man's shout and saw the youth ignore him. The newcomer shouts . . . to the waiter:

"Bring the poet's coffee, lad!"

The old poet gazes gratefully at the newcomer and says, in a sad tone:

"Thanks be to God, Dr. Booshy."

The "doctor" greets him and sits down beside him. Dressed . . . in a cloak, a skullcap and wooden clogs, he is a dentist who learned his profession from . . . [experience] having had no medical or any other schooling. Booshy began his professional life as assistant to a dentist in the Jamaliya district. He learned by observing the dentist's skill and so became proficient himself. He was well known for the effectiveness of his prescriptions, although he generally preferred extraction as the best cure! His roving dental surgery would no doubt have been considered unbearably painful were it not for the fact that his fees were so low. He charged one piaster [a few pennies] for the poor and two for the rich. . . . He relied on God . . . to prevent . . . [too much] blood from flowing! Moreover, he had made a set of gold teeth for Kirsha, the café owner, for only two guineas [about $6]. In Midaq Alley and the surrounding area, he was addressed as "doctor."

Sanker brings the coffee for the poet, as the "doctor" requested. The old man raises the cup to his lips, blowing into it to cool the drink. He then sips it and continues to do so until it is finished. He places the cup to one side and only then recalls the ill-mannered behavior of the waiter towards him. Gazing at the youth with apparent disdain, he mutters indignantly:

"Ill-mannered fellow. . . ."

He picks up his instrument and begins to pluck its strings, avoiding the angry looks Sanker gives him. He plays a few introductory notes just as the coffee-house has heard him play every evening for twenty years or more. His frail body sways in time with the music. Then he clears his throat, spits, and says: "In the name of God." Crying out in his harsh-sounding voice, he continues:

"We are going to begin today by saying a prayer for the Prophet [Mohammed]. An Arab Prophet, the chosen son of the people of Adnan. Abu Saada, the Zanaty, says that . . . ." He is interrupted by someone who enters at this point and says roughly:

"Shut up! Don't say a single word more!"

The old man lifts his failing eyes from his instrument and sees the sleepy, gloomy eyes of Kirsha, the tall, thin, dark-faced café owner looking down at him. He stares at him glumly and hesitates a moment as though unable to believe his ears. Trying to ignore Kirsha's unpleasantness, be begins reciting again:

"Abu Saada, the Zanaty, says that. . . ."

The café owner shouts in angry exasperation:

"Are you going to force your recitations on us? That's the end—the end! Didn't I warn you last week?"

A look of disappointment comes into the poet's face and he says in a tone of criticism:

"I can see you have been living fast lately. Can't you take it out on someone else?"

Even more exasperated, Kirsha shouts again:

"I know what I said and what I want, you imbecile. Do you think I am going to allow you to perform in my café if you are going to slander me with your vile tongue?"

The old poet sweetens his tone a little as he tries to soothe the angry man and says:

"This is my café too. Haven't I been reciting here for the last twenty years?"

The café owner takes his usual seat behind the till and replies:

"We know all the stories you tell by heart and we don't need to run through them again. People today don't want a poet. They keep asking me for a radio and there's one over there being installed now. So go away and leave us alone and may God provide for you. . . ."

The old man's face clouds and he remembers sadly that Kirsha's café is the only one left to him and, indeed, his last source of livelihood and one which has done him well. Only the day before the Castle café sent him away. Old as he is, and now with his living cut off, what is he to do with his life? What is the point of teaching his poor son his profession when it has died like this? What could the future hold for him and how could he provide for his son? A feeling of despair seizes him and increases in intensity when he sees the look of regretful determination on Kirsha's face. The old man pleads:

"Slowly, slowly, Mr. Kirsha. Public reciters still have an appeal which won't disappear. The radio will never replace us."

Firmly and decisively, however, the café owner replies:

"That is what you say, but it is not what my customers say and you are not going to ruin my business. Everything has changed!"

In despair, the old man insists:

"Haven't people listened to these stories without being bored since the days of the Prophet, peace be upon him?"

Kirsha brings his hand down hard on the till and shouts:

"I said everything has changed!"

At this . . . [an] absent-minded and statuesque man wearing . . . gold-rimmed spectacles and . . . [a] necktie moves for the first time. He turns his gaze to the café roof and sighs so deeply that his friends almost expect pieces of flesh to come up with the passage of air. In a dreamy tone, he says:

"Yes, everything has changed. Yes, indeed, everything has changed. . . . Everything has changed except my heart and it still loves the people. . . ."

He lowers his head slowly, moving it to the left and to the right as he does so, with movements gradually decreasing in extent until he at last returns to his previous immobile position. Once again he sinks into oblivion. None of those present, accustomed as they are to his peculiarities, has so much as turned towards him, with the exception of the old reciter who looks at him and says appealingly:

"Sheikh Darwish, are you happy now?"

The other man remains, however, as though lost to the world and says nothing. Just then another person arrives who is greeted with looks of admiration and affection, and they all respond enthusiastically to his greeting.

Radwan Hussainy is a man of impressive appearance, both broad and tall, a flowing black cloak covering his ample form, his face large and whitish with tinges of red. He wears a reddish-colored beard. His forehead seems to shine with light and its surface gleams with happiness, tolerance, and deep faith. He walks slowly, with his head slightly bent, and a smile on his lips announces his love for both people and life.

He chooses a seat next to the poet's sofa and, as soon as he does so, the old man begins to complain to him. Radwan Hussainy listens good-naturedly, although he knows well what the trouble is. Indeed, on a number of occasions he has tried to dissuade the café owner, Kirsha, from his intention to dispense with the reciter but he has always been unsuccessful. When the old man finishes his complaint, Hussainy does what he can to console him and promises to help him find a job for the poet's son. He then generously places some coins in his hand and whispers in his ear:

"We are all sons of Adam. If poverty descends on you then seek help from your brother. Man's provider is God and it is to God that any excess is due."

Going to a Koranic School

*Knowledge acquired as a
child is more lasting than
an engraving on stone.*
—Arab proverb

꙰INTRODUCTION: We have seen one source of learning in the traditional Middle East: the oral tradition in the home and in the marketplace. But many children also learned more formally by going to school, for schools have existed in the Middle East from earliest times.

Traditional schools were Koranic schools, named after the Koran, the Moslem holy book. These schools, usually located in mosques (Moslem places of worship), were concerned primarily with teaching boys to recite and interpret the Koran. The teachers were called *mullahs, fqihs* or *hocas,* depending on where in the Middle East the schools were located.

In the great cities of the Middle East there were also universities where students could learn literature, philosophy and science. Some of these universities have existed for more than a thousand years.

As Europeans began to colonize the Middle East in the eighteenth century, they established secular schools. In many cases, these European schools did not admit Moslem students. However, after the Europeans left in the 1940s and 1950s, their schools remained and began to compete for students with the Koranic schools. Today almost all Middle Eastern students go to secular schools, which in most ways are similar to American schools. But Koranic schools, with their emphasis on memoriza-

48

tion of the Koran, still exist.

The following selection, from a novel set in Morocco, describes the experiences of a young Koranic school student.[5]

Across the street from the house where Abdeslam lived
there was a mosque. Here the boys chanted their lessons
all day. When Abdeslam was six years old his father told
him it was time for him to to go and study the Koran with
the others.

The first day his father went with him and gave some
money to the *fqih*. "Look after him. Make him learn," he
said, and then he went away.

Abdeslam sat down facing the *fqih*. He did not know what
was going to happen, but he thought the *fqih* would probably give him a *hanasha*, a board to write on. Instead of that,
he made him sit with the other boys and sing the letters of
the alphabet after him: *a-lif, el-ba, et-tsa,* and so on. They
did this all day for many days, Abdeslam and the others,
singing the letters after the *fqih*. Then one morning the
fqih told them: "Today I'm going to pass out *hanashas,* so
you can learn to write and read the letters faster."

Abdeslam was delighted. He and the boys rocked back
and forth and pounded their *hanashas* while they recited
the letters. When he told his father about it, he went out
and bought him a fine board of cedar-wood from Moulay
Brahim, so he would always have something to hit while he
sang the letters. His father told him that this way the letters would go straight into his head and stay there. Some
of the other boys brought *hanashas* from home, too, made
of apple- or olive-wood, but they did not smell as good as
Abdeslam's.

The *fqih* began to teach the boys the beginning of the
Koran. In two years' time Abdeslam already had reached
the *Baqra Seghira*. His father went to the mosque and said
to the *fqih*: "I hear my son has got to the *Baqra Seghira*. Is
that true?"

"Yes," said the *fqih*. "It is true, thanks to Allah."

Two years is very little time in which to learn so much

of the Koran. Abdeslam had learned fast because his father's brother, who lived in the house with his family and could read the Koran very well, had taken him into his room each day when he got home from school and taught him more.

Abdeslam's father thanked the *fqih*. Then he and his brother went to the cattle-*souq* [market] and bought a young bull. They led it home and killed it, and invited thirty *tolba* [students] to come and recite the Koran. The *tolba* were all young men who knew it perfectly and were used to chanting it together. It was late at night when they finished. Then Abdeslam's mother and sisters served them the flesh of the bull in a *couscous* [cooked ground wheat served with a meat and vegetable sauce].

Abdeslam enjoyed his life. There was the world outside, with trees and houses and places to play, and the world of words and letters in the mosque. He felt that he was learning more every day. It was a year or so later when his father met him at the door as he came home from school one day and said to him: "Your *fqih* tells me you know the whole first part of the Book, and can read it and write it. That's good. Now you're going to go to school."

Abdeslam did not want this. He knew it was harder kind of work. "Why can't I stay at the mosque?" he said. "I want to be a *fqih*."

"You've got to learn arithmetic and French and all sorts of things. You don't know anything yet. Later you can be a *fqih*."

"But Baba, I like it at the mosque. I won't understand anything at the school. I want to learn more of the Koran."

"School," said his father.

Abdeslam sighed.

"My Mind Was Open for Information and Wisdom"

*Search knowledge though
it be in China.*
—Arab proverb

❧INTRODUCTION: Although a sizable number of boys in the Middle East have always gone to school, girls have traditionally been educated only in very small numbers. The few girls who were educated came from the wealthiest families and were either sent to small, private schools or educated at home by private tutors. A girl's place was believed to be in the home; it was not thought necessary to educate a large number of girls.

Today, however, most girls attend elementary schools, and most Middle Eastern governments are attempting to provide opportunities for them to go to high school and college as well. This revolution in women's education has come primarily in the last twenty or thirty years. In 1988 in Iraq, for example, 46 percent of elementary students and almost 40 percent of high school and college students were female. These figures, which are only slightly higher than the Middle East as a whole, represent a dramatic change in attitudes toward the education of women and point to the day when women will have to the same educational opportunities as men. In the selection that follows, an Iranian woman, Najmeh Najafi, describes how she first went to school.[6]❧

My greatest travelling in those days was down the avenue

51

and across a few streets to the school. I had been in school
since I was five, but the school had not yet begun to broaden
my life. . . . Ordinarily children in Persia [Iran] do not go
to school until they are six. There are no kindergartens in
connection with the public schools of our country. There
are the ancient *mektabs,* Moslem schools, kept for little girls
by old women whose faces are like withered apples, the fingers on their hands like winter dead twigs; for the boys by
old men.

Once when I was three, or maybe four, my mother sent
me to such a school. She and Zarah were busy and it seemed
a good idea. I remember that my mother gave me a book
before she left me seated at the feet of the old lady. I don't
remember much except that we were told to keep quiet.
Some way I got a pair of scissors and cut all the pictures
out of my book. . . . At noon we were served wheat cakes
for lunch, and after I had eaten I lay down on the carpet
and slept. It was the time for my nap. I do not remember
whether I went to the *mektab* for two days or three.

When I was five one of my friends, a girl maybe two years
older than I, maybe three, stopped at my house on the way
to school. "Come along with me," she suggested. "No one
will be angry.

"No one will be angry? They won't be angry at the
school?" I asked, to make doubly certain before I made
any decision . . . .

"No one will be angry," my friend again assured me, and
I went with her to the school.

The school, like my home, was built on three sides of a
rather large court. In the center of the court was a pool
. . . .

At the other end of the pool the school janitors had the
first room. It was a large supply closet really, but they had
stocked it with candy and other goodies which they sold to
the girls for several times the price charged in the bazaars.
I do not know how they got this concession, whether by
purchase or "gift." They were nicknamed by the girls "Father" and "Mother." The rest of that wing and the building

facing the court from the rear contained classrooms.

You ask about the lavatory? Listen, we are talking about Persia.

There was a small closet where the *aftabe* was kept. The *aftabe* is a rather large round jug with a narrow neck and a wide mouth. On one side is a spout, on the other side is a handle. The *aftabe* is for use if you need a rest room. After you have used it you carry it to the pool in the center of the court, empty it, and wash it clean. That is what the pool is really for—for the emptying and washing of the *aftabe*.

We do not mind using the *aftabe* at school. We are all girls at the school and besides we are used to the same system at home.

After my friend had shown me where the *aftabe* was kept, she took me to the first-grade room and I went in alone. No one asked, "Whose girl is this? What age is she?" I was given a seat with Nahede and Mastaneh, who today are two of my best friends, though we have gone different ways in life. Mastaneh is married and has a home and children. Nahede is a student in Teheran. Sitting there with the two little girls all day, I had a delicious sense of belonging.

Things weren't quite so smooth at home when I returned that afternoon, though. "Where have you been? Why did you go?" These were the questions. "You are too young for school —a baby," both Zarah and my mother said. Perhaps they were thinking of my three days at *mektab*.

"But I want to go to school," I coaxed. The next morning my mother went with me and signed my name on the school records. I sometimes wonder why I was so willing, even eager, to sit absolutely still for six hours a day, six days a week. There is no play in the schools of my country, and the only free day is Friday, the Moslem Sabbath. There are six grades, equivalent to the eight grades in an American elementary school. The whole approach to learning is different. First there are the twenty-five letters of our alphabet that we must learn to recognize and recite in order. Next we must learn how these letters make words. Very soon we are given a book and begin to sound out the words and see them in sentences. The back of a Persian book is the front to an American. Starting on the last page we read each line from right to left.

As soon as we begin to master the reading of Farsi, the language of Persia, we must learn Arabic, since the Koran is written in that language and it is important that each person be able to read about her religion for herself. Arithmetic is another subject that Persians are particularly quick at learning. Omar Kháyyam, the Persian poet that all English readers know, also wrote a book on algebra. The numbers we learn in school are similar to yours, since we too got them and our decimal system from the Arabs. . . .

School is tiring for the body but it is refreshing to the mind. Have you seen a fish that has just been taken from the water with its mouth open reaching for air? My mind has always been like the fish's mouth—open for information and wisdom. . . .

My favorite aunt . . . during the school vacation . . . coaxed me to spend as much time with her as I could. She loved me as she had when I was tiny. But now there was a difference in our relationship. Before, she had been my teacher, showing me how to sew, listening to me repeat my devotions; now I was her teacher. Each word I learned to read and write I taught to her. She laughed with delight when I checked her small arithmetic problems and found them correct. She clapped her hands when she read a chapter in my primer without error. She had never had a chance to attend school and she was hungry for knowledge. Perhaps it was from her that I learned that there is a joy in learning that people who take education for granted may never find.

One day—I believe I was in the third grade or perhaps in the fourth—I saw on the teacher's desk a globe with wide expanses of blue surrounding odd-shaped, varicolored patches. All morning I kept my eyes upon the globe, waiting for an explanation. At last the teacher said, "We shall study geography. This globe stands for the world."

In a second I knew that all of the blue spaces were oceans

and that the varicolored areas were the "lands and people." . . . First, of course, we found Persia; next our near neighbors; and finally, twirling the globe slowly, Western Europe and on the other side of a wide space of blue, America. I do not know whether or not my teacher was particularly gifted in the teaching of geography. I know only that the subject captivated me; maps became my favorite possessions, and I followed every strange name with the thought that some day I would see that place.

Because I dreamed always of travel, I kept my ears listening for talk about the Trans-Iranian Railway which was being built to connect the Persian Gulf with the Caspian Sea.

POSTSCRIPT: Najmeh Najafi's dream did come true; she was able to travel and see other lands. She came to the United States for university training and has had a successful career in business and social work in Iran. She has written two books in English about her native land with the help of an American, Helen Hinckley Jones: *Persia Is My Heart* (from which the above selection is extracted) and *A Wall and Three Willows*.[7]

Behavior and Morality

A bad wound heals but
a bad word doesn't.
—Persian proverb

❧INTRODUCTION: Traditionally in the Middle East, boys and girls were allowed to play together when they were young but were separated before they reached their teens. Once this separation took place, there was little contact between the sexes until marriage. However, because of the value placed on having many children, young people usually married in their early teens. The separation of the sexes, then, generally lasted no more than six or seven years. In the modern Middle East, however, marriage often does not take place until the early twenties, after a young man or woman finishes school.

In such cases, boys and girls may be separated for ten years or more. This prolonged period of separation is seen by many Middle Easterners as too long and unnatural and is beginning to break down as various dating systems are being tried out. In order to preserve the reputation of her family and to properly prepare her for marriage, the life of a young girl in the Middle East is highly regulated. What she can and cannot do are carefully spelled out. The girl's family, even after she marries, will be judged on the basis of her behavior. Qualities of character are stressed: hard work, not being a gossip, holding one's temper and not showing oneself off to men. This last quality is especially emphasized; flirtations and love affairs have serious consequences and often lead to violence or even death. A woman's actions reflect on everyone in the household, and her father or

56

brother, if she is unmarried, or her husband, if married, is bound to uphold the family honor by punishing those at fault—the man, if that is the case, or the woman herself.

A woman must therefore always act modestly and avoid drawing attention to herself in public. Traditionally women in the Middle East wore veils (*hijabs*) and long robes that touched the ground (*chadors*). In the parts of the Middle East where veils were not worn, women were expected to cover their faces with their shawls or headcloths when in sight of men. Even in the modern, Westernized Middle East, where most women do not wear veils, they are expected to keep their eyes to the ground when passing a man and to walk purposefully so as not to appear to be loitering. Any other behavior is interpreted as an invitation to the man to make an advance. For this reason, Western women, by acting in a way that is natural to them, are often signaling something quite different to Middle Eastern men.

In the following selection, a Danish scholar describes how girls were traditionally brought up in Palestine (Israel).[8]

There are many rules and much advice as to the behavior and morality of a girl. Quite early it is impressed upon her that she must learn to control herself and watch that she does nothing improper. Of how she is taught good manners Alya says:

> If she scratches her head, she is scolded.
> If she licks the ladle from the cooking-pot, she is scolded.
> If she eats out-of-doors, she is scolded.
> In the evening after the hens are shut up, the women should
>   not be out-of-doors.

Fatme Jedallah: "Except at weddings when they may go out, otherwise it is a shame." Sitt Louisa: "Indeed, weddings mean great freedom." . . . A woman has the right to be out in the morning because her work requires it. And if a man then [bothers] her, his punishment will be very severe. But already at noon it is different. She really ought to have finished her work outside. And if a man then . . . [bothers] her his punishment is not so great. But if this happens in the evening the fault is hers. Why was she out so late? She

The Middle East has traditionally been a man's world. When women needed to go out they were expected to cover their faces and make themselves as inconspicuous as possible. (United Nations)

has no right to be out in the evening. This concerns the women who are on the outskirts of the village where they must go to get water and collect wood, grass, and herbs.

Nor must a woman run about in the village or to the neighbors. This is wrong in itself, and besides leads to gossip, quarreling, and trouble of all kinds.

Alya expresses the disapproval such behavior arouses in the following way:

> Running about means gossiping and mischief-making.
> She must not be a running-about woman.
> She must not go among the women.
> She must not go from house to house.
> If she repeats what others say, she is scolded.
> If she repeats what others say, it is as if she carried dust about.

The Arabs condemn gossip by comparing it to the carrying of dust from one house to another. Nor shall gossip be carried from home to the neighbors. The woman warns her daughter: "Tell not the neighbors what we cooked!" It is considered especially improper to go and lift the lid of another's cooking pot and see what they are cooking; the neighbors shall not talk about and discuss what is being cooked in any house. It is no concern of the neighbors what happens in the family.

Least of all shall the members of the family gossip about each other. Hear again the advice given to the daughter by the mother concerning her co-wife:

"If thy father's wife speaks against me, do not tell me about it!"

The mother threatens that if the daughter does this, she will punish her. "I shall whip thee!" And her argument is very fine.

"The one who said it does not bear the shame but the one who carried it further!"

Further, a mother says to her daughter:

> Do not steal from the garden! It is shameful!
> Neither figs nor tomatoes! Do not steal anything!

A father gives similar advice to his daughter when as a
bride she leaves his house:

> Be careful and take nothing from the property of the
>   neighbors, and lay not thy hand on a stranger's property!
> Be perfect! Let not the women make fun of thee!

And the mother uses the same opportunity to repeat
some of the advice she has already many times earlier tried
to impress on her daughter.

> See my child! If she laughs [much], it is shameful!
> If she repeats what others say, it is shameful!
> If she lies, it is shameful! . . .

The mother adds:

> If she laughs with young men, it is shameful!
> If she steals, it is shameful!

In the Arabs' moral code for women, the rules and advice for their behavior toward men are very important.
Some concern their behavior toward the husband and
others their behavior toward strange men.   A woman must
not raise her voice against her husband. This is a reason for
divorce. He is her lord (*ba'el*).

The tongue of the wife shall be "sweet."

If a bride is praised for her stately figure and her beauty,
the reply may be:

> The milk is white too,
> a tree is high
> and a cow fat!

This implies that praise of a bride's beauty is superfluous.
Other qualities are necessary. The tongue is the most im-

portant. What if a woman is beautiful if she has an evil tongue? The faculty of speech distinguishes man from all other beings on earth. Much in life depends upon how the gift is used. Does not a proverb say: "A kind word can attract even the snake from his nest"?

And a woman shall speak to her husband in such a way that he shall be good-tempered. She shall not cause trouble and bring disharmony into his house.

Again, a woman shall always show her husband a happy face. Another saying is: "The woman is her husband's mirror."

To this Sitt Louisa said: "This means that the one face expresses the same as the other. If thy face smiles, it brings joy. If the wife's face is sour and angry, the husband gets bad tempered."

How the Arabs dislike a gloomy face appears from the following statement:

> My first trouble is a miserable face.
> My second trouble is blood-guiltiness.
> And my third trouble, was with my father's brother.

It is also said:

> The first evil, from which I take refuge in God,
>   is entering an unlighted house.
> And the second is the company of mad people.
> And the third is a defiant face!

... the Arab view ... [is]:

> The Prophet—upon him be prayer—said:
> "There are three things in the world which give joy."
> "What?"—"Firstly, fresh water; secondly, fresh green.
> Thirdly, a fresh and beautiful face."

This does not imply that a woman shall show a friendly face to everyone. As far as strange men are concerned a woman cannot be careful enough.

Alya: "If she talks with the men, she is scolded. Thou hast no right to speak with the men!"

If a woman must pass some men, she shall modestly draw her bead-cloth over her face, so that they cannot catch a glimpse of it. She shall also conceal her hands. . . .

The mother says to her daughter: "If thou art walking alone, and a man is behind thee, do not turn round!" The men talk in their club and say: "So-and-so walked and turned round!" . . .

Alya states: "If she does not turn out to be a well-behaved girl, the one who brought her up is cursed."The mother is blamed for all faults. Therefore a mother appeals to her daughter and says: "Dost thou not wish to protect my honor from others? Dost thou wish to shame me?"

Again, to a good daughter it is said:

> Let the womb live that bore thee!
> Let the breasts live which suckled thee!

The mother of a good girl is blessed and is wished long life on the earth.

A married woman must also be very careful in her behavior toward the men. This is especially important for a woman married in another place. . . .

When Saada, wife of Muhammad Yusef . . . was brought as a child bride from the neighboring village of el-Khadr to Artas, she went the next morning to the spring to fetch water. Hamdiye, who was also there, told me how all those at the spring saw Saada lift up her dress so high that her henna-decorated feet and legs were seen. The girl-bride was naturally so happy and proud of them that she could not help showing them. But this at once gave offense. And Hamdiye, according to what she said, went and reproached her for the raised dress.

"Remember," she said, "that thou art now in Artas!" She implied: "In thy home village people may not be so particular of women's morals. But here in Artas we demand respectable women!". . .

Her parents and the people in her village know it only too well. So they warn her already beforehand and urge her to be extremely careful not to give offense in her husband's village.

The exceptionally strict morality demanded from a stranger wife gives rise to the advice given to a daughter when being educated and to the advice and the warnings addressed to her when leaving her home, and this gives an extremely good idea of the moral standard to which the women are educated.

I give here some examples:

"As a stranger—thou must not speak to men and not lift thy dress! And not sit with the neighbors and not smile at the men. The men will take hold of thee, the men will try. Watch! Be not free with them! If they curse thee, look angry and curse them again and strike!"

And: "In thy life among strangers—do not quarrel with the people! Do not carry tales!"

And: "Be careful in thy stranger life! Let nobody speak about thee, nor the women make fun of thee! The women flatter thee to thy face and afterwards are stinging scorpions. Cleverness is needed for the men—and purity! The stranger woman must be perfect!"

This advice finishes with the wish:

"Let thy people say: Let her live and may the house from which she comes, live! Bravo for her! And let them not say: May she be cursed!"

Only a good daughter can bring her family honor and blessing.

And yet people sometimes bewail and have reason to bewail their hard fortune in being obliged to bring up a daughter only to be cursed by strangers in her husband's house later on.

Watching One's Reputation

Eat what you please, but
wear what pleases others.
—Egyptian proverb

❧INTRODUCTION: Belonging to an extended family can be difficult as well as supportive, for although you have more people to turn to for help, you also have more people to observe you to make sure you do not hurt the reputation of the family. Girls are especially watched over, for if they run away or marry without their parents' permission, the reputation of the family will be ruined. In many ways, the custom of watching over girls in Middle Eastern towns and villages is like the close notice taken of what people are doing in small towns in the United States and elsewhere. In such towns, everyone knows and talks about what his neighbor is doing, who is visiting whom, who took a walk with whom and the like.

In the selection that follows, which takes place in Turkey, we see that even when a woman is away from her family, her reputation affects the people with whom she lives and works. The main character, Feridé Hanim, is a schoolteacher from Istanbul sent by the Ministry of Education to a small town. The incident described is from her diary.[9]❧

15th May

This evening, when school was over, the headmistress asked me to come to her room; and this is what she said:

"Feridé Hanim, my dear, I am very pleased with your

64

keenness and the serious way in which you do your work. But you have one fault. You still believe yourself to be in Istanbul. There's a well-known proverb that says 'Beauty always brings trouble.' You're both pretty and young, so you ought to look after yourself better; but you've been guilty of several . . . [mistakes in your conduct]. Now, don't get into a state, my dear; I'm not saying it's your fault, but I do say that you've been incautious. For instance, this place is not so much behind the times that women can't go about smartly dressed, and that applies to our teachers as well. But what may seem quite natural to others has attracted attention in you, because, my dear girl, your youth and beauty have turned the head of every man you meet, to such an extent that there has begun to be talk in the town. I sit here as if I knew nothing, but I get news of all that's going on. From the officers in [the army] and the businessmen in the cafés, right down to the older students in the secondary school, there's not a soul that doesn't recognize you at a distance; not one that doesn't talk about you.

"And now you might ask by what right I speak to you about these things, and why I do so; and there are two reasons, my dear. The first is that you're a really good child, but after all, very inexperienced. I've become something of an expert in human nature, and so I want to be a kind of mother, or aunt, to you. And the second reason is that there is the good name of the school to be considered. Isn't that so, my dear?"

Without looking me in the face, she continued . . . "The school is a sacred place, like the Mosque. It's my most important duty to protect it from gossip, scandal, and every other kind of evil. Isn't it? But all this talk has, unfortunately, drawn attention to the school. Do you notice how many fathers and brothers have come to fetch their daughters and sisters? It may be you haven't noticed it, but I have. They come to see you, not to fetch the children. It seems that one day you tied up one of the poorer children's hair with a bit of ribbon; I don't know how the news got about, but [a] young [soldier] met the child in the street, gave her some money, took the ribbon, and went off with it. And now, from time to time, he sticks it in his buttonbole, and makes his friends laugh by saying, 'Now you've got to look up to me. I've been given a decoration by Gülbeseker' [the villagers' nickname for Feridé]. And yesterday our door-keeper, Mehmet, brought me some strange news. Some drunk men coming back from the public house the night before stopped in front of the school door, and one of them made a speech, in which he said, 'I saw Gülbeseker touch a black stone in the wall. For God's sake let us worship.'"

"So you see, my dear, these goings-on are neither good for you nor for the school. But as if all this was not enough, you've committed another indiscretion; you seem to have had a talk with Captain Ihsan in Abdurahman's house. If you had accepted Madame's proposal [of Ishan's mother that Feridé marry her son] no harm would have been done, but to meet a young man and then to refuse so good an offer attracted attention. 'Ah, she refuses Ihsan Bey, it means she loves someone else; who is it, I wonder?' That's the kind of talk going around now."

I listened to all she had to say without answering or moving. The headmistress, who was afraid at first that I should object and protest, began at last to be uneasy at my silence. With some show of hesitation she said, "What have you got to say to all this, Feridé Hanim?" I sighed deeply, and said, "It's all true, headmistress. I was beginning to be aware of it myself. I'm sorry to have to leave this lovely place, but what can I do? Write to the Department and make some excuse for having me sent somewhere else. Your greatest generosity and kindness would be not to give the real reason but to find some other excuse. You can say, 'She lacks knowledge of administration,' or 'She won't work, she is idle,' or 'insubordinate.' Say what you like, I shan't complain. But don't say, 'She's become the talk of the town!'" The headmistress said nothing, but she thought hard. I turned to the window, in order not to show that my eyes had filled with tears. I looked at the mountains opposite; they seemed like clouds slowly fading away in the darkening sky. Ah! Calikusu ["the Wren" in Turkish— Feridé's nickname for herself] was beginning to feel the wind of exile again, from those mountains. The wind of exile! It's a phrase without meaning for those who have never really experienced it. In my mind's eye, there spread out before me roads growing narrower and narrower, and more and more dreary, that seemed to have no end to them . . . .

5th June

. . . During these long holiday months I have been imprisoned . . . the headmistress said there was no chance to transfer me before September. For the present, then, I tried to let myself be forgotten. I hardly even went out, and my neighbors no longer sought me out as they had before. Maybe they were frightened by the gossip.

The Public Bath

⋟INTRODUCTION: As we have seen, girls in the Middle East did not traditionally go to school but stayed at home and learned from their mothers how to be good wives and how to raise children. Thus a Middle Eastern girl may have had ten or fifteen years' experience taking care of babies and children by the time she herself became a mother. In America, by contrast, it sometimes happens that the first baby a woman has ever held is her own.

Whether a young girl's life in the Middle East is spent at home or at school, great effort is put into planning for her marriage. Traditionally, as we have noted, girls married a cousin, for in this way extended family units within the clan could remain close and there was some assurance that the bride would become a member of a friendly family with the same customs. Furthermore, marrying a cousin meant that the bride price (dowry) would not be given to strangers.

Traditionally, and to some extent today, the final decision as to whom a child marries lay with the parents, especially the mother. Because children tended to marry young, parents felt that their superior experience and maturity were essential in choosing a partner for their child. Furthermore, traditional marriage in the Middle East was in many ways a marriage between two families, a kind of alliance that tended to ensure cooperation between these families. It is understandable, therefore, that a great deal of attention was paid to finding and appraising potential wives and husbands.

One of the places where young girls could be observed and where mothers could discuss the marriage of their children was the public bath, called *hammam* throughout the Middle East.[10]⋟

The bath house that I like best has not been changed in the memory of man. It is built of brick—as all of these houses are. The door is level with the avenue, but once you step over the threshold you must descend eight or ten steps to reach the floor level. A very thin woman sits on a sort of stool behind a high table . . . takes your money, and motions you to a seat against the wall.

No foreign people enter these ancient baths. They might not be "clean." All around the large room with its brick walls painted in steam-softened colors, perhaps fifteen by twenty-five feet, there is a brick ledge for sitting and for holding the bath case you have brought. In the center of the room is a square pool of cold water. This is not for bathing. There is a short passageway that leads from this room to the real bath, as you say, "Turkish bath." Here the air is comforting with steam. All around the room, even larger than the other, is a very low brick ledge for sitting. We have undressed in the other room and now each woman sits upon a brightly lacquered tray to be certain that she is sitting on a clean place. Now will come the attendants of the bath to wait on us. There are bright copper bowls on the floor in front of each woman. These the attendants keep filled with hot water from the large pool at the end of the room.

I have a special attendant . . . for whom I wait because I like the way she works. While she rubs over the body with her hand encased in a very soft knitted bath mitten, someone else will be washing the hair; applying the henna [a reddish substance Middle Eastern women often put on their hair and hands]. Henna is a custom in my country. It is not used for color but to make the hair strong. We are all woman and . . . we purr in the luxury of sweet-scented soapsuds, warm water, and gently massaging hands. There is much gaiety, much laughter. The best of food is sent from the homes, for this is an activity that will take several hours, and hot tea is served with the fruit and bread and other delicacies.

What do we talk about? Women things of course. Food,

and children, and clothes, and husbands. Politics, too, because now that women are attending higher schools, even
doing some work in the world of man, they are better informed about the world. Many women will quote their husbands on all important matters; men are still the head of
the house and most often do the thinking for the women
and hand down ideas as if their judgment were infallible.

But often when the young girls are at the bath the talk
is of the girls themselves. This girl has a musical laugh, this
one hair which curls even in the steam, this one a fresh
sweet skin. The women are constantly on the watch for
suitable brides for their kinsmen—their brothers, their
cousins, their sons.

From behind her copper washing bowl a dark, thin
woman with a straight-boned face half-covers her mouth as
her eyes travel over the body of a twelve-year-old. She
whispers to her neighbor, "Who is that child?" The neighbor looks and shakes her head. With a gesture the woman

Some young girls in the Middle East, especially in the big towns and cities, have adopted
Western dress, like this girl walking with her mother in Morocco. (Leon Clark)

calls the girl's bath attendant to her. "Who is that child? Of what family?"

Now the bath attendant glows with enthusiasm. She tells all she knows about the girl, information she has been [collecting] over a period of time for just such an opportunity. This girl, she says, comes from the most ancient and honorable family in Teheran. She is kin to the royal family. . . . The family has wealth. The girl arrives at the bath in a great Cadillac with two uniformed servants. The girl is unspoiled by all this family importance, all this wealth. She is simple and sweet. Her hair is of fine texture and she hasn't a tooth missing. And her skin! Like pear blossoms to the touch.

Much of the account will be exaggerated but the woman who is asking can separate the truth from the fiction. She knows that if [an engagement] comes of a visit to the home of the girl the bath attendant will expect a large tip from her.

There will be other [rewards for] the women, too. Two days before the wedding the girl will invite to the bath house twenty or thirty friends to spend the day in cleansing . . . for this function there will be a feast from the home of the bride. The attendant will share the feast. There will be a gift of a fine new dress to the woman who washes the bride.

When the attendant answers . . . she must tell all the good, conceal the not-so-good, and add as much as is credible to the story, for she is playing for great winnings.

In the city bath house and in the bath house of the village, the conversation is the same. Always in the minds of the women there is a lively interest in the young girls. For the women are the suitors of Persia. When a young girl leaves her tray to go into the hot pool or to dip screaming into the . . . cold pool, many eyes will follow her. The girl does not mind. She knows that the . . . woman in her country [must be a beautiful wife] and respected mother. She is flattered by the admiring glances and smiles inside herself at the tall tale that she is sure the bath attendant is telling.

Courtship

❧INTRODUCTION: Traditional courtship in the Middle East was carried out by the parents and relatives of the couple, not by the young man and woman themselves. In many cases, a young couple would have played together as children and would remember each other, but often they would not have seen each other for several years. Sometimes a young man, remembering a girl he had played with and liked, would ask his mother to ask her friends about the girl's character, beauty and reputation and to observe her at the public bath or visit her at her home.

Traditionally, when a girl reached marriageable age—usually between thirteen and seventeen years old—groups of women representing various families would visit the girl at her home to observe her maturity and readiness for marriage. During these visits the girl was expected to be on her best behavior, serve tea and refreshments and play an instrument or perform in some way. Often girls were unprepared for the first visit, as we see in the following selection.[11]❧

The other day I wrote a letter to a girlfriend in Persia and I told her that I still like best the Persian way of choosing a wife for a man. Women can see reality, real virtues, important things. Not for them will a pretty face cover evil temper.

The wife of a very exceptional American man once asked me, "What are you going to do when you finish school here?"

She is an intelligent woman, much interested in what is happening all over the world, so I began to tell her about my plans [to do social work in Iranian villages].

"You don't want to do that," she said. "why don't you catch an American husband?"

"Catch?" I said. "Catch?"

"Yes, I caught mine. He did not think of marrying me at first so I told him I wanted to marry him and he agreed."

I know that she is joking but still I don't like the American word "catch." At college I do not like the way American girls display themselves for the men. . . .

I have watched the courtship of my two brothers with my mother doing the courting. Both of my brothers married friends of our family. . . . My mother had known the girls since they were little children so she did not have to set an inquiry around in the bath house. But there was [another] procedure she did follow.

It is the custom for the mother, with as many female relatives as care to go along, to make the call. . . . The call is a polite one, but all eyes are open. The girl knows the eyes are upon her and she feels her knees knocking together, her smile made of cardboard on her face, her hands trembling. For this call she has prepared herself without make-up. Make-up might hide a blemish, which the mother must see if she is not to be deceived. If her hair is straight it is combed straight, not "set" in handmade waves. My curly hair was born with me so I do not need to wear my hair straight for suitors.

The girl pours tea and shows her knowledge of grace and etiquette. If she is a musician she may sing or play a musical instrument, or if she is a dancer she may dance one of the traditional dances of my country. . . .

Once outside the house there is much talking between the female suitors. "I saw —" says one. "You did!" The other rolls the eyes in disbelief. "Well, the thing I noticed was —." There is nothing left undiscussed.

If the suitors are pleased with the girl, with her accomplishments, with the wealth and position of her family, next time, very soon, the prospective groom will visit, too. The man will be older than the girl, maybe five years or so. Or maybe he will be a middle-aged or even old man looking [for a second wife].

Westerners are always interested in the harems of Islamic countries. Now they are not like the harem [of] the Arabian Nights stories. A man is allowed by Koranic law to have four wives if he can provide for them and will be just to all of them; but few can afford to keep more than one wife and her family. And to be "just" to four at once? That would be a challenge.

So most older men looking for a wife are those who have lost a wife through death. In America I heard of a widow in her middle sixties who had recently married a man of her age. I was surprised. A girl of fewer years than twenty would have been the choice of such a man in my country.

Reza Shah[King of Iran, 1925-1940] made a law forbidding child marriages. The girl, according to law, must be sixteen. But still many girls marry at eleven, twelve, thirteen [in spite of the law].

The first suitor came to my house when I was eleven or twelve. I was at home alone, barefooted, watering can in one hand and a hard chewy cookie in the other. When I saw a carriage stop in front of my home I dropped the watering can in the court and hurried into the house in full view of the . . . ladies who were [getting out].

We do not have bells but knockers on our door. "Knock, knock, knock."

I pushed back the curtain from the small peephole in the door. "What do you want?" I asked, chewing on the cookie.

"We want to see the young girl of the house," the foremost woman said in a very sweet voice.

"I am the girl," I said, still chewing and not opening the door.

"Open the door, dearie," she coaxed. "You seem like a nice child."

Suddenly the awful thought struck me that I was grown up—that these women were suitors! "I'm not ready—for that!" I cried, dropping the curtain and retreating to the back of the house. "Go to another home, please. It is not time for me!"

The summer that I was fourteen an older cousin, Efaht, was visiting me and we were bored. We spent almost a day in the bath house but there was [nothing to do in] the evening. We had heard a certain girl whom we didn't know discussed in the bath house. "Her mother," my bath attendant had told me, "is very eager to marry her daughter off. We've done all we can for her, but something goes amiss."

"There must be something wrong with such a girl," my cousin's attendant said.

Thinking about this conversation, later, gave us a project to see us over a dull evening.

We sent a servant to announce to this woman that suitors would call. When he returned the two of us dressed carefully . . . and went to pay the call.

We were treated with the greatest respect. That poor girl! She served us fruit and tea and cake—everything of the best. She sang for us. She answered questions, as did her mother. The mother told of the girl's dowry, praised her virtues, declared she had no shortcomings. Finally we withdrew. . . . The mother was reluctant to have us leave without a promise to return. She followed us to the door, still with praise of her daughter.

Afterward Efaht and I . . . laughed and giggled. Perhaps we enjoyed the whole thing because we were both reluctant to see suitors and were being subjected more and more often to such calls. We should have taken pity on the poor, white, shaking, eager girl. But we were too young to know pity.

I did not want to see suitors, but sometimes my mother consented to such calls, and I acted as gracious and grown up as I could. One day my sister Fahri called me and said, "Najmeh, I have special guests coming to my home. Will you come over and help me?"

Of course, I would be glad to.

"Come soon," she suggested. "And wear one of your nicest dresses. These are really important guests."

I hurried over and helped arrange the fruits and cakes

and other things on the table. I worked with the flowers. When the guests came I was very, very gay. Sometimes I am like that. . . . Never did I spend a more pleasant evening.

After the guests had gone Fahri looked at me from under lowered lids as if she were ashamed of something. "Those were suitors," she said. "They wanted to meet you."

"You did this to me!" I cried, arranging my hands to fit around her neck. "To me!"

Now her blue eyes were wide open, laughing with a white light shining through her face. I laughed, too. No danger about those suitors returning!

But the next day they came back. They were pleased with the girl. She was so gay, so unself-conscious!

I decided not to marry. At least not for a long, long time. But it would be exciting to be [engaged]. I was almost envious of my friends who were happily preparing for marriage. . . .

After the call by the female relatives, after the boy (or man) has visited the home and has said that he is satisfied, then the parents of both the boy and girl get together to talk about the dowry of the girl, the gifts of the boy, the wedding, the ceremony, other matters.

The first gift of the groom's parents to the bride will be, most likely, a diamond ring . . . if the parents can afford it. . . . After this will come the handwritten, beautifully illuminated copy of the Koran. This too is a very expensive gift. Later there will be such gifts as silver candlesticks done with the care and creative precision of the Persian artisan, silver mirrors, lacquered chests—the gifts are reflections of the artistic culture of Persia.

For two or three months, maybe even for a year, the bride will remain in the home of her mother getting her dowry arranged. In my country this is a happy time in the girl's life and in the mother's too, when the two work together for the lifelong happiness of the girl.

As I grew older there were many suitors coming to my home. This does not mean that I was the most attractive girl in Teheran. Ordinarily suitors visit many girls before

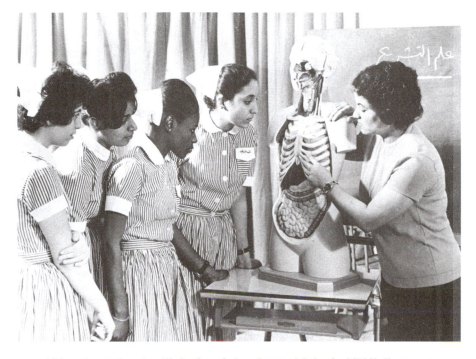

Although marriage is still the first choice of most girls in the Middle East, many now wish to postpone it until they are established in a career. These young Kuwaiti women are studying to be nurses. (Embassy of Kuwait, Washington, D.C.)

they make a choice. Sometimes, nowadays, the men themselves select a girl and ask their female relatives to make the first call. Of the many who called at my home there were several who wanted to call again. But I was not satisfied. Ordinarily the girl is not asked if she is satisfied. It is her business to satisfy! But my family understood me. My mother would have liked to have me marry well as Fahti and Fahri did, but she knew that a man who would make an excellent husband for 90 percent of Persian girls would not be happy with me. I must have something more than a good man, a kind man, a man of good family, and position and means. I must have a husband who can read my heart if I open it to him. Who understands what I must do because I am I. . . .

But no. I was not yet ready. I had many dreams, many

wishes still unfulfilled. . . . I prayed, "God, let me be just myself, just Najmeh, until I have done the things that I must do."

Removing the Veil

Salt will never be worm-eaten.
—Arab proverb

&INTRODUCTION: Throughout the world, including the Middle East, the status and role of women are changing, and men and women are beginning to work out new relationships with each other. Until relatively recently, in the United States as elsewhere, a woman's place was considered to be in the home, and it was only in 1920 that American women first won the right to vote.

One of the signs of the changing status of women in the Middle East is the removal of the veil. The veiling of women was a custom that was borrowed by the Moslems from the Christians of Constantinople, where it was considered a stylish way to distinguish the sophisticated city women from the women of the country. The veil is disappearing in the Middle East at rates varying greatly from country to country. As we see in the next selection, the veil was being removed in Turkey as much as fifty years ago. In Lebanon as well, the majority of women in the large cities have been without veils for many years. In these same countries, however, women from small towns may still be veiled most of the time or may cover their face when passing a man.

In other parts of the Middle East, change has been slower. In Afghanistan, women were not officially allowed to remove the veil until 1959 and have done so only in the larger cities, where the veil has been replaced by scarves or dark glasses. Even in places where the veil has been removed, women most often walk modestly and avoid looking directly at men. Dating does occur, but it is usually chaperoned.

In the following selection, a Turkish writer describes what happened when his mother decided to remove her veil. The struggle between tradition and change, so obvious here, is typical of what continues to take place in many parts of the Middle East today.[12]🔊

My mother was rebelling against life. . . . Her rebellion, unexpectedly enough, was against wearing the veil, for she had noticed that none of the foreign women wore them and that even a few of the more daring Turkish women from good families had ceased the practice. . . . She used to complain about it to my grandmother, declaring that she was sick and tired of keeping her face covered. I would interrupt from the lofty perch of my ten years, saying that I would not have her going about the streets with her face open. I would [criticize] her, too, for her many goings-out.

"You are never at home," I would declare; and although usually I was told to mind my own affairs, one day I was very surprised when my grandmother actually agreed with me." It is quite true," she said heatedly. "You are always out these days. And it is not right for you to complain that you have to wear the veil. Why, many women . . . never see the color of the sky except from behind their veils. . . . It is a wonder to me that you were accepted in this street, for you behaved exactly like a fast woman looking for another husband or like a prostitute. Yes, you did!" she assured my mother's astonished face. "And now you talk of leaving aside your veil. Why, I lived for thirty years with my husband, and I never went out without his permission and I had to keep my face covered all the time. If I went out in the carriage with Murat, immediately all the windows were closed and sometimes the blinds were drawn too. I say it is a scandal that women today are revealing their faces. God will punish them! Do not let me hear another word from you, my daughter, for surely the sky will open on you for such impiety."

Never had I heard my grandmother talk at such length

or with such obvious passion.

My mother replied: "You are talking a great deal of old-fashioned nonsense, Mother! My place is not in the home these days. If I were to sit at home all day, or you either for that matter, who would go to market for us? Do you expect me to stay here all day, reading the Koran and wearing my veil for fear the passersby should see me from the street? I tell you again: From now on I shall go without my veil!"

She angrily tore the pretty veil from her face and threw it . . . on the floor.

My grandmother lifted her hands to heaven.

"I never thought I should live to see this day," she said.

"Ach! Times are changing," said my mother.

"They will say you are a prostitute!" wailed my grandmother, genuinely distressed. . . .

"If they do, it will not worry me," retorted my mother. "Their words will not bring bread to me. And from now on, you will throw aside your veil too, Mother."

"Oh, no, no, no!" said my grandmother in . . . horror. "God forbid that I should invite punishment upon myself!"

But the next morning, when my mother went into Beyoglu with a box of embroidered articles under her arm and her lovely face naked to the world, she was stoned by some children near Bayazit and received a nasty cut on the side of her head.

After that she was cautious about going anywhere alone; but she was obstinate about reveiling herself, and Mehmet or I would go with her to Beyoglu, my grandmother steadfastly refusing to be seen with her. The reaction to her in the street was mixed. The older ones were stricken with horror, more especially since they had always recognized my mother as a good woman; now their faith in her was badly shaken. She was still young and attractive—she was twenty-five—and despite the shadows that lingered now and then in her eyes, she was so unusually beautiful that people could not help staring at her. Certain sections of the street wondered if she were trying to catch a husband. They came in droves, the old men as well, to [complain to] my grandmother, urging her to put a stop to this terrible thing; and my grandmother, thoroughly enjoying herself, would groan to them that she had no authority left in this wayward family of hers. But the younger women sided with my mother, and some of them even began to follow her example. Their fathers, however, in the absence of dead husbands, took a stick to them, muttering piously that no woman in their families would so disgrace themselves. So they put their veils on again in a hurry.

Not a few wished to apply the . . . stick to my mother also. They gave my grandmother sympathy until she was sick of it, prophesying gloomily . . . that my mother would come to a bad end.

And indeed she very nearly did!

For one day in Bayazit, when she was alone, an impressionable Frenchman attempted to flirt with her. She tried walking hurriedly on, but this had no effect at all; or, if anything, it had a worse effect, for the gallant Frenchman became more than ever aware of the swing of her silk skirts and the little dark curls . . . at the nape of her neck. Naturally, he followed her. All the little boys of the district became aware, as is the way of all little boys, of the one-sided flirtation that was in progress. And naturally enough, they followed the tall Frenchman, so there was that day in Bayazit the very, very unusual sight of a young Turkish woman, with open face, followed by a foreigner and innumerable small, dirty-nosed boys. When my mother made the mistake of stopping, trying to explain in her entirely inadequate French that the gentleman was making a great mistake, he took off his hat, bowed elegantly, and declared with obvious feeling, "Vous étes ravissante!" ["You are ravishing!"]

The small boys, who could not understand a word of what he said, cheered or jeered . . . and my mother—very properly—hurried on, blushing and breathless and perhaps wishing a little for the security of her veil.

When she came down our street, with her procession behind her, the neighbors were more scandalized than ever and ran into their houses to tell the ones inside. But when my mother called out to them in Turkish that she was being followed, and very much against her will, they set to with a vengeance and brought out sticks and brooms, shooing off the . . . [Frenchman] in no uncertain manner. Mehmet and I, who were watching the whole proceedings from the window, were bursting with laughter, but my poor grandmother was quite ready to die of shame.

"Such a disgrace!" she kept saying. "We shall never be able to live in this street again." But in this she was wrong, for when the street [was finally clear] of the . . . Frenchman, and a few old men had, in fact, chased him halfway to Bayazit with tin buckets in their hands to break his head, the street settled down again [saying] my mother [was not to] blame—all except the old women, that is.

The Dream

Whatever you sow, you reap.
—Persian proverb

&INTRODUCTION: As we have seen, the habits and traditions of the past are in a constant and ongoing interaction with new ideas and ways of doing things in the Middle East. Some people in the Middle East believe that the old, religious way of life and the new, secular and scientific way are not incompatible and can exist side by side without friction. Not everyone agrees that this can be done, however, and the old and the new are often seen as pitted against each other; one or the other will win out.

We have also seen what changes occur when traditional people are exposed to new ideas from the city. But changes are taking place in the villages and small towns as well, as new technology and people trained in modern ways move out from the cities. In the selection that follows, a short story from Syria, we see the competition between the old way, represented by the religious Sheikh Mohamed Sa'id, and the new way, represented by the narrator-schoolmaster of a secular government school.[13]&

In his dream Mohamed Weess saw himself praying. There was nothing extraordinary in this for in his waking hours he was continually praying and never put off performing one of the [five daily] prayers. He saw himself reciting out loud, during his first prostration,* the *Sura* [chapter] of

---

* Moslems pray on their knees, with their heads to the floor or ground.

84

al-Nasr from the Koran, and on coming to the end of it he had woken up in a state of terror. "God's word is the truth!" he had said, sitting up in bed and wiping his eyes.

Mohamed Weess could not remember why it was that this of all his dreams should have fixed itself in his mind. However, when morning came he set off in search of Sheikh Mohamed Sa'id, the village elder. Around noon he ran him to ground and told him of his dream. The Sheikh, head lowered and with knotted brows, kept silent for a long time before asking:

"Are you sure that you were reciting the *Sura* of *al-Nasr?*"

"Absolutely," replied Mohamed Weess. "I recited it right through in full: 'When there comes God's help and victory, and thou shalt see men enter into God's religion . . . then celebrate the praises of thy Lord, and ask forgiveness of him, [for] He is [merciful]!'"

"God's word is the truth!" said Sheikh Mohamed Sa'id. "Celebrate the praises of thy Lord, O Mohamed Weess, and ask forgiveness of him . . . [for] He is [merciful]."

"O Sheikh. . . . What do you make of my dream?"

Sheikh Mohamed Sa'id grasped hold of his thick, broad beard and ran his fingers through it. He appeared hesitant. . . .

"O Mohamed Weess," he said eventually, "ask forgiveness of thy Lord, [for] He is [merciful]. The reciting of this *Sura* in one's dreams is a sign that one's end is near."

Of a nervous disposition at the best of times, Mohamed Weess felt a shudder . . . through his entire body.

"What are you saying, O Sheikh?"

"It pains me to face you with this," replied the Sheikh. "However, your consolation is that God's mercy will soon be yours. . . . No one who has this dream, Mohamed Weess, lives for more than another forty days."

Having . . . said this . . . the Sheikh hurried off to [wash] for the midday prayer, leaving Mohamed Weess seated on the ground in a daze, his legs completely incapable of bearing the weight of his body.

"Forty days," he muttered through a parched throat.

"God give me strength!"

The village in which Mohamed Weess and Mohamed Sa'id lived was a small one and by evening everyone knew of Mohamed Weess's dream and of Sheikh Mohamed Sa'id's interpretation of it. The village was one whose people believed in the interpretation of dreams and so by the following evening everyone was firmly convinced that Mohamed Weess would be dead within forty days. Singly, then in groups, the men paid visits to Mohamed Weess; he was thus forced to keep to his house to receive those who came, in anticipation of his death. . . .

The womenfolk of Mohamed Weess's household came in search of news, casting telling glances at him. They found him in perfect health but with his features set in an abstracted air; mourning and wailing, they [cried to] God to intervene with the Angel of Death who was seeking to snatch him away while still as fit as ever. Though Mohamed Weess felt no pain or discomfort, the many [visits made] him [expect] pain and discomfort. He stuck it out for the first ten days and continued going and coming between his house and the cattle market. Soon, however, he was unable to hold out any longer; his nerves gave way and people began paying their visits to him during the daytime, whereas previously they had only found him at home in the evening.

Twenty days from the date of his dream Mohamed Weess . . . now remained in [his bed] night and day. When thirty days of the allotted period had passed, the various plates of his favorite foods, prepared specially for him by his family, [lay at] his bedside untouched. Dressed in an all-white garment and having let his beard grow, be spent his time in prayer. He wept, not from fear of death or in regret for life, but out of terror for the punishment that lay beyond the grave, and in dread lest God should not forgive him the many times be had taken His name in vain at the cattle market or had cheated the peasants from neighboring villages. As the days melted away, drawing nearer to the fateful fortieth, so the store of fat which surrounded

Mohamed Weess's stomach, empty with hunger, melted away. . . . People—those of his own village and those from round about—talked of the spiritual glow that emanated from his face and of the mystical and mysterious phrases which fell from his lips as he [prayed]. Thirty-nine of the forty days passed, and on the evening of the thirty-ninth I made my appearance.

And who, you may well ask, am I?

I am the schoolmaster of the village in which Mohamed Weess works . . . at the cattle market and in which Sheikh Mohamed Sa'id is regarded as the holy man. I used to spend my summer vacations in Damascus [the capital of Syria] and my return to the school coincided with the thirty-ninth day. . . . I was acquainted with Mohamed Weess in the same way as I knew all the [people] of the village and when Mohamed Atallah, the elderly school porter, informed me about him I was at a loss to know whether to laugh or feel sorry for him. I therefore set off with Mohamed Atallah to comfort him. . . .

The courtyard, usually filled with the livestock which Mohamed Weess bought from the market, was now crowded with people who had come to witness the slow creeping of death into his soul. In one corner were the men, in another the women, while in the third stood the sheep and goats which Mohamed Weess's friends had brought during his lifetime that they might be slaughtered on the [day of his death]. On entering the room in which Mohamed Weess awaited the Angel of Death, I found him—Mohamed Weess, not the Angel—seated on his bed in a corner praying, while Mohamed Sa'id sat in another corner reciting the Koran in rolling tones. I was struck by the change that had come over the face of the Mohamed Weess I had known: his rounded, ruddy face had become long and . . . pale. . . . There was no similarity between this saint of God whose whole face exuded a spiritual glow and that other Mohamed Weess whom I used to hear each morning under the school window swearing. . . . I had visited Mohamed Weess in a mood of skepticism and curiosity, but the extreme change

that had come over him . . . persuaded me that he would
in fact die on the morrow as fate had decreed. I was filled
with anger as I listened to Sheikh Mohamed Sa'id loudly
reciting the Koran and glancing sideways at me.

Between myself and this Sheikh, whose nature was com-
pounded of simplicity, stupidity, and cunning, there existed an age-long [hatred]. I fought against the . . . trickery
with which he gained control of the souls of the ignorant
villagers, while he never missed an opportunity to set them
against me, accusing me of teaching blasphemy to my students and filling their minds with disobedience against God
and His Prophet. His zeal in his attacks against me [were
not] lessened on learning from people that I came of a
family which traced back its ancestry to Zain al-Abidin,*
the grandson of the Prophet's son-in-law. On the contrary
he made this a justification for being hostile to me and
used to say, "Look at this man, descended from Zain al-
Abidin, who claims that the world turns round [by] itself;
yet," he would say, "I put it to you, has ever any one of you
seen the door of his house which was facing east suddenly
turn to the west?"

I was, as I said, filled with anger on seeing Sheikh
Mohamed Sa'id. I almost shouted out that he was a murderer, that he was killing Mohamed Weess with . . . the
poison of [putting] in his mind the thought that he would
die within forty days. I recollected, however, that I had
never succeeded in getting the better of Mohamed Sa'id
by being annoyed or angry, for he was always able to win
over the village folk by [his] argument . . . that the earth
did not turn. Had it ever happened that a villager had seen
the door of his house facing toward the west after it had
faced eastwards? [Therefore] the earth did not turn. God
have mercy on him for his [anger] against me, and God,
too, have mercy on Mohamed Weess should he remain
under the crazy power of Sheikh Mohamed Sa'id till tomorrow morning. Heavy of heart with sorrow and anger, I went

* Descendants of the Prophet Mohammed are especially revered in the Middle East.

off to my room in the school building.

Mohamed Atallah, the school porter, woke me at dawn as I had asked. I had placed three prickly pears, brought with me from Damascus, under the water-jar which stood in the path of the cooling breeze. I took one of these and hurried off to Mohamed Weess's house. The courtyard was empty except for the sheep and goats awaiting their owner's death and so, in turn, their own. The women's quarters were lit up and a low sound of wailing issued forth. The door of Mohamed Weess's room was shut, so I glanced in through the closed window and saw that he was asleep, no doubt exhausted after his long night of praying in readiness for death. I knocked loudly several times, then pushed open the door shouting:

"Give praises to God, Mohamed Weess."

He started up from sleep in alarm. "What is it?" he cried.

Here the traditional and the modern mix naturally—men eating separately and out of a communal dish but wearing Western dress and drinking Coca-Cola. (United Nations)

"I'm Naji the teacher. Don't be afraid, Mohamed Weess, and listen to me."

I saw the tears trickling down Mohamed Weess's cheeks as he sat there tongue-tied with terror. Fearful that he would die of fright before hearing me out, I said:

"I have come to you because I have just been awakened by my ancestor Zain al-Abidin, God bless him, who said to me: 'Go to Mohamed Weess and tell him that God has tested him and found that he is a repentant servant of His. Give him this, one of the fruits of Paradise, and order him to pray with you and make two prostrations before the rising of the sun; in the first of the prostrations he should recite the *Sura* of *al-Nasr* and God will so extend his days that he shall live to see his children and his children's children.'"

Mohamed Weess swallowed. . . . It seemed to me that his brain had not taken in all I had said to him as he gazed at the prickly pear I held in my hand. (I was sure that no one in the village had ever seen a prickly pear before.) I peeled it and stuffed it in his mouth, inviting him to swallow it, seeds and all. I then dragged him to a corner of the room.

"Prepare for prayers, Mohamed Weess, before day breaks."

I prayed standing behind Mohamed Weess. We made two prostrations, during the first of which he recited the whole of the *Sura* of *al-Nasr.* Then I went back to the school to await daybreak.

Within an hour the whole village had heard the new story about Mohamed Weess. All those people who had filled the courtyard of Mohamed Weess's house yesterday were now crowding the schoolyard, all tumbling over themselves to learn how it was that my ancestor, Zain al-Abidin, had come to me bearing God's pardon for Mohamed Weess. At that moment I felt that here at last I had scored a decisive victory over Sheikh Mohamed Sa'id, for neither had Mohamed Weess died nor had the sheep and goats in his courtyard been slaughtered—they had been turned over to me, a present from Mohamed Weess's friends to that saint of God, schoolteacher Naji, the direct descendant of

Zain al-Abidin!

But was it in fact a victory? In truth I am not sure. My doubts as to the value of this victory are increased by the fact that I have been unable to reduce by one single person the number of [religious people] who take part in communal prayers behind Sheikh Mohamed Sa'id; on the contrary, I have increased his congregation by one: the village teacher, which is to say myself! To preserve the honor of my forefather, about whom I had [invented] my dream, I [for the first time have] to attend in person behind Sheikh Mohamed Sa'id at all prayers!

The Life of Mohammed

📖INTRODUCTION: At the center of any discussion of modernization in the Middle East lies the question of the future role
and form of the Moslem religion, Islam, which can be translated
as "submission" or "resignation" to the will of God (Allah). Basic
to the study of Islam as a religion and a way of life is the life of
Mohammed, his role in narrating the word of Allah to his
people and the transcription of his narration into a holy book,
the Koran.

It is important to understand that Moslems conceive of
Mohammed as a man, not a god. According to Islamic belief,
Moses and Jesus were also prophets of Allah, but their word was
misunderstood by the peoples of the earth, and the resulting
religions, Judaism and Christianity, although close to the truth,
are in some respects in error. God needed a final prophet to
clear up the remaining misunderstandings, and Mohammed was
that prophet, the last and greatest of God's prophets.

To refer to the Moslem religion as Mohammedanism implies
that Moslems "believe in" Mohammed as Christians believe in
Christ. This would be a great heresy, for in Moslem eyes there is
only one God, Allah, and Mohammed is only a man, although
an exceptional one, who was chosen by God to be transmitter of
His word. One of the misunderstandings that Allah needed to
clear up, in fact, was the Christian belief in the trinity, the idea
that God consists of three parts. According to the Koran, there
is only one unified God. He cannot be divided. The next selection is based on many accounts of Mohammed's life.[14]📖

One of the most exciting periods in the history of the
world began with the birth of Mohammed in A.D. 570. At
the time of his birth there was no Arab nation as such, no

religion called Islam and no Koran. Yet within 200 years, Islam and the Arabs had created an empire reaching from Spain to India and established a religion that today is practiced by more than 700 million people, one-fifth of mankind.

Prior to Mohammed's birth, each of the Arab tribes of the Arabian Peninsula was ruled independently, and throughout the peninsula a great many religions were practiced, including some that believed in more than one god as well as Judaism and Christianity. Whether he was a desert dweller or a trader of the town, no Arab had much trust in the members of other tribes, for all were loyal only to themselves and distrusted those who were not related to them by blood or religion.

Mohammed was born into a well-respected tribe charged with the duty of guarding the sacred shrine, the Kaaba, in the town of Mecca, a center for pilgrimages in pre-Islamic times. As Mohammed's father had died before his birth and his mother was ill, he was sent as an infant with a nurse to an oasis in the desert, where it was hoped he would benefit from the pure desert air. On his mother's death six years later he returned to Mecca, where he was brought up by his grandfather and uncle.

Mohammed, like many town boys, became a merchant, and in his early twenties he was hired by a wealthy widow, Khadija, to lead a camel caravan loaded with goods to Syria for trading and selling. Mohammed's honesty, intelligence and thrift in carrying out this venture impressed his employer, and, as the two came to know each other, they decided to marry.

Mohammed now had little need to spend his days earning money. Although illiterate, he turned more and more to philosophy and mysticism. Perhaps he had heard stories in the desert as a boy, or perhaps during his travels as a merchant he was exposed to many of the religions practiced by the various tribes of Arabia and Syria. His mind filled with different ideas and philosophies, Mohammed struggled to unify them in some way, to decide what to keep and what to reject, to know what was truth. He frequently wandered off by himself, seeking seclusion and a place to meditate. His favorite spot was an isolated eave on Mount Hira, just outside of Mecca. Mohammed's meditations went on for years. Then one day when Mohammed was meditating inside his cave, the Angel Gabriel came to him and told him to "recite in the name of the Lord." The experience was so charged with emotion that, trembling all over, Mohammed returned home and asked his wife to cover him, for he feared that he was ill. But even as she was doing as he asked, a voice spoke within him saying, "O Thou, enwrapped in thy mantle, arise and warn." As the revelations continued, Mohammed gradually became convinced of the terrifying task before him. He had been chosen by God to be His prophet and to reveal a creed, to be written down in a holy book, for His people and all mankind.

The message Mohammed received was clearly understandable: There is one God, Allah, and Mohammed is His prophet. God is the Creator of all things, and His will must be done. On Judgment Day He will be merciful to those who follow Him but merciless to those who follow false gods.

For years Mohammed had been a recluse, a quiet man of meditation and philosophy. At this point, he probably did not foresee the degree to which he was to become a leader of men in a political as well as religious sense. But with the first revelation came the start of a vast unification process in which the tribes of Arabia would begin to see themselves as one people, a people destined to take the message of Allah as far as their horses and camels could carry them.

Mohammed's earliest converts were those closest to him, his wife and her cousin, his cousin Ali and another relative, Abu Bakr. But from most others in Mecca Mohammed met scorn and ridicule, for the people were content to worship idols as before. Gradually, however, Mohammed gained converts, mostly from slaves and the lower classes. As his converts grew in number, the controversy surrounding him grew more intense until it became dangerous to be a Moslem. When he received an invitation to settle in the nearby town of Medina, his mother's birthplace, Mohammed decided to move to this more friendly environment. With his followers, he evaded his enemies and successfully journeyed to Medina. Eight years later, Mohammed was to return to Mecca at the head of an army of thousands. This *hegira,* or flight, from Mecca in A.D. 622 was later declared to be the official starting point of the Moslem era, and in the Moslem calendar it is the year 1.

In Medina, Mohammed finally found a receptive climate for his teaching. As his converts grew rapidly, it was necessary for him to become a political and social leader as well as a religious one. And with so many enemies, it was soon necessary for him also to become a military leader. Hearing of a richly loaded and heavily guarded caravan heading from Syria to Mecca, the city that had so recently forced him to leave, Mohammed and his followers decided to attack it. Mohammed explained to his followers that to weaken those who opposed the spread of God's word was a virtue, and that those of his men who fell in battle would be rewarded in heaven. Outnumbered three to one, Mohammed's men won a quick victory. The courage shown by Mohammed's soldiers and the decisiveness of the victory were seen by the people of Medina as signs that Allah was with them. With the Prophet leading, Islam had won its first military victory. It was no longer just a religious movement, it was a social and political one as well.

This victory also established the idea of the *jihad,* the holy war of the Moslems against unbelievers. To die in the cause of Islam became a great virtue, and the pleasures of heaven for true believers were stressed. Although Mohammed and his fledgling army were to suffer defeats in the future, Islam as an expansionist force was established.

As conflicts with both Jews and Christians increased in number, Islam became more and more distinct from the other two monotheistic religions of Arabia. Friday was de-

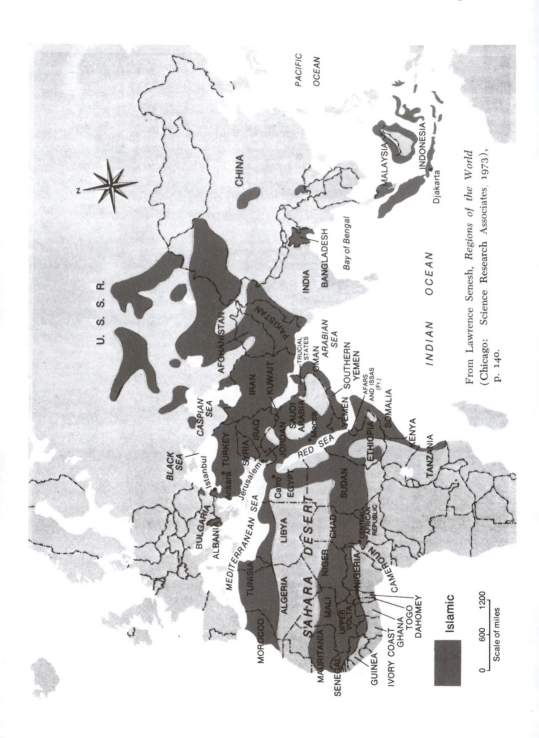

From Lawrence Senesh, *Regions of the World* (Chicago: Science Research Associates, 1973), p. 140.

clared the Sabbath in Islam, and Mecca, the home of the sacred Kaaba stone, replaced Jerusalem as the holy city. Soon Islam became the religion of all the Arab tribes, except Mohammed's own, the Quraysh, who lived in and around Mecca. It was clear to Mohammed that he had to return to the town of his birth. Mohammed, leading an army of thousands, triumphantly returned to Mecca, where he had all the pagan idols of his tribesmen smashed. The people of Mecca, giving in to an irresistible force, converted to Islam.

After the conquest of Mecca, Mohammed returned to Medina. With the nearby Arab tribes under his control he next took to consolidating the total area, and in A.D. 631 he successfully completed peace treaties with the Christians to the west and the Jews to the south. He now was ready to spread the word of Islam to faraway tribes and other countries. The payment of a tax and the verbal profession of faith in Islam were enough to enlist a tribe under the rapidly spreading banner of Islam. Thus on the eve of Mohammed's death, Arabia, which had never before been united, now extended to the borders of the Roman Empire in Palestine to the west, and Mohammed's messengers had established contact with the great Persian empire to the north and east.

Mohammed's last major action in the cause of Islam was to head the annual pilgrimage to Mecca from his home in Medina in A.D. 632. He died three months later at the age of sixty-two. All his life Mohammed lived simply and piously in the midst of his people. He left what material goods he had to the state, but his chief legacy was the collection of *surahs,* or chapters of the Koran, transcribed over the years as Mohammed had experienced each of his many revelations. These *surahs* were collected into a book during the reign of Mohammed's successor, Abu Bakr, the first caliph or leader of Islam, and were completed in the present-day form of the Koran during the reign of the second caliph, Omar.

Islam, as is revealed in the Koran, brought a whole new

basis for the social organization of Arabia and what was to become the Arab Empire. For the first time, religion rather than blood ties became the organizing force of the Arabs. Henceforth, there were only two kinds of people: the believers, who had seen the light, and the unbelievers, who lived in darkness. Once converted, all people were considered brothers: "Know ye that every Moslem is a brother to every other Moslem, and that ye are now one brotherhood." It was on this foundation that the spread of Islam was based. There was originally no religious hierarchy. All men were the same before God, and the leader in prayer and the leader of the state became the protector of the believers against the unbelievers. It is easy to see how appealing this new religion was to the Arabs, for it was based on a belief in the fundamental equality of all men and a straightforward, simple religious code. Under Mohammed's successors—the caliphs of Islam—Islam continued its dramatic spread. Within the next century and a half, the horsemen of Islam swept across North Africa to the west, into Spain, and across Persia and Afghanistan to the east, to the steppes of Russia and the gates of India. And in following centuries Islam continued to expand—to Indonesia and the Philippines, across the Sahara and into black Africa, and even across the ocean to America. Today, from minarets all over the world, one hears the profession of faith of one-fifth of mankind: *"La ilaha illa-'llah Mohammedun rasulu-llah"* ("There is no God but Allah, and Mohammed is His prophet").

Letters on Islam

ᴀINTRODUCTION: The Middle East is the cradle of three of the great religions of the world: Judaism, Christianity and Islam. These are all "revealed" religions, in which the word of God is given to a prophet and is written down in a holy book—the Torah for Jews, the New Testament for Christians and the Koran for Moslems, and all are monotheistic, based as they are on the belief in a single God.

There are many other similarities among the three Middle Eastern religions. Many Old Testament stories appear in the Koran in identical or similar form. Adam, Noah, Abraham, Ishmael, Joseph, Moses, David, Solomon, Job, Jonah and others are all mentioned in both books. From the New Testament, John the Baptist, Jesus and many others are mentioned. This and the fact that Jesus and Moses are considered prophets by Moslems makes Jews and Christians much closer to the Moslem faith than to Hindus and those who believe in more than one God.

To have no religion is much worse in Moslem eyes than to have the wrong religion. For this reason, Moslems are very skeptical of communism and other systems that are based on a philosophy of godlessness.

The following letters examine the fundamental principles of Islam. These letters were written by a father, Mohammed Fadhel Jamali, who had been jailed in Iraq for political reasons, to his son Abbas, a university student in Lebanon. Notice the rather formal tone of the letters. Letters are usually more formal and stylized in the Middle East than they are in the West. In addition, the father feels it his duty to give guidance to his son. In return, the son is expected to pay due respect to his father and to obey his wishes.[15]ᴀ

99

Because the representation of the human figure was forbidden in early Islam, calligraphy and design became highly developed, as can be seen in this hand-illustrated copy of the Koran. (John Siceloff)

Baghdad,
March 25, 1961

Dear Abbas,

After presenting you my good greetings, I pray for your safety, success, and guidance.

I have not yet received a letter from you this week, but I am writing to you as usual.

My health is all right, praise to Allah. Your mother visited me with several relatives and friends every day of the blessed Feast.

I have read again your letter dated February 11. In it you say: "What is religion? Let us take Islam as an example of a religion. . . ." I answer you with the following:

(1) I have already referred in a previous letter to what I think is the meaning of religious experience . . . and I told you that the highest stage which the spiritual evolution of man has reached is faith in Allah, the One and Only, the Allah of Abraham, Moses, Jesus, and Mohammed, peace be on them. . . .

(2) Islam is clear and simple, easy to understand, and no two who are guided by Allah and whose hearts have been enlightened by the light of faith could disagree about it.

(3) Literally Islam means man's surrender of himself to Allah and his complete submission and resignation to the guidance of Allah. If man submits and surrenders to the will of Allah the Almighty, spiritually, intellectually, physically, and in action, then he is a Moslem in the literal sense.

(4) Legalistically a Moslem is one who says, "I witness [say publicly] there is no Allah but Allah, and Mohammed is the messenger of Allah." On this all Moslems are agreed.

(5) Realistically Islam is a divine order which directs the life of the Moslem in all its phases—spiritual, social, political, and economic—for it consists of:

(a) a creed

(b) rituals

(c) a social order

(d) morality

I may describe the religion of Islam as a totalist religion . . . . It differs from those religions which care for the spiritual aspects of man only and leave [out] the physical and mundane [everyday] aspects. . . .

FADHEL

Baghdad,
April 28, 1961

Dear Abbas,

I was greatly delighted with your letter of April 17. It brought to me memories of over thirty years ago when I used to pursue the subjects you are studying now. The study of philosophy is delightful indeed, but the important thing is that one should not forget the forest and who brought it into being while one is studying the tree. . . .

Today I am going to take up the rituals, which are usually called duties *(faraidh),* which are the acts which a Moslem must perform. They are acts intended to feed the soul. For, just as the body . . . grows with material food, so the soul . . . grows with worship. Worship makes man turn . . . to Allah . . . and dedicate his life to the service of Allah. If we liken the faith of a man to a tree, then worship is the water which irrigates the tree and the food which makes it grow. . . . If we liken faith to a building, then worship are the pillars upon which the building stands.

The duties of Islam consist of:*

(1) Prayer

(2) Fasting [during the month of Ramadan]

(3) Tithing [giving money to the state and to the poor]

(4) Pilgrimage [to Mecca]. . . .

I am reading the Koran for the thirty-fifth time since entering the prison and every time I read it I discover wisdom and hidden things to which I had not been attentive in previous readings. The enjoyment of the blessings of the Koran requires persistence in reading it, and it also requires a good knowledge of the Arabic language, for the Koranic expression possesses beauty and grandeur which has not been approached. . . .

My greetings to those who ask about me.

Keep safe for your father.

FADHEL

P.S. Today happens to be your birthday. I wish you a long life filled with goodness and happiness.

---

*   There are usually five duties or "pillars" listed. He leaves out the "profession of faith": There is no God but Allah and Mohammed is His Prophet (or the Messenger of God). See the following chapter.

The Five Pillars of Islam

❧INTRODUCTION: As we have seen, Islam means submission to the will of God. In many Moslem countries, there is no separation of church and state in an official sense, as there is in America. Islam thus permeates all aspects of a person's life. The writings of Islam, the Koran, the Shari'a (the legal system of Islam) and the *hadith* (the collected thoughts and sayings of Mohammed) together deal with all phases of existence.

In spite of these prescriptions, however, man still has freedom of action, for not everything a person does is punished or rewarded by God, according to the holy writings. Professor Abdulla Lutfiyya of the American University of Beirut stated that there are four main categories of action in Islam: (1) lawful actions, those rewarded by God; (2) forbidden actions, those punished by God; (3) good actions, those that are good but not rewarded; and (4) bad actions, those that are bad but not punished by God. It is believed that two angels keep track of all these actions in order to determine whether or not a person will go to heaven.

There are five principal duties that a Moslem must perform: (1) making the initial public statement to the world that he is a Moslem; (2) praying toward Mecca five times a day; (3) giving money to the poor; (4) fasting during the month of Ramadan each year; and (5) if it is within his means to do so, making the annual pilgrimage to Mecca at least once in his lifetime. These duties are known as the five pillars of Islam. In the selection that follows, Philip Hitti, one of America's foremost scholars on Arab history, describes what these five essential duties entail.[16]❧

The acts of worship, or religious duties, of the Moslem center on the so-called five pillars of Islam.

The profession of faith, which is the first pillar, is summed up in the tremendous formula *"La ilaha illa-'llah; Mohammedun rasulu-llah"* ("There is no God but Allah, and Mohammed is His Prophet"). These are the first words to strike the ear of the newborn Moslem babe; they are the last to be uttered at the grave. And between birth and death no other words are more often repeated. They occur in the *muezzin's* [crier's] call to prayer, chanted many times daily from the tops of [a mosque's] minarets. Islam has generally satisfied itself with only a verbal profession; once the formula is accepted and reproduced the person is . . . a Moslem.

Five times a day—dawn, midday, midafternoon, sunset and nightfall—is the faithful Moslem supposed to turn his face toward Mecca and recite his prescribed prayer. Prayer is the second pillar of faith. A bird's-eye view of the Mos-

The Friday noon prayer brings unity to Moslems and a sense of oneness before God. (Robert Pearson)

lem world at the hour of prayer would present the spectacle of a series of concentric circles of worshipers radiating from the Kaaba at Mecca and covering an ever-widening area from [West Africa to Indonesia and from Russia to South Africa].

The Friday noon prayer is the only public one and is obligatory for all adult males. . . . In dignity, simplicity, and orderliness it is unsurpassed as a form of collective worship. Standing erect in self-arranged rows in the mosque and following the leadership of the *imam* [the leader of the prayer] with precision and reverence, the worshipers present a sight that is always impressive. As a disciplinary measure this congregational prayer must have had great value for the proud, individualistic sons of the desert, developing in them a sense of social equality and a consciousness of solidarity. it promoted [a] brotherhood of believers. . . .

Almsgiving constitutes the third pillar of faith. It evolved into an obligatory tax on property. . . . Its exact amount varied, but generally it averaged 2 1/2 percent. . . . Later, with the disintegration of the purely Islamic state, it was again left to the Moslem's conscience. . . .

Though . . . fasts are prescribed a number of times in the Koran, Ramadan as a fasting month is mentioned only once. Abstinence from all food and drink . . . is [required] from dawn till sunset during Ramadan. [This] became the fourth pillar.

Pilgrimage is the fifth and last pillar. Once in a lifetime every Moslem of either sex who can afford it is supposed to undertake at a stated time of the year a holy visit to Mecca. . . . Down through the ages this institution has continued to serve as the major unifying influence in Islam and the most effective common bond among the diverse believers. It [made] almost every capable Moslem . . . a traveler for once in his lifetime. The socializing influence of such a gathering of the brotherhood of believers from the four quarters of the earth is hard to overestimate. It afforded opportunity for Negroes, Berbers, Chinese, Per-

sians, Syrians, Turks, Arabs—rich and poor, high and low—
to fraternize and meet together on the common ground of
faith. Of all world religions Islam seems to have attained
the largest measure of success in demolishing the barriers
of race, color, and nationality—at least within the confines
of its own community. The line is drawn only between
believers and the rest of mankind. These gatherings have
undoubtedly contributed an important share toward the
achievement of that result.

The Pilgrimage to Mecca

⋙INTRODUCTION: As Hitti says, the pilgrimage or *Hajj* to Mecca is one of the most colorful and unifying institutions of Islam. People taking the trip to Mecca are honored beforehand by parties of rejoicing. On their return they are revered for their holiness and purity and given the title "Haji" meaning a holy one who has completed the *Hajj*. For those who cannot afford the trip to Mecca or who live too far away, numerous minor pilgrimages to local shrines are considered roughly equivalent. However, if at all possible, a once-in-a-lifetime trip to Mecca is obligatory.

The American black leader Malcolm X was a member of the Black Muslims, a group that turned to Islam as a religion and as a way of life. Malcolm X originally belonged to a Black Muslim group headed by Elijah Muhammed of Chicago, who believed that white men were devils and that black men, after centuries of oppression, would rise again to the glory that had once been theirs.

Although their creed differs in many respects from orthodox Islam—for example, in their belief that the races should be separate—the Black Muslims in America share with Middle Eastern Moslems a belief in Allah, an abhorrence of alcoholic beverages and an emphasis on the virtue of cleanliness. The Black Muslims in America have thus been able to reform a large number of drug pushers and alcoholics who, under their influence, have gone straight and worked, like Malcolm, for the betterment of black people in America. A central tenet of the Black Muslim sect is the separation of the races, with the final goal the creation of a separate black state in America.

In the selection that follows, from *The Autobiography of Malcolm X*, we see the process of conversion from the Black Muslim sect to orthodox Islam, as practiced in the Middle East, that

107

took place when Malcolm X took the *Hajj* to Mecca. For the first time in his life, Malcolm X found himself treated as an equal by whites. As a result of this experience and his exposure to orthodox Islam, he began to doubt many of the beliefs of the Black Muslims who followed Elijah Muhammed. On his return to the United States he started a reformed Moslem sect based on orthodox Islamic principles. Soon thereafter he was assassinated, presumably by a member of Elijah Muhammed's group. The United States now contains two major Moslem groups, the Black Muslims of Elijah Muhammed and the followers of Malcolm X, known as Sunni Moslems.

The selection from Malcolm X's autobiography shows the tremendous impact of the *Hajj* on all the Moslem pilgrims who go to Mecca.[17]🙿

Allah always gives you Signs, when you are with Him, that He is with you.

When I applied for a visa to Mecca at the Saudi Arabian Consulate, the Saudi Ambassador told me that no Muslim converted in America could have a visa for the Hajj pilgrimage without the signed approval of Dr. Mahmoud Shawarbi. But that was only the beginning of the sign from Allah. When I telephoned Dr. Shawarbi, he registered astonishment. "I was just going to get in touch with you," he said, "by all means come right over."

When I got to his office, Dr. Shawarbi handed me the signed letter approving me to make the Hajj to Mecca, and then a book. It was *The Eternal Message of Muhammad* by Abd ar-Rahman Azzam. The author had just sent the copy of the book to be given to me, Dr. Shawarbi said, and he explained that this author was an Egyptian-born Saudi citizen, an international statesman, and one of the closest advisors of Prince Faisal, the ruler of Arabia. "He has followed you in the press very closely." It was hard for me to believe.

Dr. Shawarbi gave me the telephone number of his son, Muhammad Shawarbi, a student in Cairo, and also the number of the author's son, Omar Azzam, who lived in Jedda, "your last stop before Mecca. Call them both, by all means."

. . .

"The Cairo airport was where scores of Hajj groups were becoming *Muhrim,* pilgrims, upon entering the state of lhram, the assumption of a spiritual and physical state of consecration. . . .

Driving to the airport with our Hajj group, I began to get nervous, knowing that from there in, it was going to be watching others who knew what they were doing, and trying to do what they did.

Entering the state of lhram, we took off our clothes and put on two white towels. One, the *Izar,* was folded around the loins. The other, the *Rida,* was thrown over the neck and shoulders, leaving the right shoulder and arm bare. A pair of simple sandals, the *na'l,* left the ankle-bones bare. Over the *Izar* waist-wrapper, a money belt was worn, and a bag, something like a woman's big handbag, with a long strap, was for carrying the passport and other valuable papers, such as the letter I had from Dr. Shawarbi.

Every one of the thousands at the airport, about to leave for Jedda, was dressed this way. You could be a king or a peasant and no one would know. Some powerful personages, who were discreetly pointed out to me, had on the same thing I had on. Once thus dressed, we all had begun intermittently calling out "*Labbayka! Labbayka!* " ("Here I come, O Lord!"). The airport sounded with the din of *Muhrim* expressing their intention to perform the journey of the Hajj. Planeloads of pilgrims were taking off every few minutes, but the airport was jammed with more, and their friends and relatives waiting to see them off. Those not going were asking others to pray for them at Mecca. We were on our plane, in the air, when I learned for the first time that with the crush, there was not supposed to have been space for me, but strings had been pulled, and someone had been put off because they didn't want to disappoint an American Muslim. I felt mingled emotions of regret that I had inconvenienced and discomfited whoever was bumped off the plane for me, and, with that, an utter humility and gratefulness that I had been paid such an honor and respect.

Packed in the plane were white, black, brown, red, and yellow people, blue eyes and blond hair, and my kinky red hair—all together, brothers! All honoring the same God Allah, all in turn giving equal honor to each other.

From some in our group, the word was spreading from seat to seat that I was a Muslim from America. Faces turned, smiling toward me in greeting. A box lunch was passed out and as we ate that, the word that a Muslim from America was aboard got up into the cockpit.

The captain of the plane came back to meet me. He was an Egyptian, his complexion was darker than mine; he could have walked in Harlem and no one would have given him a second glance. He was delighted to meet an American Muslim. When he invited me to visit the cockpit, I jumped at the chance.

The co-pilot was darker than he was. I can't tell you the feeling it gave me. I had never seen a black man flying a jet. That instrument panel: no one ever could know what all of those dials meant! Both of the pilots were smiling at me, treating me with the same honor and respect I had received ever since I left America. I stood there looking through the glass at the sky ahead of us. In America, I had ridden in more planes than probably any other Negro, and I never had been invited up into the cockpit. And there I was, with two Muslim seatmates, one from Egypt, the other from Arabia, all of us bound for Mecca, with me up in the pilots' cabin. Brother, I knew Allah was with me.

I got back to my seat. All of the way, about an hour's flight, we pilgrims were loudly crying out, "*Labbayka! Labbayka!*" The plane landed at Jedda. It's a seaport town on the Red Sea, the arrival or disembarkation point for all pilgrims who come to Arabia to go to Mecca. Mecca is about forty miles to the east, inland.

The Jedda airport seemed even more crowded than Cairo's had been. Our party became another shuffling unit in the shifting mass with every race on earth represented. Each party was making its way toward the long line waiting to go through Customs. [When] the clerk saw that I was handing him an American passport . . . he held it, he looked at me and said something in Arabic. My friends around me began speaking rapid Arabic, gesturing and pointing, trying to intercede for me. The judge asked me in English for my letter from Dr. Shawarbi, and he thrust it at the clerk, who read it. He gave the letter back, protesting—I could tell that. An argument was going on, *about* me. I felt like a stupid fool, unable to say a word, I couldn't even understand what was being said. But, finally, sadly, the judge turned to me.

I had to go before the *Mahgama Sharia*, he explained. It was the Muslim high court which examined all possibly non-authentic converts to the Islamic religion seeking to enter Mecca. It was absolute that no non-Muslim could enter Mecca . . . .

Right outside the airport was a mosque, and above the airport was a huge, dormitory-like building, four tiers high. It was semi-dark, not long before dawn, and planes were regularly taking off and landing, their landing lights sweeping the runways, or their wing and tail lights blinking in the sky. Pilgrims from Ghana, Indonesia, Japan, and Russia, to mention some, were moving to and from the dormitory where I was being taken. I don't believe that motion picture cameras ever have filmed a human spectacle more colorful than my eyes took in. We reached the dormitory and began climbing, up to the fourth, top tier, passing members of every race on earth. Chinese, Indonesians, Afghanistans. Many, not yet changed into the *Ihram* garb, still wore their national dress. It was like pages out of the *National Geographic* magazine. . . .

As the sleeping Muslims woke up, when dawn had broken, they almost instantly became aware of me, and we watched each other while they went about their business. I began to see what an important role the rug played in the overall cultural life of the Muslims. Each individual had a small prayer rug, and each man and wife, or large group, had a larger communal rug. These Muslims prayed on their rugs there in the compartment. Then they spread a

To symbolize their belief that all men are one before God, Moslems dress in simple white clothes while on the pilgrimage. Here they circle the Ka'ba, a house in the Great Mosque, which is the chief destination of the pilgrimage. (Ministry of Information, Riyadh, Saudi Arabia)

tablecloth over the rug and ate, so the rug became the dining room. Removing the dishes and cloth, they sat on the rug—a living room. Then they curl up and sleep on the rug—a bedroom. . . . Later in Mecca, I would see yet another use of the rug. When any kind of a dispute arose, someone who was respected highly and who was not involved would sit on a rug with the disputers around him, which made the rug a courtroom. In other instances it was a classroom.

Our tier [in the building where I was waiting for permission to go to Mecca] gave an excellent daylight view of the whole airport area. I stood at the railing, watching. Planes were landing and taking off like clockwork. Thousands upon thousands of people from all over the world made colorful patterns of movement. I saw groups leaving for Mecca, in buses, trucks, cars. I saw some setting out to walk the forty miles. I wished that I could start walking. At least,

I knew how to do that. . . .

I had just said my Sunset Prayer, *El Maghrib;* I was lying on my cot in the fourth-tier compartment, feeling blue and alone, when out of the darkness came a sudden light. . . .

In a matter of a few minutes, I was downstairs and rushing to where I had seen . . . four officials. One of them spoke functional English. I excitedly showed him the letter from Dr. Shawarbi. He read it. Then he read it aloud to the other three officials. "A Muslim from America!" I could almost see it capture their imaginations and curiosity. They were very impressed. I asked the English-speaking one if he would please do me the favor of telephoning Dr. Omar Azzam at the number I had. He was glad to do it. He got someone on the phone and conversed in Arabic.

Dr. Omar Azzam came straight to the airport. With the four officials beaming, he wrung my hand in welcome, a young, tall, powerfully built man. I'd say he was six foot three. He had an extremely polished manner. In America, he would have been called a white man, but—it struck me, hard and instantly—from the way he acted, I had no *feeling* of him being a white man. "Why didn't you call before?" he demanded of me. He showed some identification to the four officials, and he used their phone. Speaking in Arabic, he was talking with some airport officials. "Come!" he said.

In something less than half an hour, he had gotten me released, my suitcase and passport had been retrieved from Customs, and we were in Dr. Azzam's car, driving through the city of Jedda, with me dressed in the *Ihram* two towels and sandals. I was speechless at the man's attitude, and at my own physical feeling of no difference between us as human beings. I had heard for years of Muslim hospitality, but one couldn't quite imagine such warmth. . . .

That [next] morning was when I first began to reappraise the "white man." It was when I first began to perceive that "white man," as commonly used, means complexion only secondarily; primarily it described attitudes and actions. In America, "white man" meant specific attitudes and actions toward the black man, and toward all other non-white men. But in the Muslim world, I had seen that men with white complexions were more genuinely brotherly than anyone else had ever been.

That morning was the start of a radical alteration in my whole outlook about "white" men. . . .

The Azzam family were very elated that I was qualified and accepted to go to Mecca. I had lunch at the Jedda Palace. Then I slept again for several hours, until the telephone awakened me.

It was Muhammad Abdul Azziz Maged, the Deputy Chief of Protocol for Prince Faisal. "A special car will be waiting to take you to Mecca, right after your dinner," he told me. He advised me to eat heartily, as the Hajj rituals require plenty of strength.

I was beyond astonishment by then.

Two young Arabs accompanied me to Mecca. A well-lighted, modern turnpike highway made the trip easy. Guards at intervals along the way took one look at the car, and the driver made a sign, and we were passed through, never even having to slow down. I was, all at once, thrilled, important, humble, and thankful.

Mecca, when we entered, seemed as ancient as time itself. Our car slowed through the winding streets, lined by shops on both sides and with buses, cars, and trucks, and tens of thousands of pilgrims from all over the earth were everywhere.

The car halted briefly at a place where a *Mutawaf* [guide] was waiting for me. He wore the white skullcap and long nightshirt garb that I had seen at the airport. He was a short, dark-skinned Arab named Muhammad. He spoke no English whatever.

We parked near the Great Mosque. We performed our ablution and entered. Pilgrims seemed to be on top of each other, there were so many, lying, sitting, sleeping, praying, walking.

My vocabulary cannot describe the new mosque that was being built around the Ka'ba. I was thrilled to realize that it was only one of the tremendous rebuilding tasks under the direction of young Dr. Azzam, who had just been my host. The Great Mosque of Mecca, when it is finished, will surpass the architectural beauty of India's Taj Mahal.

Carrying my sandals I followed the *Mutawaf.* Then I saw the Ka'ba, a huge black stone house in the middle of the Great Mosque. It was being circumambulated by thousands upon thousands of praying pilgrims, both sexes, and every size, shape, color, and race in the world. I knew the prayer to be uttered when the pilgrim's eyes first perceive the Ka'ba. Translated, it is "O God, You are peace, and peace derives from You. So greet us, O Lord, with peace." Upon entering the Mosque, the pilgrim should try to kiss the Ka'ba if possible, but if the crowds prevent him getting that close, he touches it, and if the crowds prevent that, he raises his hand and cries out "*Takbir!* " ("God is great!"). I could not get within yards. "*Takbir!* "

My feeling there in the House of God was a numbness. My *Mutawaf* led me in the crowd of praying, chanting pilgrims, moving seven times around the Ka'ba. Some were bent and wizened with age; it was a sight that stamped itself on the brain. I saw incapacitated pilgrims being carried by others. Faces were enraptured in their faith. The seventh time around, I prayed two Rak'a [prayer or prayers], prostrating myself, my head on the floor. The first prostration, I prayed the Quran verse "Say He is God, the one and only"; the second prostration: "Say O you who are unbelievers, I worship not that which you worship." . . .

The *Mutawaf* and I next drank water from the well of Zem Zem. Then we ran between the two hills, Safa and Marwah, where Hagar wandered over the same earth searching for water for her child Ishmael.

Three separate times, after that, I visited the Great Mosque and circumambulated the Ka'ba. The next day we set out after sunrise toward Mount Arafat, thousands of us, crying in unison: "*Labbayka! Labbayka!* " and "Allah Akbar!" Mecca is surrounded by the crudest-looking mountains I have ever seen; they seem to be made of the slag from a blast furnace. No vegetation is on them at all. Arriving about noon, we prayed and chanted from noon until sunset, and the *Asr* (afternoon) and *Maghrib* (sunset) special prayers were performed.

Finally, we lifted our hands in prayer and thanksgiving, repeating Allah's words: "There is no God but Allah. He has no partner. His are authority and praise. Good emanates from Him and He has power over all things."

Standing on Mount Arafat had concluded the essential rites of being a pilgrim to Mecca. No one who missed it could consider himself a pilgrim. . . .

About twenty of us Muslims who had finished the Hajj were sitting in a huge tent on Mount Arafat. As a Muslim from America, I was the center of attention. They asked me what about the Hajj had impressed me the most. One of the several who spoke English asked; they translated my answers for the others. My answer to that question was not the one they expected, but it drove home my point.

I said, "The *brotherhood!* The people of all races, colors, from all over the world coming together as one! It has proved to me the power of the One God." . . .

The *color-blindness* of the Muslim world's religious society and the *color-blindness* of the Muslim world's human society: these two influences had each day been making a greater impact, and an increasing persuasion against my previous way of thinking. . . .

Here is what I wrote from my heart:

> Never have I witnessed such sincere hospitality and the overwhelming spirit of true brotherhood as is practiced by people of all colors and races here in this Ancient Holy Land, the home of Abraham, Muhammad, and all the other prophets of the Holy Scriptures. For the past week, I have been utterly speechless and spellbound by the graciousness I see displayed all around me by people of *all colors.*
>
> I have been blessed to visit the Holy City of Mecca. I have made my seven circuits around the Ka'ba, led by a young *Mutawaf* named Muhammad. I drank water from the well of Zem Zem. I ran seven times back and forth between the hills of Mt. Al-Safa and Al-Marwah. I have prayed in the ancient city of Mina, and I have prayed on Mt. Arafat.

There were tens of thousands of pilgrims, from all over the world. They were of all colors, from blue-eyed blonds to black-skinned Africans. But we were all participating in the same ritual, displaying a spirit of unity and brotherhood that my experiences in America had led me to believe never could exist between the white and the non-white.

America needs to understand Islam because this is the one religion that erases from its society the race problem. Throughout my travels in the Muslim world, I have met, talked to, and even eaten with people who in America would have been considered "white"—but the "white" attitude was removed from their minds by the religion of Islam. I have never before seen *sincere* and *true* brotherhood practiced by all colors together, irrespective of their color.

You may be shocked by these words coming from me. But on this pilgrimage what I have seen, and experienced, has forced me to *re-arrange* much of my thought-patterns previously held, and to *toss aside* some of my previous conclusions. . . .

During the past eleven days here in the Muslim world, I have eaten from the same plate, drunk from the same glass, and slept in the same bed (or on the same rug)—while praying to the *same God*—with fellow Muslims, whose eyes were the bluest of blue, whose hair was the blondest of blond, and whose skin was the whitest of white. And in the *words* and in the *actions* and in the *deeds* of the "white" Muslims, I felt the same sincerity that I felt among the black African Muslims of Nigeria, Sudan, and Ghana.

We were *truly* all the same (brothers)—because their belief in one God had removed the "white" from their minds, the "white" from their *behavior*, and the "white" from their *attitude*.

I could see from this, that perhaps if white Americans could accept the Oneness of God, then perhaps, too, they could accept in *reality* the Oneness of Man—and cease to measure and hinder and harm others in terms of their "differences" in color. . . .

All praise is due to Allah, the Lord of all the Worlds.

Sincerely,
EL-HAJJ MALIK EL-SHABAZZ
(MALCOLM X)

"If God Wills It"

Fear not the man who fears God.
—Arab proverb

❧INTRODUCTION: Although many Moslems in the Middle East, like many Christians in America, do not keep the duties of their faith perfectly, religion is a more important part of everyday life in the Middle East than it is in the United States. It exerts a great influence over the behavior of most people, and it can be said that the average person's philosophy of life is a religious one.

The following selection examines the way in which Islam permeates everyday life in a village. The author, a professor at the American University of Beirut, Lebanon, feels that the main characteristics of the villager's philosophy of life are a feeling of dependency on God, fear of God's punishment on earth and after death and a deep-seated respect for tradition and the past. In addition, the villager is traditionally polite and generous to all.

Professor Lutfiyya studied a traditional village in Jordan, but much of what he says pertains to city dwellers as well.[18]❧

DEPENDENCY ON GOD

"*In sha'a Allah,*" or "if God wills it," looms large in the thinking of the average inhabitant of Baytin. Implicit in this saying is the fatalism which is characteristic of most villagers. One hears this phrase repeated constantly. A visitor may ask a villager: "Are you going to send your son to school next year?" The inevitable answer is: *"In sha'a Allah."* No further explanation is added or needed. One is apt to hear a mother telling her son who is on his way to school: "If God wills it, you will succeed in passing your examination today." His reply then would be: "If God wills it."

If a villager loses something of value, he does not stop to examine the causes for the loss but merely sighs philosophically, *"Hathihi mashi 'atu Allah,"* or "This is the will of God." Friends who come around to offer sympathy merely reinforce this belief by repeating the same saying. The author recalls once listening to an old man telling another villager who had just lost his sick cow, the only property he had, "This is the will of Allah. By taking your cow, Allah has tested your faith. Be thankful to Allah and you may be given a better cow." "You are right," replied the second villager, "this is *mashi atu Allah,* there is no God but He, and let Him be praised in all circumstances." . . .

Every villager utters certain traditional sayings several times each day to invoke the blessing of God. When he begins a task, he says aloud that he is doing it "in the name of God, the Merciful, the Compassionate." When he has finished, he offers his "thanks to God the Lord of all people" for enabling him to complete the job.

If a villager receives some aid in accomplishing a certain task, he thanks his helper by telling him, "May God pay you (*hasanat*) for the work you have done for me." The helper then answers: *"Samabak Allah,"* or "May the Lord forgive you (for me)." If the villager simply uses the phrase "thank you" to his helper, the helper reminds him, "Let your thanks be to God (*"al-shakru li-Allah"*) for He is the one who caused me to help you."

FEAR OF GOD'S PUNISHMENT

The Muslim villager, as noted above, feels that God keeps a very close watch over him. God is interested in his everyday behavior; he will be punished for his "bad" acts, and rewarded for his "good." Consequently, before the vil-

lager will commit a sin or undertake a move which might
be construed as sinful, he asks himself the question: "Would
God be pleased or displeased with my behavior?" If he
proceeds to commit the sin, he lives in fear of God's punishment and hopes that he might appease Allah by repentance
and doing good deeds in the future. . . .

In another case where a family lost its wealth, villagers
were quick to point out that the family fortune had been
acquired in a dishonest way in the first place. . . .

If a villager suffers misfortune but cannot attribute it to
any sin or wrong doing, he is apt to ask: "God, what have I
done wrong that you should punish me?" Such an attitude
is evident in the remarks made by parents who are
mistreated by their offspring.

[A] simple conversation between two friends might run
as follows:

> "Have you seen my son Ahmad today?"
> "Wa-Allah! [by God] no."
> "We have been looking for him all day. Wa-Allahi we do
> not know where he has gone."
> "What seems to be wrong with him? Wa-Allahi he strikes
> me as a good boy."
> "Wa-Allahi we do not know. He asked us to buy him a
> bicycle last night, and we said no. This morning he disap-
> peared. Wa-Allah we do not know where he has gone!"
> "That's it. If you don't get them what they want they get
> angry with you. Wa-n-Nabi [by the Prophet], children these
> days need a big stick to be broken on their backs. Wa-Allah
> al-ghazim [by God the greatest] if I were in your place I
> wouldn't look for him. When he gets hungry, he'll go home.
> Come, let me buy you a cup of coffee."
> "May God heap his abundance upon you. Wa-Allahi one's
> heart does not leave him [from worrying in such a case]. I'd
> better look for him."
> "May the Lord accompany you [in your search]."
> "And [may he be] with you." . . .

The villager often tries to appease God and to avoid His
punishment by vowing to offer Him a *dahiyya,* or a sacrifice.

Sacrifices are also offered on behalf of a dead relative. This is done with the hope that the sacrifice will please God. . . .

A DEEP-SEATED RESPECT FOR
TRADITION AND THE PAST

Muslims are taught to look to the [Koran] for inspiration and guidance in whatever they do. This holy book is said to be the most complete source of truth and wisdom. But Islam also sanctions traditional behavior and gives it precedence over innovations . . . "[A]nything of the past has precedence [over innovations]." . . .

There is a constant yearning to get back to "the good old days." Innovators are always the objects of shame and ridicule. Invariably there is an outright rejection of anything new that appears to conflict with tradition. There is always a deep respect reserved for the aged, and a heavy reliance upon sayings and proverbs in everyday conversation. . . .

The villagers are taught from childhood to show great respect for their elders. Children are often instructed to kiss the hands of older people when they are introduced to them, to be polite in the presence of elders, and to stand up and offer them their seats. They are to remain standing until the older folks are all seated. Young people are encouraged to listen to and learn from their elders. Only from older people who have lived in the past can one learn anything of value, they are told. The wisdom of the elders is seldom questioned. If one deviates from this norm and dares to challenge the ideas of an older person, he is put in his place immediately by the latter, who tells him: "How would you know that? You were only born yesterday."

POLITENESS AND GENEROSITY

. . . The filial piety demanded and expected of all Muslims is considered a religious duty. Ill-treatment of parents or disobedience to them constitutes a sin. The child is considered to owe his parents a great debt for bringing him up. . . .

Children, on the whole, are very obedient to their parents. Only the most impolite child dares to cross his legs, smoke, or utter profanity in the presence of his parents. No child dares to sit down while his father is still standing, or to start eating before his father. The polite child faces his parents with utter humility. He does not talk back if rebuked, or raise his hand in retaliation if struck . . . .

This complete obedience to parents does not end at an early age. It continues even after the child is married and lives away from his father and mother. . . .

Tradition and religion combine to instruct the villager on how to be a good relative and neighbor. Every one is expected to visit his neighbors and relatives at their homes on religious holidays. . . .

The etiquette of greeting and salutations is also highly formalized. When villagers meet in the street, the young must invariably greet the old first out of respect. Upon entering a house, the guest is required to give it his blessing. . . .

The villagers often quote a saying that runs: "If guests do not enter a house, angels do not enter it." This is their way of indicating that such a house is not blessed by God. In view of this traditional understanding, the villager usually puts aside any work that he might be doing for the moment, regardless of how pressing the work might be, in order to welcome any guests. . . . He then shakes hands with each guest several times. The guests are then led into the house, offered the best seats, and every effort is made to provide for their comfort. A cool reception in [the] eyes of the villagers is considered bad taste and reflects bad manners.

The host feels it his duty to make the guest feel welcome. He will say that he is delighted and honored by the visit and inquire why his guest has not visited more often. The host will do everything in his power to give [the] impression that he has no work to do, so as to spare his guest the feeling that he may be imposing. For fear that his guest might feel lonely, the host will not leave him except under very unusual circumstances.

The ritual of hospitality commences by offering coffee to the guest immediately after his arrival. The guest accepts the coffee readily because it would be an insult to his host to reject it. . . .

The first [offer] of hospitality is followed by offering food to the guest. The guest shows more restraint when food is brought. He politely tells his host that he is full and at the moment has no desire to eat. He further volunteers the information, whether or not it be true, that he has eaten very recently. The host on the other hand, will appear very apologetic for the simplicity of the food he has to offer. But he will insist that his guest partake of all the food he desires.

The guest will be served the very best of food as long as he remains. . . .

★POSTSCRIPT: Many Middle Easterners believe that much or all of what happens in the world is the result of God's will. This belief does not necessarily conflict with the idea of free will as described in the following excerpt[19]:

> People ask me if I believe in Fate—Kismet.
> Suppose you are on board a ship, a very enormous ship. In that ship you may do as you please. You may sleep, wake, eat, bathe, play, walk in the way that you wish to. You may go where you wish to go. But there is one limit to your freedom. If you go too far you are lost in the sea. To me Kismet is like that. There is freedom, liberty, room for initiative; but each of us is placed on a certain ship, and the ship we are placed on determines our limits. . . .
> When we pray we must ask God to help us to do the things that are our particular destiny.★

The Grocer and the Chief

&sINTRODUCTION: As we have seen, the traditions in the Middle
East are strong and have served an important function in the
lives of the people. As long as the culture remained relatively
stable, the tried and tested ways of the past were useful in
preserving a sense of security. However, as technological changes began to take hold in the Middle East, along with new ideas
from cultures outside the area, the old ways began to give way to
new ways, and new values began to take root. The process of
modernization is complex and no one is quite sure how to
measure it. Nor is there agreement on which aspects of modernization are good and which are bad. Industrialization, for example, is usually considered an important part of the
modernization process, yet we all suffer from the effects of pol-
lution, a by-product of industrialization. Modernization, then, is
a mixed blessing, leading to a better society in some ways but
not in others.

During the modernization process attitudes, values and behavior change. Old ideas are modified and new ways of doing
things become accepted. A man whose mother was housebound
and wore the veil all her life may send his daughter to college. A
girl may break tradition and insist that she, not her parents,
should be the one to choose her husband. Such alteration in behavior and values are characteristic of social change.

In the following selection, the process of social change is
symbolized by two characters, the grocer and the chief. The
author is an American scholar who has studied social change in
the Middle East by using trained local interviewers to ask identical questions of sample groups of people in several Middle
Eastern countries. The selection describes two visits four years
apart to the same village in Turkey by different inter-

124

viewers.[20]ᐧ

The village of Balgat lies about eight kilometers [five miles] out of Ankara [the capital], in the southerly direction. It does not show on the standard maps and it does not figure in the standard histories. I first heard of it in the autumn of 1950 and most Turks have not heard of it today. Yet the story of the Middle East today is encapsulated in the recent career of Balgat. Indeed, the personal meaning of modernization in underdeveloped lands can be traced, in miniature, through the lives of two Balgati— the Grocer and the Chief. . . .

The Chief was a man of few words on many subjects . . . . He was also a man of many words on a few subjects . . . . Only when the issues involved first principles of conduct did he consider the occasion appropriate for pronouncing judgment. . . .

The Chief has so little trouble with the first principles because he desires to be, and usually is [the spokesman for], traditional Turkish virtues. His themes are obedience, courage, loyalty—the classic values. . . . For the daily round of village life these are adequate . . . and as the Chief has been outside of his village only to fight in two wars he has never found his austere code wanting. . . . When [Tosun, the interviewer] asked what he wished for his two grown sons, for example, the Chief replied promptly: "I hope they will fight as bravely as we fought and know how to die as my generation did."

With his life in Balgat the Chief is contented. At sixty-three his desires have been quieted and his ambitions achieved. To Tosun's question on contentment he replied with another question: "What could be asked more? God has brought me to this mature age without much pain, has given me sons and daughters, has put me at the head of my village, and has given me strength of brain and body at this age. Thanks be to Him."

The Grocer is a very different style of man. Though born and bred in Balgat, he lives in a different world, an expan-

A traditional village meeting, in which village leaders sit together in a circle, is still the most common method of resolving local issues in the Middle East. (United Nations)

sive world, populated more actively with imaginings and fantasies—hungering for whatever is different and unfamiliar. Where the Chief is contented, the Grocer is restless. To Tosun's probe, the Grocer replied . . . : "I have told you I want better things. I would have liked to have a bigger grocery shop in the city, have a nice house there, dress in nice civilian clothes." [A]fter each respondent had named the greatest problem facing the Turkish people . . . Tosun asked [each one] what he would do about this problem if he were the president of Turkey. Most responded by stolid silence—the traditional way of handling "projective questions" which require people to imagine themselves or things to be different from what they really are. Some were shocked by the impropriety of the very question. "My God! How can you say such a thing?" gasped the shepherd. "How can I . . . I cannot . . . a poor villager . . . master of, the whole world!"

The Chief . . . made . . . reply to this question with another question: "I am hardly able to manage a village, how shall I manage Turkey?" . . . When the Grocer's turn came, he did not wait. . . . As president of Turkey, he said: "I would make roads for the villagers to come to towns to see the world and would not let them stay in their holes all their life."

To get out of his hole the Grocer even declared himself ready—and in this he was quite alone in Balgat—to live outside of Turkey. This came out when Tosun asked another of his projective questions: "If you could not live in Turkey, where would you want to live?" The standard reply of the villagers was that they would not live, could not imagine living, anywhere else. The forced choice simply was ignored.

When Tosun persisted ("Suppose you had to leave Turkey?") he teased an extreme reaction out of some Balgati. The shepherd, like several other wholly routinized personalities, finally replied that he would rather kill himself. The . . . peasant can more easily imagine destroying the self than relocating it in an unknown, i.e., frightful, setting.

The Chief again responded with the clear and confident voice of traditional man. "Nowhere," he said. "I was born here, grew old here, and hope God will permit me to die here." To Tosun's probe, the Chief replied firmly: "I wouldn't move a foot from here." Only the Grocer found no trouble in imagining himself outside of Turkey, living in a strange land. Indeed he seemed fully prepared, as a man does when he has already posed a question to himself many times. "America," said the Grocer, and, without waiting for Tosun to ask him why, stated his reason: "Because I have heard that it is a nice country, and with possibilities to be rich even for the simplest persons."

Tosun had been instructed to ask each person whether others ever came to him for advice, and if so what they

wanted advice about. Naturally, the Balgati whose advice
was most sought was the Chief, who reported: "Yes, that is
my main duty, to give advice." (Tosun: "What about?")
"About all that I or you could imagine, even about their
wives and how to handle them, and how to cure their sick
cow."

Rather more surprising was Tosun's discovery that some
Balgati went for advice also to the disreputable Grocer.
What did they ask his advice about? "What to do when they
go to Ankara, where to go and what to buy, how much to
sell their things for." . . . This suggested . . . a new role for
the Grocer as cosmopolitan specialist in how to avoid
wooden nickels in the big city. Also, how to spend the real
nickels one got. For the Grocer was a man of clear convic-
tions on which coffee-houses played the best radio
programs and which were the best movies to see in Ankara
. . . .

Movies . . . were his avenue to the wider world of his
dreams. It was in a movie that he had first glimpsed what
a real grocery store could be like—"with walls made of iron
sheets, top to floor and side to side, and on them standing
myriads of round boxes, clean and all the same, dressed
like soldiers in a great parade." This fleeting glimpse . . .
had provided the Grocer with an . . . image of how his fan-
tasy world might look. It was here, quite likely, that he had
shaped the ambition earlier confided to Tosun, "to have a
bigger grocery shop in the city." . . .

BALGAT REVISITED: 1954

I reached Ankara in April after a [trip] through the Middle East. . . . I called a transportation service and explained
that I [and my interviewers] wanted to go out the following day, a Sunday, to a village some eight kilometers south
that might be hard to reach. As I wanted to spend the day,
would the driver meet me at eight a.m. and bring along his
lunch? . . . [The next morning when the car arrived] we
got in and settled back for a rough haul. Twenty minutes

later . . . the driver said briskly: "There's Balgat."

We looked puzzled at each other until Tosun's words of 1950 recurred to us: "It could have been half an hour to Ankara if it had a road." . . . Feeling strange, we made our way along the erratic path through the old village, led and followed by a small horde of children, to the house of the Chief. . . .

The Chief looked as I had imagined. His cheeks a bit more sunken, perhaps, but the whole presence quite familiar. Tall, lean, hard, he walked erect and looked me straight in the eye. His own eyes were . . . black and did not waver as be stretched out a handful of long, bony fingers. "*Gun aydin, Bey Efendim,*" he said. "Good day, sir, you are welcome to my house." . . .

The Chief heard me through gravely, and when he spoke I knew I was in. He bypassed the set of formulas available to him—for rejecting or evading my implied request—and responded directly to the point. I was right to have come to see Balgat for myself. He remembered [Tosun] well . . . . Much had changed in Balgat since that time. Indeed, Balgat was no longer a village. It had, only last month, been incorporated as a district of Greater Ankara. This was why they now had a new headquarters of metropolitan police, and a bus service, and electricity, and a supply of pure water which would soon be in operation, Where there had been 50 houses, there were now over 500, and even he, the *Muhtar* [chief], did not know any more all the people living here.

Yes, he had lived in Balgat all his life and never in all that time seen so much happen as had come to pass in these four years. . . . Tahir [my interviewer] and I, he said, could walk about Balgat entirely as we wished and speak with whomsoever it pleased us to honor. . . . We set out for a stroll around Balgat. Our next goal was to find the Grocer.

After a couple of bends and turns, we came to a coffeehouse. . . . We stopped at the door and bade the proprietor "*Gun aydin!*" He promptly rushed forward with two chairs. . . . In a matter of minutes, the male population of Balgat was assembled around our two chairs, squatting, sitting on the ground, looking us over with open and friendly curiosity. . . . [M]any changes had occurred in Balgat. [Our respondent's] inventory included . . . all the by-now familiar items: road, bus, electricity, water. . . .

Other voices were finally raised. . . . [A] farmer undertook to explain why he was no longer a farmer. He had retired, over a year ago, because there was no one left in Balgat to do an honest day's work for an honest day's lira. Or rather two lira—the absurd rate, he said, to which the daily wage of farm laborers had been driven by the competition of the . . . Ankara labor market. Now, all the so-called able-bodied men of Balgat had forsaken the natural work praised by Allah and swarmed off to the Ankara factories where, for eight hours of so-called work, they could get five lira a day. . . . Surprised, we asked whether it was indeed true that there were no farm laborers left in Balgat any more. "How many of you," we quickly rephrased the question, " work on farms now?" Four hands were raised among the twenty-nine present, and all of these turned out to be small holders working their own land. . . . [It] became clear that most of the male population of Balgat was now . . . working in the factories and construction gangs of Ankara—for cash. . . .

How did they spend the cash they earned? Well, there were now over 100 radio receivers in Balgat as compared to the lone receiver Tosun had found four years earlier. There were also seven refrigerators, four tractors, three trucks, and one Dodge sedan. Most houses now had electric lights and that had to be paid for. Also, since there was so little farming in Balgat now, much of the food came from the outside (even milk!) and had to be bought in the grocery stores, of which there were now seven in Balgat. . . . How was the Grocer doing? "Which one?" The original one, the great fat one that was here four years ago? "O, that one, he's dead!" . . .

"What a lousy break," growled Tabir . . . as we started

back toward the house of the Chief. He was speaking of the Grocer. I didn't know what to say. . . . I felt only a sense of large . . . regret. . . .

THE PASSING OF BALGAT

While dressing slowly the next morning, I planned my strategy for lunch with the Chief. Had he learned anything from the Grocer?

Most villagers were closer to his [the Grocer's] situation than to the Chief's. The Grocer then was my problem and, as symbol . . . my man. It was he who dramatized most poignantly the personal meaning of the big change now under way throughout the Middle East. . . .

Maybe [he was like] the eighteenth-century field-hand of England who had left . . . to find a better life in London or Manchester. . . . [or] the nineteenth-century French farm lad . . . who had gone off to San Francisco to hunt gold and, finding none, had then tried his hand as mason, mechanic. . . . [Once] in Balgat I reported directly to the Chief. . . .

Things had changed . . . [the Chief told us again] and a sign of the gravity of these changes was that he—of a lineage that had always been *Muhtars* [chiefs] and landowners—was no longer a farmer. Nor was he long to be *Muhtar*. After the coming election, next month, the incorporation of Balgat into Greater Ankara was to be completed and thereafter it would be administered under the general municipal system. "I am the last *Muhtar* of Balgat, and I am happy that I have seen Balgat end its history in this way that we are going." The new ways, then, were not bringing evil with them?

"No, people will have to get used to different ways and then some of the excesses, particularly among the young, will disappear. The young people are in some ways a serious disappointment; they think more of clothes and good times than they do of duty and family and country."

And as his two sons were no longer to be farmers, what

of them? The Chief's voice did not challenge, nor did his eyes cloud over, as he replied:

"They are as the others. They think first to serve themselves and not the nation. They had no wish to go to the battle in Korea, where Turkey fights before the eyes of all the world. They are my sons and I speak no ill of them, but I say only that they are as all the others."

I felt at this moment a warmth toward the Chief. . . . His sons had not, after all, learned to fight bravely and die properly. . . . Yet the old Chief bore stoically what must have been a crushing disappointment. These two sons through whom he had hoped to relive his own bright dreams of glory had instead become shopkeepers. The elder son owned a grocery store and the younger one owned Balgat's first clothing store. . . .

We went first to the elder son's grocery store. . . . The central floor space was set out with merchandise. . . . Built into [the counter] was a cash drawer and above each surface a hygienic white porcelain fixture for fluorescent lighting.

Along the walls . . . rows of shelves running from "top to floor and side to side, and on them standing myriads of round boxes, clean and all the same, dressed like soldiers in a great parade." The Grocer's words of aspiration came leaping back as I looked admiringly around the store. His dream house had been built in Balgat—in less time than even he might have forecast—and by none other than the Chief! . . .

[W]e walked in quartet, the Chief and I ahead, the sons behind, to the clothing store of the younger son. . . . The stock inside consisted mainly of dungarees, Levis, coveralls . . . . There was a continuous and growing demand for these goods, the Chief stated solemnly, as more and more Balgati went into the labor market of Ankara. . . . In a corner of the store there was also a small stock of "gentleman's haberdashery"—readymade suits, shirts, even a rack of neckties.

The younger son, who maintained . . . a steady silence

in the presence of the Chief, replied to a direct question from me that he had as yet sold very few items from this department of the store. . . . A few, indeed, had purchased . . . neckties which remained to be exhibited in public . . . . I remembered Tosun's rather nasty comment about the Grocer: "He even wore some sort of a necktie." As one saw it now, the Grocer had shown the way, and it was now only a hop, skip, and jump through history to the point where most men of Balgat would be wearing neckties. . . .

The afternoon was about over before I got an appropriate occasion to ask about the Grocer. It came when the talk returned to the villagers' favorite topic of how much better life had become during the past four years. . . . Again they illustrated the matter by [mentioning] the new shops in Balgat and the things they had to sell that many people could buy. There was even a new barber shop, opened last month. . . . "How are these new grocery shops better than the old grocery shop of years ago owned by the fat grocer who is now dead?" I asked. [T]he question served to lead to another: What sort of man had the Grocer been?

The answers were . . . [short], consisting mainly of pro forma expressions of goodwill toward the departed. . . . How had the Grocer dressed? Why had he been so interested in the life of Ankara? The light finally shone in one of the wiser heads and he spoke the words I was seeking:

"Ah, he was the cleverest of us all. We did not know it then, but he saw better than all what lay in the path ahead. We have none like this among us now. He was a prophet . . . ."

The ancient village I had known for what now seemed only four short years was passing, had passed. The Grocer was dead. The Chief—"the last *Muhtar* of Balgat"—had reincarnated the Grocer in the flesh of his sons.

A Lebanese Family

☙INTRODUCTION: In "The Grocer and the Chief," we saw how rapidly change can come to a traditional community. In a few short years, a substantial portion of a community can change many of its customs. Such rapid social change most often occurs in connection with economic changes, for example, industrialization of an area.

In certain parts of the Middle East, especially in the big cities, the kinds of change described in "The Grocer and the Chief" have been going on for thirty or forty years. As a result, the lifestyles of many urban dwellers in the Middle East are very similar to the lifestyles of Westerners. The family introduced in the following selection lives in Beirut, Lebanon, but it might just as well be a family in Istanbul, Cairo, Teheran or other cities in the Middle East. The selection depicts part of a typical day in their lives.[21]☙

"*Habeebty* Samar, it's past six o'clock and your aunt did so want to see you, especially as you promised to be home early. . . . Samar, dear, you told me you would be here by five, latest."

"I'm sorry."

Her mother sighed, put down her sewing and lit a cigarette from the box on the round damascene wood table in front of the sofa on which she was sitting. . . .

"I'm sorry I was late. I was drawing."

"You spend so much time with this art of yours . . . and then you come back and study all evening, The family never sees you, so I was very sad that you —"

134

"I forgot the time, Mama."

"I wish you would pay attention when I tell you something, dear. I know you don't do it on purpose, and it would be all right if you were living alone, but you must help me sometimes. You're big, now. I had a very tiring day shopping, and I told you only at lunchtime that your aunt would be coming for tea and I needed your help."

"I'm sorry." She took her coat off and went to hang it up in the small, dark vestibule. Her mother did not look up when she reappeared.

"You're a good girl, Samar, but you're always in the clouds . . . . . Samar, are you listening?"

"Yes, Mama." She had only been hearing. . . .

"What are you always thinking about, Samar?"

"Nothing special." She felt very tired, there was Hegel [to study] and she wanted a cigarette, for both of which she had to be alone in her room.

"Where are you going, dear?"

"To my room. I have some work for tomorrow."

"Well, supper is quite soon, when your father comes. Tell Farid, he's in his room."

"Yes, Mama."

[The door of her own room] was locked.

She gave a polite knock. After some time the key turned and the door was flung open. Her brother, his long form enveloped in cigarette smoke, had made himself [at] home on her bed, with his books strewn over the floor and the dark green . . . rug kicked halfway under the bed. Both the overhead and the small bedside lights were on, and the window was wide open.

"And what, may I ask, is wrong with *your* room?" She put her books on the large desk in the corner and automatically began arranging them with the others.

"Someone broke one of my windows," Farid mumbled, regaining the bed. "Shhh. I have an exam tomorrow."

"Who broke one of your windows?"

"I did. Shut up, woman."

"And whose cigarettes are you smoking?" She opened

Many modern Middle-Eastern women are indistinguishable from their sisters in the West. This young woman is listening to language tapes at a U.N.-assisted teacher-training college in Libya.
(United Nations)

the white-painted cupboard, which took up half a wall, and bent down. The rubber boot which usually contained her cigarette packet was empty. "May I ask for one of my cigarettes, please?" . . .

"How dare you accuse me of pinching your cigarettes—who bought them for you, anyway? And besides, [mother] knows you smoke."

"Of course," she murmured with rising apprehension, knowing her mother's quick temper.

"She does, she does. She told me she'd found ashes under your bed. So what does your dear brother do? He moves in here and smokes and claims the ashes as his own.

"She thinks you're in your room." . . .

"Sit down, dear, sit down." She did so, in the large chair of which she was particularly proud, having bought it second hand with her own money. "You've been smoking like a chimney, right? For over six months, right? And there's nothing Mama doesn't find out about, right?"

"I don't care."

"I'll bet you don't."

"Thank you, Farid," she said, after a short silence, during which they had been scrutinizing each other, "thank you. But I must study." . . .

"All right. All right. And anyway, Father has just come. So supper [will be soon]."

He shut the door behind him with a bang and she surveyed the crumpled bed spread, the ashes on the floor, on the bed, on the bedside table, the smoke in a thick, tiered cloud.

With a tired sigh she smoothed the bed, picked up Hegel (sixty interminable and interchangeable pages from *Phenomenology of Spirit*) and began to read. Thirty minutes later she had fifty-five pages ahead of her and her hair down— she had been pulling strand after strand of straight black hair from her once neat plait.

Farid barged in noisily, remarked something about disheveled females, and added that supper was ready.

All three were seated and had begun the usual meal of olives, tomatoes, cold meat, cheese, and bread, when she finally appeared.

"And how is Samar?" Her father enquired as usual, getting the usual reply.

"You look pale —"

"Exams, Father," she volunteered hesitantly. He [carefully] searched her face for a few moments and then asked for the cheese. Her mother had always claimed that Samar had inherited her absentmindedness from her father. He was a good man, everybody agreed; having been in the same job in an insurance company for twenty-five years; moreover, he was honest, kind, had the accepted political beliefs of a man of his age . . . and was settled at the age of forty-seven with too much fat and too little hair.

"Really, Fuad, can't we do anything about these neighbors?"

The news blared forth, monotonous and loud, from all the open windows.

"What can you expect, dear? If we ask them, they get insulted; if we warn them, they start a feud. I'd rather bear it for a few minutes."

"I still think —"

"Father," Farid broke in, looking for the olives which Samar passed silently, "Professor Hani told me you and he had been classmates."

"Oh yes, Antoine Hani. . . . We saw him at that cocktail party we went to last week, didn't we, dear?"

"I think I remember. . . . Samar, will you pass the water?"

The meal was very much as usual. Once or twice remarks were addressed in her direction, and she replied appropriately. She was thinking about her father, and that very little intimacy had ever emerged between them. . . . What she would remember of him were his very rare but destructive outbursts of fury, which were immediately followed by tenderness (rarely an apology). She had been the recipient of one, two years before, when she had inadvertently revealed that she had read *Lady Chatterley's Lover.* His fury had nailed her to the wall, and there had been no tenderness to follow, because she had been too dazed to play her part in the small game of kissing him lightly, receiving a pat, and forgetting the whole thing. She had not even locked herself into her room but had started a loud, raucous card game with Farid, who had been sympathetic and cooperative, having himself frequently been the target of such outbursts. . . .

"I have a confession, Father," Farid began, his eyes bright, fingers playing with a knife.

"Well?"

"You'll find the paint a little scraped on the right door of the car. I'm sorry."

"I see. And when did this happen?"

"This afternoon; I was backing out, and —"

"—And the other fellow didn't see you? Yes. I seem to have heard this before." A muscle began to twitch in Farid's cheek, but he said nothing, keeping his eyes on his father. "It's all right by me—after all, it's high time I got used to it.

He laughed with genuine amusement, and Farid looked surprised but wary. "As long as you pay for the repairs."

"But—I haven't got the money—I was hoping —"

"I know you were, son. But remember our agreement. If you take the car you're responsible."

"Yes, but —"

"Fuad, never mind this once." With a pleading look at her husband she got up and began to fuss with the plates. Samar rose to help; it was the maid's evening off.

"You get a decent allowance, and if you choose to squander it foolishly you will have to look for a job. I'm sorry, but you're almost twenty-one, and I think it's high time you grew up." He pushed his chair back with a pleasant smile. Farid kept his face clear of all expression. . . .

"If you've a class at seven-thirty tomorrow, dear, you'd better eat something." His mother hovered about the table.

"It's an exam, not a class," he replied irritably.

"All the more reason to eat something."

"I have eaten!"

"You know, I agree with your father. He started working at seventeen —"

"Oh, we all know he's a paragon." His voice was low, and did not travel to the sitting-room, where the subject of the conversation was reading a newspaper.

"Farid . . ." Samar murmured.

"You shut up! And keep out of this."

She removed his plate with great calm, took the tablecloth, shook it out of the window, folded it, and put it in the drawer with the napkins.

"And your martyred silences don't impress me," he finished savagely, stood up, uttered a loud and cheerful "Goodnight," and slammed three doors in succession.

"He has become so difficult her mother [said] . . . having returned the farewell. . . .

"He's spoilt."

"A little, maybe, but he can be such a good boy. Samar placed a vase of flowers on the table. . . .

"Never mind, Mama. Goodnight."

The Islamic Backlash

&INTRODUCTION: As we have seen in the last two selections, change has come rapidly to many parts of the Middle East, exposing traditional Moslem cultures to modern Western attitudes and practices. The lifestyle described in "A Lebanese Family," for example, could be found in almost any European or North American family. But rapid social change often brings a reaction, and this is exactly what has happened in the Middle East in recent years.

Since the mid-1970s, a movement to revive traditional Moslem beliefs and laws, often referred to as Islamic fundamentalism, has been gaining momentum throughout the Middle East. Largely a backlash against Western influence, the movement has been especially critical of capitalism and communism, both seen as Western systems that foster a secular, materialistic way of life.

The most extreme form of the backlash took place in Iran in 1979 when a full-scale revolution overthrew the king, Shah Mohammed Reza Pahlavi, whose ancestors had ruled Iran for more than 2,000 years. In the Shah's place, the revolution implanted an Islamic government under the control of religious leaders. In the eyes of the revolutionaries, the Shah was a pawn of American capitalism, which in turn was seen as the "devil," bringing temptation in the form of "flashy" consumer goods, "corrupt" music and art and scantily clad "liberated" women.

For almost thirty years, Iran had been going through a rapid process of modernization, financed by oil money and encouraged by the Shah. Western consumer goods, including television, brought European and American customs into many Iranian homes, and modern education brought many Iranian women out of the home and into the workplace beside men, as

141

in the case of Najmeh Najafi, the young woman in the selection
"My Mind Was Open." Such changes alarmed many Iranians
who favored the old ways. Religious leaders, called *mullahs,*
warned the people that their traditional way of life was under attack. These concerns corresponded with growing fears among
Iranians that the Shah was becoming less and less tolerant of
political opposition. While the Shah encouraged social and
economic modernization, he refused to share any of his political power with the people, and jailed and tortured thousands
who opposed his autocratic rule. One estimate is that between
1953 and 1973 about 125,000 Iranians died either by torture or
by execution.

The hopes of the people focused on an exiled *mullah,* the
Ayatollah Khomeini, who led the opposition to the Shah from
his temporary residence in France. This opposition movement
came to a head in 1979 when the Iranian people rose up and
forced the Shah to abdicate his throne. The Ayatollah, upon his
triumphant return to Iran, immediately set about turning back
the clock. Political power was turned over to the *mullahs;* people
believing in secular democracy or socialism were labeled "communists" and either jailed or killed. The universities were closed
to rid them of Western influence, and Westernized women, a
small minority, were forced to abandon cosmetics and Western
dresses and to cover themselves from head to foot in a *chador,* a
tent-like cloak designed to hide the shape of the body. Only the
hands and face may be seen in public.The Ayatollah intended to
make Iran a "pure Islamic republic," and anyone promoting
other ideas was considered the enemy.

In October of 1979, when the U.S. allowed the exiled Shah
to come to New York for medical treatment, student supporters
of the Ayatollah captured the American Embassy in Tehrân and
took ninety hostages, sixty-three of them American. Two weeks
later all women and blacks were released. Despite worldwide
criticism for breaking international law, the Iranians held fifty-
three Americans for one year and seventy-nine days, indicating
how deeply they believed in the wisdom of their revolution. The
capture of the hostages was Iran's message to the world: we will
resist any outside influence in telling us what to do or believe.
Since the release of the hostages, Iran has continued to go its
own way in the world, and in 1980 it went to war with neighboring Iraq, in part to further the cause of its Islamic revolution.

In 1984, vice squads patrolled Tehrân in a renewed campaign against "corrupt" Western influences. The director of the Office for Propagation of Virtues and Inhibition of Vices was quoted as saying the patrols would first attack "blatant offenses," such as breaches of the Islamic dress code, but would also deal with "concealed offenses," such as parties attended by both men and women, alcohol consumption and drug abuse.

"Under the rules of the new campaign, women insufficiently clothed will be stopped and asked to conform. If they refuse, they can be tried in a court with the power to impose up to 75 lashes in serious cases," according to a Reuters news story. "Many women have found subtle ways to rebel, such as allowing a fringe of hair to show under headscarves or wearing loose-fitting smocks instead of the traditional *chador* to cover the body."

The then president of Iran, Ali Khamenei, was quoted as saying: "Suspicious hands are at work. Some people are making calculated moves to gradually encroach on the chastity and

Iranian women, wearing the traditional chador, *chant their support for the Ayatollah Khomeini.* (Wide World Photos)

modesty of our women and restore the prerevolutionary situation. Of course, it is impossible, but our enemies are busy at it."

The campaign, which applied equally to foreigners, also concentrated on "decadent" Western rock music, video tapes and gambling. "From now on," according to Reuters, "a woman will no longer be able to dine in public with a man other than her husband. Nor will she be able to go for a drive with a boyfriend without a chaperon."

Such restrictions may seem harsh to Westerners, but they are quite acceptable to most Iranians. In the following selection, Ayatollah Khomeini, the spiritual leader of the Iranian revolution, explains some of the motives behind the Islamic backlash; these same motives help to explain the puritanical laws now being applied in Iran.

This selection is taken from a speech given by Khomeini in September of 1979, approximately eight months after the Shah was overthrown and two months before the American Embassy was taken. Notice Khomeini's ingenious use of the word "Westoxication," suggesting both the toxic influence of the West and the Iranians' intoxication with things Western, implying a drunken stupor or loss of control. The backlash was precisely a renunciation of "Westoxication."[22] ✒

God is the Guardian of those who believe
He taketh them out of darkness into light
and those who disbelieve, tyrants are their guardians and
they take them out from the light into darkness
They are the companions of the fire, therein shall they abide.
                                                    —Koran, 2:257

These are two subjects which oppose each other—"the taking out of darkness into light" and "the taking out of light into darkness"—the doing away with darkness and the taking of people to the light and, opposing this, doing away with light and taking people to darkness. This latter is the profession of the tyrants. All disharmony is darkness, all backwardness is darkness, all "westoxication" is darkness; those who turn their attention to the West and foreigners, have taken the West to be their direction of prayer. They have moved into darkness and their saints are idols.

Eastern societies which, by means of internal and external propaganda and by the orders of internal and external agents, have turned to the West, have lost themselves. They do not know themselves. They have lost their gloriousness and honor and in [their] place have put a Western mind. Their saints are idols. They have entered darkness from the light.

All the problems of Easterners and, among them, our problems and miseries, are caused by our losing ourselves. In Iran, until something has a Western name, it is not accepted. Even a drug store must have a Western name. The material woven in our factories must have something in the [L]atin script in its selvedges and a Western name is put on it.

Our streets must have Western names. Everything must have a Western color to it. Some of these writers and intellectuals either put a Western name on the books they write or, when they express an idea, they do so on behalf of a Westerner. The defect is that they are also "westoxicated" and so are we. If our books did not have these titles, or our material did not contain that script and if our drug stores did not have that name, we would pay less attention to it. When we turn to a book, a great deal of attention is paid to finding foreign words. We forget our own phrases and the word itself.

Easterners have completely forgotten their honor. They have buried it. In place of it, they have put others. These are all darknesses which a tyrant transforms us to from light. It is these very tyrants—of the past and present—who have reached out towards "westoxication." They take all their subjects and sources from the West and have given them to us. Our universities were at that time Western universities. Our economy, our culture were Western. We completely forgot ourselves.

I recall that a member of the family of the deposed, accursed Mohammad Reza got tonsillitis and they brought a surgeon from Europe, while for the doctors here it is a

simple operation. You know what damage this does to
Iranian medicine. This is traitorous to the people of Iran
that they are introduced to the belief that, in all of its
country, there is no doctor to operate on someone's ton-
sils. How much this helps colonialism and the West! How
much self-respect of our country is lost with this way of
thinking!

When I was young, I remember my eyes weakened—they
are still weak—and at that time, Amin ol-Molk, God's Mercy
be upon him, was an eye doctor. I went to Tehrān to have
him treat my eyes. A person who knew him and me suggested I go to see Dr. Amin ol-Molk. He said, "One of the
Daulahs [of the court] had become near-sighted. He had
gone to Europe to see a doctor. The doctor asked him,
"Where are you from?" In answer, he said, "I am from Iran."
The doctor had asked, "Isn't Amin ol-Molk there?" He had
answered, "He may be, but I do not know him." That professor had then said, "Amin ol-Molk is better than we are."

We have good doctors but our minds have become
Westernized. We and they have both lost our self-respect
and our sense of nationality. If this nation does not come
out of this "westoxication," it will never find independence.

The attention of some of our women is turned to the
idea that such and such a mode must come from the West
and such and such an ornamentation must come from
there, here, so that whenever something is found there, it
is imitated here. As long as you do not put aside these im-
itations, you cannot be a human being and independent.
If you want to be independent and have them recognize
you as a nation, you must desist from imitating the West.

As long as we are in this state of imitating, we do not
wish for independence. As long as all of the words of our
writers are Western, we do not hope to have our nation be
independent. As long as these names appear on our streets
and our drug stores and our books, and our parks and in
all our things, we will not become independent. It is only
the mosques which do not have Western names and that is
because the clergymen, until now, have not succumbed.

The Ayatollah Khomeini.
(Wide World Photos)

"And those who disbelieve," disbelieve in God's blessings and realities are dark and covered in darkness. Their saints are idols. "They take them from light into darkness"—from absolute light, from guidance, from independence, from nationalism, from Islam—they take these too and put them into darkness. We have now lost ourselves. Until the lost be not found, we will not become independent. Search and find it. Search for and find the East.

As long as we are as we are, as long as our writers are as they are, as long as our intellectuals think that way, as long as our freedom-seekers seek that kind of Western freedom, it will remain as it is. They cry out that here is suffocation, there is no freedom. What has happened that there is no freedom?

They say, "these clergymen do not allow men and women to turn somersaults together in the water. These clergymen do not let our young people go to bars or gambling houses and seek out prostitutes. They do not allow our radio and television to show naked women and that type of ugly lewdness. They do not allow our children and young people to be entertained." This is an imported kind of a freedom which has come from the West. It is a colonialistic freedom, that is, colonialist countries dictate to those who are traitors to their own countries so that they can promote these freedoms. They are free to take heroin. They are free to smoke hashish. They are free to go to gambling houses. They are free to go to houses of entertainment and, as a result, our young people, who must be active in relation to the fate and destiny of their country, become indifferent.

An indifferent person cannot think for a country. Those who are and have been deceived from abroad are foreign agents and they promote prostitution. The promotion of these actions pulls our young people towards corruption. As a result, thoughts about what goes on in this country are put out of their heads. In place of serious minds, silly minds appear. As a result, the person who should be a human being, who thinks about his own destiny, this thought is taken away from him. This is a type of freedom which we have to call colonialist freedom. This is other than the freedom which must be amidst a people. This is a type of freedom which has come from abroad.

A young person who forms a habit with these kinds of things no longer thinks about who takes our oil, our steel, our gas. He says, "What's it to me! Leave me alone to my pleasures. Do I have time to waste, putting efforts into those things?" This is how they brought us up.

If these writers do not save our young people from these kinds of thoughts and do not promote a healthy kind of freedom and do not prevent their steps and their pens from writing about these corrupt freedoms, there is no hope that we will have an independent and free country. This hope must be taken to the grave.

Moses was appointed to take his tribe from darkness to light. The assignment of all of the prophets was that they take people away from darkness and from these things which oppose the way of humanity and enter them into the light.

An enlightened heart cannot stand by silently and watch while traditions and honor are trampled upon. An enlightened heart cannot see its people being drawn towards baseness of spirit or watch in silence while individuals around Tehrân live in slums. Yet the West wants to bring you up in such a way that you remain indifferent in all of your affairs. They do not ask why these poverty-stricken people remained in poverty and why others take our oil. It never appears in your mind that we have such problems. Look at how your hearts were fifteen, twenty years ago when there was no perseverance.

The second command which God gave to Moses was to "remind people of the Days of God." All days belong to God but some days have a particularity and because of that particularity are called the Days of God. The day that the great Prophet of Islam migrated to Medina is one of the days that is called the Day of God. The day that he conquered Mecca is one of the days called the Day of God. It is the day that God showed His strength as when an orphan who everyone rejected and who could not live in his home, after a short time, conquered Mecca. He brought the tyrants, the wealthy and the powerful under his influence and he said to them, "You are free." Thus such a day is one of the Days of God. The day of Khawareh is a day when Hazrat Ali unsheathed his sword and did away with these corrupt and cancerous tumors. This was also one of the Days of God.

These are all Days of God and they are things which relate to God. One of the Days of God is the 15th of Khordad when a people stood against a force and they did something which caused almost five months of martial law. [Khomeini here is referring to June 5, 1963, when thousands of unarmed people resisting the Shah's reforms were murdered in the streets and bazaars of Tehrân. Massacres also took place in other cities. Khomeini was arrested and exiled to Turkey and then Iraq.] But because the people had no power, they were not consolidated, they were not awake, they were defeated. Of course, they were defeated on the surface, but actually, that was a point of victory for the people.

The 17th of Shahrivar was another one of the Days of

Copyright © Cartoonists & Writers Syndicate, 1993. (Plantu)

God when a people, men, women, young people and older
people, all stood up and, in order to get their rights, were
martyred. [The 17th of Shahrivar, also known as "Black
Friday," took place on September 8, 1978. Religious leaders
and political opponents of the Shah had asked the people
to respect the martial law imposed the day before and to
stay home, but hundreds of thousands of demonstrators
flooded the streets of Tehrân. Troops opened fire and
killed more than 3,000, including 700 women. The Shah
was overthrown four months later. This speech by Khomeini
was given on the first anniversary of "Black Friday."]

    You must recall these Days of God as you have and you
must not forget them. It is these days which build human

beings. It is on these days that our young people leave their places of entertainment and enter the battlefield. These are the Divine Days. These Days awoke our people. God commands that you enter the Days of God into the minds of people.

Do not forget this great Day which passed for our people and were Days of God like the 15th of Khordad, the 17th of Shahrivar and the Day that that wicked man [the Shah] left. A nation, which had nothing, broke a force in such a way that nothing remained of it. Not only was that power opposing you, but all of the powers of the world as well. I was aware that the whole world had supported him. America was holding him up with both hands. . . .

One of the great Days of God, the Most High and Exalted, was the night when they had planned a coup d'etat when we were in Tehrân. They announced a 24-hour martial law so that even in the daytime people should not come out. Later they informed us that they had intended that night to kill [the religious] leaders of Qom [the holy city in northern Iran] and finish them off and end the job. God did not want it to be so. That was an enlightened insurrection of a responsible nation which took place and we were victorious. This was one of the Days of God which you, the enlightened and noble people of Iran, with your hearts filled with faith, should not fear. Even though they had announced martial law that day, you went into the streets and did away with that which they had wanted. They had wanted the streets to be empty so that they could bring in tanks and place them everywhere and at night be busy with their crime. God, the Most High and Exalted, answered the cries of this nation. That day is one of the great Days of God.

Do not forget that we had a 15th of Khordad and this is the beginning of the Islamic movement of Iran. Do not forget that we had a 17th of Shahrivar and we must not forget that on that day, we gave so many martyrs and so much blood and the nation arose against foreigners and their agents. Blood was spilt, but it was victorious and also all the other innumerable days.

Recall days that they attacked us with complete cruelty and you, with complete courage, your men and women, stood against them. Someone told me, "I saw, with my own eyes, that a child of ten or twelve was riding a motorcycle and went towards the tanks. The tank ran over and killed him." A spirit was born which prompted a child to do such an act. Empty handed, a monarchial empire of 2,500 years, 2,500 years of criminals, was done away with.

Do not forget your honor. Our intellectuals and writers and all of our groups of scholars should turn their attention to their own honor and glory. They should not prostrate themselves so much towards the West and writers of books. You yourselves have things to say. What difference does it make to you what so and so from the West said? Why do you quote from a foreigner so that the spirit of our young people becomes melancholy? You people must protest and not buy anything from a drug store with a foreign name until they change its name. These beloved university students of ours should pay attention to the fact that when a writer quotes from a foreigner, do not buy that book and do not read it. If you do this and buyers pull back, they will stop doing it. They want customers. When a commodity has not customers, it is discontinued.

Push away and turn your backs on things which pull you to the West and trample upon your honor and in place of it put Western things. I pray for you. May God continue His Mercy upon this nation in the way that He Blessed this nation and showed it Mercy and saved us from foreigners and their agents. May God save you from those kinds of freedoms which are colonialistic and come here from abroad.

Peace be upon you, and the Mercy and Blessings of God.

☙POSTSCRIPT: Many Americans think that the kind of Islamic fundamentalism represented by the Ayatollah Khomeini in Iran has taken control of the Middle East. This view has been reinforced by the strict rule of the Taliban in Afghanistan where women were not allowed to work and the people were forbidden to watch television or listen to the radio. While it is true that Islamic fundamentalists are a force to be reckoned with in many Middle Eastern countries, they still represent a minority and actually control only one Middle Eastern country: Iran.

A more accurate generalization about governance in the Middle East is that power tends to be centralized—in the hands of mullahs in Afghanistan and Iran, in the hands of kings in Saudi Arabia, Kuwait, Jordan, and Morocco, in the hands of dictators in Iraq and Libya, and in the hands of powerful presidents in Syria, Egypt, and Algeria. Only Tunisia and Turkey resemble modern democracies.

It could even be argued that Islamic fundamentalism is on the wane in the Middle East. The Algerian military has fought off a strong fundamentalist movement in Algeria, and in Egypt and Turkey a strong secular tradition of government has kept the fundamentalists at bay. In Jordan and Morocco, young kings have brought about the kinds of reforms that keep their people from turning to fundamentalism for answers to their problems, and in Syria, with the death of strongman president Assad, reforms are likely under the new president, his son, a doctor trained in England. And even in Iran, the election of moderate mullah president Khatami in 1997 and again in 2001 has led to many freedoms not allowed under the Ayatollah Khomeini.

Part of the push for change in Iran has come from the large number of young people: 65 percent under 26, 40 percent under 15. While reform is resisted by the old guard, democracy seems to be gaining ground. There are now only 33 mullahs in the 290-seat parliament, and freedoms are increasingly permitted, such as the installation of satellite dishes to bring in foreign T.V. shows, a relaxation of the strict dress code, increased freedom of speech in public and in the media, the freedom to listen to rock music in the home, and even the public exchange of valentines between sweethearts.

Thus, only in Afghanistan and Saudi Arabia could it be said that there is a rigid conservatism with few signs of moderation in the social and religious life of the country. In the rest of the Middle East, the struggle is not to create Western-style democracies but rather to create constitutional monarchies or presidencies consistent with the traditions of Islam and the norms of centralized governmental power.

Part Two

Past Glories, Future Hopes

Introduction

In Part One, we learned about some of the traditional values of the Middle East and how they were passed on from parents to children. We also learned about some of the changes taking place today in the traditional way of life, for the Middle East, like many parts of the world, is going through a period of modernization. In other words, it is becoming more Western, at least in some ways. Once the modernization process starts, a new perspective is needed to deal with the rapidly changing world. The development of industry and technology demands modern schools and new ways of doing things.

But in the Middle East, modernization means not merely an imitation of the Western world but a merging of Middle Eastern and Western ways. The Middle East has its own traditions and its own historical triumphs. There was a time when the rest of the world looked to the Middle East for the most advanced technology. In this section, we shall consider these glories of the past and the attempts of the nations of the Middle East to regain a position of importance in the world.

We begin by looking at European colonization in the Middle East, which led directly to the development of Turkish, Persian and Arab nationalism. Although the Turks, Persians and Arabs differ ethnically and linguistically, they share a common religious and cultural tradition. Surrounded by evidence of past glories, from the pyramids and the magnificent Islamic architecture to their great clas-

BASIC DATA: THE MIDDLE EAST

Country	Year of Independence	Present or Former Colonial Authority
Afghanistan	since ancient times	—
Algeria	1962	France
Bahrain	—	Great Britain
Iran	since ancient times	
Iraq	1932	Great Britain
Israel	1948	Great Britain
Jordan	1946	Great Britain
Kuwait	1961	Great Britain
Lebanon	1944	France
Libya	1951	Italy
Morocco	1956	France
Saudi Arabia	1913	Ottoman Empire
South Yemen	1967	Great Britain
Syria	1944	France
Tunisia	1956	France
Turkey	since ancient times	—
United Arab Rep. (Egypt)	1922-1936	Great Britain
Yemen	1918	Ottoman Empire

sical poetry and art, all three Moslem peoples can look back to a time when they were renowned throughout the world for their cultural and military achievements. All are well aware of their fallen place in the world and are determined to regain the status they had before their humiliation at the hands of European colonialists.

In their efforts to understand what happened to them, Middle Easterners blamed both the effects of colonization and internal corruption in their decaying empires. Turkish, Persian and Arab nationalists saw a need for both an external revolution against their colonial oppressors, and an internal revolution against their own corrupt and outdated institutions. The best of the traditional beliefs, which had given rise to the great Middle Eastern civilizations of the past, had to be welded to the progressive social, economic and political systems of the West. As a reaction against what they saw as the excessive greed of the colonialists, some Middle Eastern countries rejected capitalism and turned to a kind of Islamic socialism that avoided the godless aspects of socialism and communism. But whatever political or economic system was developed, the changes we describe in this section were an attempt to establish a new "golden age" in the Middle East. The prospects for the development of a new golden age improved greatly with the discovery of vast quantities of oil in the Middle East. We therefore look at some of the extraordinary changes taking place as a result of the Middle East's virtual monopoly of the world's oil supply.

The Middle Easterners, especially the Arabs, have another source of humiliation in addition to their fall from eminence: the establishment of the state of Israel in the heart of the Arab lands. From the point of view of the Arabs, Israel is a creation of the Western colonial powers forced upon them during the colonial period and maintained through a kind of neocolonialism. Needless to say, the Israelis do not see their nation in this light. In Part Two of this volume, we consider the events that led to the return of the Jewish people to their homeland and the official establishment of the Jewish state of Israel. The clash of Jewish and Arab nationalisms is one of the great tragedies of the modern world, for in the broadest sense it is a conflict of two equally valid historical forces.

There is, of course, much more to understand about Israel than the political disputes surrounding its birth. We take a brief look at life today in this complex culture, with its varied languages, nationalities and perspectives. In examining some of the factors and philosophies that went into the making of Israel, we hope to convey some of the spirit as well as the tensions of this diverse country.

Colonialism and the
Making of a Revolution

‮INTRODUCTION: Until the 1940s and 1950s, most Middle Eastern countries were under some form of control by European countries. France had colonies in Morocco, Algeria, Tunisia, Syria and Lebanon; Britain had control in Palestine, Iraq and Egypt. Libya was an Italian colony. There were some differences among the British, French and Italian systems of colonization, but these systems shared the same underlying premises: that European culture was superior, and that the colonized peoples were not yet ready to participate fully in running their own countries. At best, the colonized people were seen as potential equals who needed to be civilized; at worst, they were viewed as inferior savages who never could be equal to Europeans.

This attitude was understandably resented by the colonized peo-ples and led to the growth of nationalistic feelings and to the demand for self-government. When this demand was ignored and it became evident that only force could bring change, revolutionary movements were born throughout the Middle East.

The most violent of the revolutions against European powers took place in Algeria, which was under the control of France. The conditions that existed there at the start of the revolution were typical of conditions in many other colonized countries in the Middle East. Although the French had come to Algeria more than a hundred years before, they had done little to better the lives of the people. In 1954, only 10 percent of Algerian children went to school, as opposed to 100 percent of the French children. As a result, 95 percent of Algerian men were il-

160

literate, and 90 percent of the commerce and industry was controlled by the French. In addition, 50 per cent of Algerian men were employed fewer than a hundred days a year. The French, in short, ran the country for their own benefit and exploited the cheap labor of the uneducated Algerians.

As a result of this kind of treatment, the Algerians became a desperate people who would do anything to gain their freedom. When their neighbors, Morocco and Tunisia, won independence from France in 1956, the Algerians intensified their struggle. The FLN (National Liberation Front), the secret Algerian revolutionary command, which had the full support of the people, launched wave after wave of massive peaceful demonstrations, terrorist attacks and guerrilla warfare against the French colonial government. The French met the challenge to their rule with torture and escalated violence, killing as many as 40,000 Algerians in one retaliatory action. But each repressive action brought renewed determination. After eight years of violence, the French saw that they could not continue to resist the wishes of the masses of Algerians, and in 1962 Algeria gained its independence.

One of the leaders of the Algerian revolt was a young man named Ahmed Ben Bella, who was to become the first leader of independent Algeria. In 1985, Ben Bella was overthrown by his fellow revolutionary Colonel Houari Boumedienne, who ruled Algeria until the end of 1978.

In the selection that follows, Ben Bella tells of his boyhood in Algeria and his gradual conversion to revolutionary action.[1]⤴

I was born on the 25th December 1918 at Marnia, a small market town in the Oran district, quite close to the Moroccan frontier. My father was a *fellah* [peasant] and owned a small property of about seventy acres, a mile outside Marnia. But the soil was poor and there was no water supply, so my father's main source of income was the small business he ran in Marnia, where we lived. . . .

[After] I passed [primary school] it was decided that I should go to the nearest town for further education. A friend of my father's who lived in Tlemcen was generous enough to offer me hospitality for the time it would take [to go to secondary school].

At Tlemcen, the gulf between the French world and the Algerian world was obvious. Discrimination hit you in the face, even at school. At Tlemcen I felt, for the first time, that I belonged to a community which was considered inferior by the Europeans. For the first time I realized that I was a foreigner in my own country.

I think I was fourteen when . . . an incident occurred which made a deep impression on me. One of the teachers was called Benavidès . . . he was French and an excellent teacher when he did not bore us with long digressions on the religions of the world. . . . Faith in his own religion made him believe that all others were bad and despicable.

One day during school, he did not hesitate to go for his Moslem pupils, launching a violent attack on Islam. "Your prophet Mohammed," he shouted at the end of this diatribe, "was nothing but an impostor!"

I stood up, pale with anger. "Sir," I told him, "you must understand that to us our religion is sacred. No, no, it is wrong of you to speak like this." I cannot remember my exact words, because I was trembling with rage—I may have been even more outspoken. Of course Benavidès blew up. It was terrible. I was punished, dismissed from the class, and even threatened with expulsion. But I stuck it out, and gradually the scandal died down. And it was a double scandal, as I well knew. Firstly, for a pupil to tick off a teacher was bad enough. But for a "native" to stand up to a European made me a thousand times more guilty.

I remember this incident because it made me feel ill for over a fortnight and left a lasting impression on me. But it was not isolated. At school and in the town, dozens of small insults reminded me every day of the discrimination against us. I made up my mind that I myself would never submit to it, and it was from that moment that, deep in my heart, I felt myself becoming a rebel. . . .

It was at this period that I made contact with nationalist groups. The *Union Nationaliste des Musulmans Nord-africans* . . . had just been founded. This National Union had attracted to itself all those Algerians who were determined that colonialism could no longer be tolerated as a necessary evil. It consisted mainly of ardent and dedicated young men, one of whom, Abdelkrim Baraka, initiated me. He was a year older than me, and was studying at a *médersa* [a Moslem religious school]. The wave of nationalism at that time was surging through the *médersas,* with their 100-percent Moslem students, with far greater force than in the French schools. . . .

In 1934 . . . I had already made up my mind; I was certainly not going to intrigue for some comfortable job as a minor government official, let myself sink into a cozy routine and turn my back on the vast unhappiness of my people. . . . I [left school and] decided to go back to Marnia. I found employment but did not definitely commit myself to anything. . . . I put my name down for voluntary military training at Marnia, obviously not from any excess of enthusiasm, but because I felt that the experience gained would be useful to me some day.

In 1937 I was called up for military service and posted to the 141st Alpine Infantry Regiment at Marseilles. . . . During the summer of 1943, [I was] posted to the 6th Algerian Infantry Regiment at Tlemcen. What a contrast to the 141st Regiment [in France, which treated Frenchmen and Algerians equally]! The discrimination practiced between Algerians and Frenchmen in the ranks was flagrant. There were two completely separate officers' messes and two separate sergeants' messes. Our plates were not allowed to fraternize with the plates of Frenchmen of the same rank. We were not allowed to touch glasses with them, even though their glasses were filled with wine and ours with water. I will not dwell on the awkwardness and the humiliations which were the result of this segregation.

The Algerians were becoming more and more resentful of this discrimination. To all people living under colonial rule, the year 1940 [and the start of World War II] had burst like a clap of thunder. The course of history had broken loose from its traditional boundaries and was gathering speed. Frontiers had been overrun, states were

disintegrating, everything was chaotic. We felt that Algeria
could not stand aside from the great upheavals of the century. . . .

In the 6th Infantry, a movement against segregation, of
which I was the chief organizer, had begun to take place
in the Algerian ranks. . . . My superiors had no doubts as
to the part I played in this matter, and a few months later
I was transferred, without a word of explanation, to the 5th
Moroccan Infantry Regiment [at Oudja]. It was a clever
move. I found myself the only Algerian among Moroccans
. . . .

It was at Oudja that rumors reached me of the events of
1945 [when, in retaliation for an uprising in which scores
of Frenchmen were killed, forty thousand Algerians were
massacred]. I was profoundly shocked by the fierce repressive measure which followed the rising. According to the
evidence it was quite clear that, when the war was over,
colonialism was not going to cede anything to the Algerians,
and that rule by fear would prevail.

I was meditating on this bitter lesson when my chiefs suggested that I should stay on in the French army. . . . I refused
the offer, giving as my reason the fact that my family was
in distress. . . . In reality, it was the events of Constantine
[where the Algerians were slaughtered] which made me
decide to refuse. . . .

No sooner had I returned to Marnia than my compatriots
asked me to put my name down on a list of candidates for
the municipal elections. . . .

In the whole of Algeria, ten million Algerians elected
one-third of the municipal councilors [known as the *Second
Collège*], whereas one million Europeans elected the other
two-thirds [known as the *Premier Collège*].

The electors of the *Second Collège!* This delightful euphe-
mism was used to describe the Algerians. The *Premier Collège*,
naturally, was composed of Europeans: first they were, and
first they intended to remain. . . . In each parish, the elected members of the *Second Collège* . . . were . . . resigned and
powerless, passive onlookers of the administration of the

Premier Collège. They were perpetual yes-men who were intended to provide the colonial system with the semblance of democracy. I must confess to feelings of deep skepticism when those same politicians who invented this splendid institution of the two *collèges* accuse present-day [independent] Algeria of not being sufficiently democratic. . . . As for the [French colonial] democracy, with its readymade electoral laws, its intrigues, its *Deux Collèges*, and its clever carving-up of districts, we prefer to leave that kind of democracy. . . .

At the very first meeting of the town council of Marnia, it was clear to us that the members of the *Premier Collège,* secure in their superior numbers, had no intention of delegating any authority to the members of the *Second Collège.* It meant that we were denied even the smallest share in the administration of the little town and consequently we were unable to be of use to our electors. The members of the *Second Collège* resigned in a body and were immediately re-elected, in a body, by the electors of the *Second Collège.* . . . The *Premier Collège* could neither vote for nor administer the budget by itself, and although they were in the majority, they were unable to move without us. But we, the minority, only had the right to agree—and in order to disagree, we had to resign. The alternatives were to agree to everything, or to turn everything down.

The Mayor, Monsieur Gerbaud . . . was a decent fellow, but in order to obtain a minimum of administrative power [from him] it took us three elections. He gave in at the third one—or rather, he thought up a plan. We wanted administrative power: all right, he would let us have it—in full measure! He was convinced, like all Europeans in Algeria, that we "didn't know how to do anything" and that we "couldn't do without them." He thought that he would overwhelm us with hard work and the weight of our responsibilities. What a blow was in store for him! We took on all the tasks he assigned to us, and they did not overwhelm us at all. . . .

As well as being a town councilor, I was also a militant

member of [one of the nationalist parties]. The way in which I carried out my daily tasks on behalf of my fellow citizens of Marnia had, in a few months, attracted new supporters to my side, and had turned Marnia into a party headquarters. The chief colonial administrator and his henchmen . . . could not forgive me for this.

One day my brother-in-law, who lived in Marnia, came to see me, looking worried. "Ahmed," he said to me, "So-and-So has moved into your farm and is claiming that it belongs to him." "I will go and fling him out," I answered. "Be careful," my brother-in-law replied, raising his right hand in warning, "I have a feeling that this is a trap. The man himself is not particularly dangerous, because he is a legless cripple. But his cousins are brigands, real killers . . . . May Allah protect you!"

I went to see the cripple, who was indeed in possession of my house. He received me as though he were quite at home, with a wife on either side. He reeled off a long and complicated story which was meant to prove that my farm really belonged to him. Needless to say, he had not even the shadow of documentary proof. But, unfortunately, neither had I anything in writing to protect my rights, as land that had already belonged to native families before the conquest of Algeria never carried any title deeds. Property was owned by right of long occupation; my land was mine because my father had cultivated it, and he had inherited it from his father, and so on. There [were quarrels and the] colonial administration made the most of these quarrels, sometimes even creating them in order to favor those whom they considered to be "good natives" against the "bad natives." . . .

The more I listened to him, the more I was convinced that my brother-in-law was right, and that the whole business had been rigged by the administration. If I gave in, I would be dispossessed of my rights and discredited in the eyes of my fellow citizens. If I resorted to violence, the cousins were there to eliminate me physically. They would be tried as a matter of form, but the murder of a "native"

As the Algerian revolution progressed, the French administration sealed off Moslem quarters. Moslems entering European quarters were carefully searched. (Wide World Photos)

by another "native" was of no importance. Ten witnesses would be found who would swear great oaths that the murderer had acted in self-defense.

I tried by every possible legal means to recover my property, but I was up against a brick wall. My final step was to ask for an interview with the [French] administrator. The way in which he received me left me devoid of hope: he was triumphant. His eyes sparkled with malice and he never once dropped his sarcasm, even when I reminded him of my war record. . . . I got up to go and said to him: "Tell me, *monsieur l'administrateur,* what exactly are you driving at?" He answered in the same ironic voice: "You will see all right," and then added: "You think you're pretty smart, Ben Bella, but we will show you that we are even smarter than you." As I left, I realized that I had lost the farm. . . .

[Afterwards] I went to Algiers, and changed my name. This was in 1947, and from that date onwards I became a clandestine fighter, and remained one until the day of my arrest.

The Arab Golden Age:
Harun Al-Rashid's Baghdad

۰INTRODUCTION: As we have seen, the colonization of the Middle Eastern countries and the refusal of the colonizers to treat the Middle Easterners as equals created a great deal of resentment against Europeans. The Arabs found the feelings of superiority expressed by the Europeans especially hard to tolerate, for they had had a flourishing civilization stretching from Iran to Morocco and Spain at a time when Europeans were still wearing animal skins. Furthermore, they looked upon themselves as a special people, for Mohammed, who was used by God to communicate His word and to correct the misinterpretations of the Jews and the Christians, was an Arab. Thus, in connection with their nationalistic feelings, the Arabs began to look back to their Golden Age for inspiration, to the ancient glories of Baghdad (Iraq) and to the refined Arab civilization in Spain and Morocco known to the West as "Moorish."

The following selection looks at the Baghdad of Harun Al-Rashid, the setting for the famous *Tales of the Arabian Nights.*[2]۰

The sweep of the armies of Islam out of the Arabian peninsula following the death of Mohammed was to lead to the development of many great Islamic civilizations, from the famous Moorish civilization in Spain to the civilization of the Moguls in India, the builders of the Taj Mahal. After the death of the prophet, in A.D. 632, the center of gravity of the growing Arab Empire shifted from Mecca to Damascus, Syria. For the next hundred years

Damascus was the home of the Umayyad caliphate, the official religious governing body of Islam. Following the temporary decline of the Umayyad caliphate in A.D. 750, the center of the Islamic civilization gravitated to Iraq with the rise of Abul Abbas, the founder of the new Abbasid caliphate. His brother and successor, Mansur, built a new capital, Baghdad. The zenith of the Abbasid caliphate and the Arab Golden Age came with the ascendancy of Mansur's grandson, Harun Al-Rashid, the famous Caliph of the 1,001 Arabian nights.

Harun's Baghdad is perhaps best known for the wealth and luxurious lifestyles of its inhabitants. As a commercial center, it was unsurpassed. Ships from all over the world brought their rich cargoes to the Persian Gulf and up the Tigris River to Baghdad. Silks and porcelain from China, spices and precious metals from India, and ivory, gold dust and black slaves from Africa were shipped to Baghdad by sea. Caravans brought jewels overland from Turkey, pearls from Arabia and furs and white slaves from Scandinavia and Russia. Taxes in the form of money or goods flowed into the capital from all the provinces of the empire, and wealthy merchants developed trade networks on land and sea linking the commercial centers of Europe, Asia and Africa. The Middle East, because of its geographical position, became the center of world trade. As a result, the ruling classes were able to live on a scale that the world had rarely seen before. Harun's wife, Zubeidab, who set the fashions of the city, wore jewel-studded shoes and had workmen design and construct a tree of mechanical chirping birds made of pure gold. At the wedding of her son, Mamun, Zubeidah arranged for the couple to be showered with pearls while they sat on a carpet gold-studded with jewels. Many of the guests in attendance were honored with the gift of an estate or a slave, given to them by means of a ticket hidden in the perfumed gifts distributed during the wedding.

Luxurious living was not confined to the ruling classes. With Baghdad and the Middle East as the center of world trade, a new and wealthy middle class of artisans, merchants and professional men arose whose services commanded high salaries. Indeed, the economic boom affected all classes; few lives were left untouched.

Although wealth was perhaps the most spectacular aspect of Harun's Baghdad, its cultural and scientific achievements were more significant. Harun wanted Baghdad to be the center of world learning, and to this end he invited famous poets and scholars from all over the Middle East, including Turks and Persians as well as Arabs, to come to Baghdad to work and live.

The intellectual ferment began with the translation of books from all over the world into Arabic. One of these books was an Indian text on astronomy and the Indian system of numbers. Borrowed by the Arabs, this system has in turn been adopted by the Western world and is used in the West today. What we know as Arabic numerals, the decimal system and the use of the number zero have come to us by way of Harun's Baghdad. A large number of Greek texts were also translated, including the works of Aristotle and Plato as well as works on medicine, mathematics and astronomy. The medical works of Galen and Hippocrates, Euclid's *Elements of Geometry* and Ptolemy's astronomical writings were among the books translated from Greek into Arabic, with the help of Syrian Christians who could read both Greek and Arabic. Much of Greek learning that otherwise might well have disappeared was thus saved for the world. The resurgence of interest in Greek civilization today owes much to these unknown translators of Harun's court. Under Harun's son, Mamun, the translation of documents continued with the establishment of a House of Wisdom, which had a vast library with an academy for scholarly learning and also sponsored original research.

Original research in the field of medicine included the dissection of apes by the Christian physician Yuhanna and the production of a ten-volume treatise on the eye by his student, Hunayn. There were many famous practicing physicians as well, such as Al-Razi, known to the West as

Rhazes. Al-Razi, when asked to pick a site for a new hospital in Baghdad, had strips of meat hung from poles around the city, and chose as the site for the hospital the place where the meat had decayed the least. Al-Razi wrote books on smallpox and measles as well as his most famous work, an encyclopedia that catalogued all Greek, Hindu and Persian medical knowledge as well as the results of his own medical research.

An equally famous physician, Ibn Sina, known to the West as Avicenna, codified all Greek and Arabic medical knowledge into a volume that became the standard medical textbook in the Arab world and in Europe for the next 800 years. Works on dietetics and pharmacology were published by others. The first pharmacies date from this period, during which there were more than 800 registered pharmacists in Baghdad.

Original scientific research was also conducted in the field of astronomy. Because of their desert tradition, the Arabs had always been interested in the stars; the Sabean Arabs had even been star-worshipers prior to the coming of Islam. With the translation of Ptolemy's astronomical works, interest in astronomy increased, leading to the construction of an observatory in Baghdad that was to calculate accurately the length of the solar year. And 500 years before the Western world accepted the fact that the earth was round, Arab astronomers conducted experiments to determine the length of a terrestrial degree on the earth; their estimate of 56 2/3 miles was within a half-mile of the correct answer. Other astronomers studied the moon's influence on the tides, and corrected errors in Ptolemy's observations of the orbit of the moon and planets. A mathematician, Al-Khwarizmi, designed the first set of astronomical tables in Arabic and wrote a book on algebra that was widely used in Europe and thus introduced the word algebra into English. Other original research was done in the fields of chemistry, zoology, music and philosophy.

The expansion of the Arab Empire contributed greatly

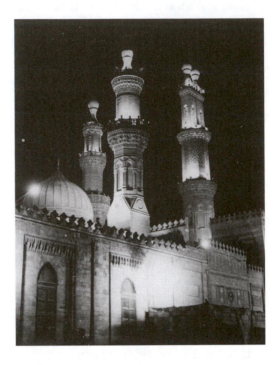

The mosque of Al Azhar University in Cairo, with its graceful minarets, is representative of the magnificent architecture of the Arab Golden Age. (Egyptian Tourist Office, New York)

to the development of the field of geography. Moslem merchants had reached China in the seventh century A.D., long before the reign of Harun, and Arab traders had journeyed as far as Russia, Zanzibar, Morocco and Spain. These travelers kept records, and as a result an interest in geography developed. The greatest geographer of his time, Yakut, organized existing geographical knowledge into an encyclopedia, including cultural, historical and geographical data on the entire known world.

Learning in Baghdad was not confined to the scholarly work of the House of Wisdom. There were elementary schools for both boys and girls. Theological colleges were established for the advanced study of Islam and became the models for the religious colleges of today in the Middle East, such as the famous religious university of Al Azhar in Cairo. There were public as well as private libraries, and many bookstalls were to be found on the streets of Baghdad.

The development of an empire brought the need for an efficient government and communication system. A well-trained police force was organized to keep order in the towns, and a standing army, drawn from all the tribes and provinces, helped keep the countryside under control and safe for travel. For the benefit of travelers, inns and hostels were maintained in various parts of Harun's domain, and a system similar to our pony express assured mail delivery throughout the provinces. The delivery of mail was supplemented by a carrier-pigeon service for the speedy exchange of messages.

To assure maximum food supplies, ancient canal systems established in Babylonian times were restored, and irrigation was extended throughout the land. Increased food production meant increased wealth for the nation, for taxes were often paid in food or goods as well as in cash. It also made more ambitious military conquests possible, and these in turn brought new lands under cultivation.

By A.D. 710, Arab armies had crossed North Africa to Morocco, and from there, with the help of the Moroccan Moors, they crossed the Straits to the Jebel Al Tariq, the Rock of Gibraltar and Spain. The revival of the Umayyad caliphate in Spain led to another glorious period in Arab history, which reached its peak during the reign of Abdur Rahman from A.D. 912 to 961. The Arab, or Moorish, civilization of Spain is perhaps more familiar to Westerners than that of Harun's Baghdad. Tourists today still visit some of the great Moorish cities in Spain, such as Cordova and Grenada. It was not until 500 years later—in 1492, the year that Columbus sailed in search of a new route to India— that the Moors were finally forced out of Grenada by the Spanish Christians. Soon thereafter, they retreated back across the Strait of Gibraltar to Morocco.

For 700 years, the Arab and Moslem civilizations had dominated the Middle East and North Africa, and in Harun's Baghdad and Moorish Spain their way of life represented the highest civilization of its time. With the fall

of Baghdad to the Seljuk Turks in A.D. 1055 and the final
ouster of the Moors from Grenada in 1499, Arab influence
in the Middle East and in world affairs dwindled, and the
initiative in world affairs passed to the Europeans. In the
Middle East, the Arabs increasingly came under the control of another Moslem power, the Ottoman Turks, who
were to reign supreme for more than 400 years, until their
final downfall as an international power as a result of World
War I.

The Ottoman Empire

INTRODUCTION: The heir to the power and magnificence of the Arab Golden Age in the Middle East was the Ottoman Empire. The Ottomans rose to power in Turkey during the fourteenth century and by 1453 had conquered the Byzantine Christian city of Constantinople (Istanbul) and were in control of southeastern Europe as far as the Danube. Once their foothold in Europe was secure, the Ottomans pushed southward into the Arab lands. By the middle of the sixteenth century they were in control of Syria, Palestine, Arabia, Egypt and most of North Africa. This empire, which they were to hold for the next 350 years, continued the influential role of Islamic civilizations in the history of the world. It was not until their defeat in World War I that the Ottomans lost control of their empire and were forced back to the borders of present-day Turkey.

The Ottomans are best known for their military prowess and their administrative skills. Their most famous governing device was *devshirme*, a system by which conquered Christian villages were forced to contribute young boys to the state for special training and service in the military and in government. Although these boys were in most ways considered to be slaves, their advancement in the service of the Sultan was based on merit alone rather than on the system of hereditary connections common to most governments of the world at that time. The most capable boys rose to positions of great importance in the military and in the Sultan's palace government. It was with the collapse of this system and the gradual introduction of corruption in the government that the Ottoman Empire began to decline in the eighteenth and nineteenth centuries.

The first part of the following selection suggests the strength and pageantry of the Ottoman armies under the

175

leadership of Suleyman the Magnificent as they entered Aleppo, Syria, on their way to battle the Persians. This eyewitness account by an Englishman, Anthony Jenkinson, demonstrates how impressive the Ottoman Turks were to the average citizen of that time.[3]

The second part of the selection supplies a picture of the daily lives of the people of Istanbul in 1638, at the height of the Ottoman period. In the account, Sultan Murad IV gives orders for a complete description of the resources of Istanbul in preparation for the coming campaign against Persia.[4]😎

AN EYEWITNESS ACCOUNT

There marched before the Great Turk [Suleyman] 6,000 light horsemen, very brave, all clothed in scarlet.

After marched 10,000 men clothed all in yellow velvet, with great velvet hats two feet long. They were carrying bows in their hands made in the Turkish fashion.

After them marched four captains, men of arms, clothed all four in crimson velvet, each captain having under his banner 12,000 men of arms, well equipped with helmets on their heads, marching in good order, with short swords by their sides.

After came 16,000 Janissaries, called the slaves of the Great Turk, all on foot, with strange hats on their heads with foot-long silver and gold cones studded with jewels and topped by plumes that waved up and down most bravely when they marched.

After this there came 1,000 pages of honor, all clothed in gold, carrying bows and quivers of arrows, marching in good order.

Then came three men of arms with helmets on their heads and spears at the ready.

After them came seven pages of honor, clothed in silver, riding on seven white horses, covered with cloths of silver, garnished with emeralds, diamonds, and rubies.

After them came six more pages of honor, clothed in gold with bows in their hands.

Immediately after them came the Great Turk himself,

with great pomp and magnificence, riding majestically. On either side of him was a page clothed in gold; he himself was mounted on a fine white horse and was dressed in a robe of gold embroidered with precious stones. On his head was wound a turban of silk at least fifteen yards in length, at the top of which were white ostrich feathers.

After marched the Great Pasha, chief conductor of the whole army, clothed in a robe of crimson, and about him marched fifty Janissaries on foot, also clothed in crimson velvet.

Then after came three other Pashas with slaves about them numbering 3,000.

After came a company of horsemen, brave to behold, all well armed, who numbered 4,000.

All of this army, most amazing to behold, was in number 88,000 men, encamped about the city of Aleppo, Syria. The Great Turk, the Sultan, was himself lodged within the town in a fine castle situated upon a high mountain, at the foot of which ran a goodly river, which is a branch of that famous river, the Euphrates.

The whole army, including the part that went by the mountains as well as that which came to Aleppo, with horsemen and footmen and those who guided the camels and those who prepared the food, numbered 300,000 men. The camels which carried the ammunition and food totaled 200,000.

THE SULTAN'S EDICT

In order to assist me in this great expedition, I desire that all guilds [organizations of people in the same trade] of Constantinople, both large and small, shall [come] to my Imperial camp. They shall exhibit the number of their men, shops, and professions. . . . They shall all . . . on foot, and on horseback, with . . . music, pass before Alaykōshk, that I may see how many thousand men and how many guilds there are. It shall be an *alay* [procession] the like of which never was seen before. A general description shall

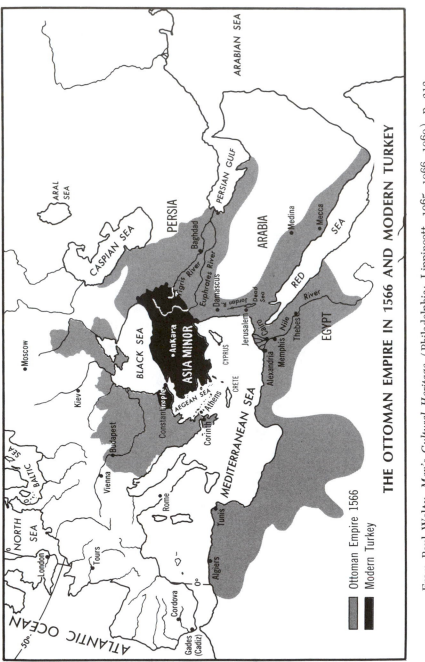

THE OTTOMAN EMPIRE IN 1566 AND MODERN TURKEY

Ottoman Empire 1566
Modern Turkey

From Paul Welty, *Man's Cultural Heritage* (Philadelphia: Lippincott, 1965, 1966, 1969), p. 213.

be made of all the . . . mosques, . . . colleges, houses for
reading the Koran, and houses for reading the tradition,
schools, convents, . . . baths, magazines [stores],
caravanserais [inns for people and their animals], palaces
of the vezirs [government officials] and great men, fountains, establishments for distributing water, conduits,
cisterns, quarters of Moslems, Christians, and Jews, chur-
ches and synagogues, ovens for bread and biscuits, water,
wind and horsemills, halls . . . of all the houses, gardens
. . . and all the monuments to be found in the four districts
. . . . Those who make the description shall be men of im-
partial character; if the contrary should be found I shall
order them to be quartered. . . .

The description of Constantinople and all its suburbs
and villages on both sides of the Bosphorus was completed
in three months. It formed a complete book, bearing the
title *Description of Constantinople.* The historiographer
Solakzade read it day and night in the presence of the Sultan, who exclaimed, "O my God! Let this town flourish to
the end of time." . . .

The following is [an excerpt from] the description of
the excellent town of Constantinople.

Under the four Mollas of Constantinople . . . justice is
transacted at 670 tribunals. Great mosques of the Sultans,
74. Great mosques of the Vezirs, 1,985. Small mosques of
the town quarters, 6,990. Other mosques great and small,
6,665. Dining establishments for the poor, 19. Hospitals,
9. Primary schools, 1,993. Houses for reading the Koran,
55. Houses for delivering the tradition [of the Prophet
Mohammed], 135. Great convents, 557. Cells and rooms
of *Dervishes* [religious mystics], 6,000. Sick-houses for
strangers, 91. Caravanserais, 997. Khans [hotels] of merchants, 565. Khans for single men, 676. Quarters of Moslems, 990. Quarters of Greeks, 354. Quarters of Jews, 657.
Quarters of Franks, 17. Quarters of Armenians, 27. Palaces
of Vezirs, 6,890. Baths public and private, 14,536. Foun-

tains public and private, 9,995. Water-pipes, 989. Establishments for distributing water, 200. Fountains sweet and bitter, 100. Wells, 60,000. Cisterns, 55. . . . Covered markets,
3. Flour-halls, 37. . . . Repositories for grinding coffee, 22.
Repository for silk, 1. Repository for wax, 1. Repository for
gold-wire, 1. Repository of the customhouse, 1. Repository
of the land customhouse, 1. Repository for oil, 1.
Repository for fish, 1. Repository for salt, 1. Repository for
biscuits, 1. Repository for wine, 1. Repository for powder,
1. Repository for prisoners, 1. The Imperial Mint, 10.
Magazine for cloth, 1. Magazine for corn, 1. Magazine for
barley, 1. The magazines of Bayezid, of Suleyman, of wood,
of horses, of flour, and of hay; of each, 1. The stables of
the palace and at Wefa, 1. The Armory, 1. Prisons of State,
4. Prisons for criminals, 4. Ovens, 600. Windmills, 600.
Watermills, 28. Houses of the inspectors of provisions, of
vegetables, of mutton, of the Inspector of the town, of the
Inspector of the kitchen, of salted meat, of slaughter-
houses. Barracks of the Janissaries, old and new, . . . 162.
Barracks of . . . the armorers and the caulkers. The Arsenal
and the barracks of the bombardiers. . . . One house for
yoghurt. The paper factory of Battal, 1. The royal lion-
house, 1. Houses for dyeing, 70. Houses for silverware, 10.
The musket factory, 1. Leaden-hall, 1. The music-house, 1.
House of the tent-pitchers, 1. . . . House of the painters, 1.
House for the water-carriers, 1; for the gunners, 1; for the
founders, 1; for the tailors, 1; for the waggoners, 1; for the
fireworkers, 1; for the exercise of the Janissaries, 1; for the
Samsunji, keepers of the great dogs, 1; for the Zagarji, or
keepers of the pointers, 1; . . . for the falconers, 1; for the
head of the goldsmiths, 1; for the kettle-makers, 1; for the
button-makers, 1; for the saddlers, 1; for the glass-makers,
1; for the head of the merchants, 2; for the vinegar-makers,
1; for the confectioners of sour fruits, 1.

Ataturk's Reforms

❧INTRODUCTION: When the Ottoman Empire was defeated during World War 1, it was not entirely destroyed but was pushed back to the borders of modern-day Turkey. Its archaic institutions and corrupt leadership proved unable to deal with the collapse of the empire and invasion by the Greeks. The future looked dim for Turkey until the meteoric rise of a young man named Mustafa Kemal. Mustafa, later known as Ataturk, "father of the Turks," formed and led a people's army that drove the Greek invaders out and declared Turkey a republic.

A brilliant, charismatic and sometimes ruthless leader, Ataturk came to wield almost absolute power in Turkey. With an iron will, he set out to modernize his country. By alternating persuasion and force, Ataturk, in the period from the end of World War I to his death in 1938, brought radical changes to Turkey, shaking his country out of the corruptions and superstitions of the dying Ottoman Empire and bringing it again to life in a modern, Western mold. One of his major changes involved the abolition of the caliphate, the religious administration of Islam, which had wielded great political power through the theocratic Ottoman period. By abolishing the caliphate, Ataturk separated church and state and provided the basis for the secular Turkey of today.

In the following selection, a Turkish journalist recounts the bold means by which Ataturk confronted the reactionary institutions in his country and gives a summary of Ataturk's major reforms.[5]❧

Ataturk was ill—dangerously ill. What would happen? The outside world held the opinion that his achievements

were purely personal, that there would be no continuity to
new Turkey after his death. . . . Patriotic Turks loved him
for saving the country and making possible a new national existence, and they excused any error he might have
committed. Although they had faith in the continuity of
their national life, the danger of losing Ataturk filled them
with deep anxiety in addition to their sorrow. . . .

I left Turkey in October, 1938, for America. . . .

When we [Turks] arrived in Milan, on our way to Paris,
a railway conductor gave me the terrible news of the death
of Ataturk.

Mustafa Kemal Ataturk dead! That such a man of inex-
haustible vitality, creative power, iron will, and humane
heart should cease to exist among those who lived sounded
unbelievable. His long illness had prepared us for the end.
Still, the actual news was a shock. We wept; all the Turks
on the train wept; an entire nation wept for months. . . .

Although the whole world has heard of Ataturk and admired his great work, the meaning and scope of his accomplishments have not been fully understood. . . .

[A summary of his major reforms follows.]

I have already described the manner in which he
abolished the caliphate and the . . . authority of religion,
opening wide the avenues of reason for the advance of
science, education, and justice, hitherto saddled with
religious dogma. He made secularism a going policy in
Turkey, more so than in most advanced countries, leaving
religion its proper function as a source of altruism and
love, but preventing it from being used as an unfair and
reactionary tool in politics.

Religion had hampered the freedom and equality of
women by depriving them of opportunities for public activity. Ataturk gave them equal political rights with men
and opened all professions and offices to them. . . . In
Turkey today there is a larger proportion of women judges,
lawyers, architects, engineers, chemists, and high-ranking

government officials than anywhere else in the world.
Usually people are surprised to learn that the assistant head
of the aviation school run by the Turkish Air League, confined exclusively to military aviators during World War 1,
was for some time a woman pilot with an iron sense of discipline and duty.

After the reforms in religion and the status of women,
a sweeping change in personal attire, itself a symbol of the
old, narrow life, was introduced. The Turks had adopted
European dress for men about one hundred years earlier,
but had kept the red fez [a tall, red cylindrical hat] as a
sign of Ottoman distinction. The conservative mind clung
to it as its last symbol of religious and political difference
from the Christian West. Ataturk, on the contrary, thought
that there should be no symbol of difference. The fez had
to go. . . .

Ataturk chose a remarkable way for eliminating the fez.
He singled out Kastamonu, a town north of Ankara reputed
to be the most conservative community in Turkey, as the
place to inaugurate this phase of his program and arranged
there a meeting with noted reactionaries of the town.

"I have brought you some nice presents," he told them
on arrival. "Look at them. They are called hats, a much
more suitable headgear than the fez as protection against
sun and rain."

The men were startled and terrified at the prospect of
wearing hats. All of them said they could not accept the
gifts. "But why?" asked Ataturk. . . .

When a group of pious conservatives led by Ataturk, all
wearing hats, took a stroll through the main street of the
town, people could not believe their eyes. . . . [Afterward]
in all communities the radicals started to wear hats. . . .
Then a law was passed forbidding the wearing of the fez.
Here and there the law met silent resistance, but there was
no open manifestation of it. A reform thought impossible
had taken place simply and smoothly. . . .

The change in the alphabet was another sweeping
reform by Ataturk. The complicated Arabic characters, so

long used by the Turks, were one of the main causes of illiteracy. Adoption of the Latin alphabet had been a wish in the hearts of a few radicals, perhaps, but it was hardly a subject for public discussion. To change the alphabet would be a tremendously difficult and unpopular job. But Ataturk called a conference of writers and leading authorities to consider language problems. The majority approved the adoption of Latin characters.

"How long a period of transition do you foresee?" Ataturk asked them.

"About fifteen years," was the almost unanimous answer.

"No," said Ataturk. "'It must be completed in six months."

The entire country became a school to teach the new alphabet. Evening classes were compulsory for men up to sixty and women up to fifty years old. Ataturk was one of the teachers. From partly Arabic and partly Latin, the newspapers went, in a few months, to entirely Latin characters. . . .

As a rule, Turks had no family names and were called by their given names. There were no surnames to denote a common family bond. . . . To differentiate a man from others with the same given name, it was necessary to add detailed information about him, such as "son of," "native of," and so on.

A law passed in 1935 made it compulsory for every Turk to adopt and register a family name. Mustafa Kemal was given the name of Ataturk by the Grand National Assembly. Ataturk gave General Ismet the surname "Inonu," in honor of his victory in the battles of Inonu. Everyone used his imagination and wits in selecting his own name. I spent hours searching in a dictionary for a . . . name [with a beautiful sound] without a poor meaning. "Yalman," meaning "the highest summit of a mountain," seemed to be all right. It sounded pretentious, but most people were taking pretentious names. As long as they could choose, they took the best.

During the period of these reforms, much had been achieved in the economic field through two five-year plans and by the creation of government banks as holding institutions for a number of separate industrial undertakings on a public-utility basis. A new generation of Turks interested in economics was reared, and the experiment was successful, at least in its honeymoon stage, while effort was concentrated on following the better practices of private business and avoiding red tape. Unfortunately, the new business techniques practiced in the government banks— the selection of men on the basis of fitness and efficiency, and the system of paying living wages and encouraging initiative and merit by prompt increases in salary and position—were not applied even to a small degree in the government bureaus. This lack of harmony in two different fields of government activity was one of the reasons why the progressive measures were short-lived. . . .

Ataturk saw the necessity for an opposition party. An attempt was made on two occasions to encourage another party, but the whole thing was done badly and half-heartedly. Ataturk insisted he was not neutral as the head of state, that he had to insure control by his own side. Under such circumstances, a free system could hardly be expected to have a chance.

Ataturk struggled fiercely not to become a dictator in spite of his personal power and prestige. The one purge, made under the pressure of a crisis which seriously threatened the regime, resulted in so much disgust and unpopularity that it was never repeated. On the contrary, all Turks living outside of Turkey were granted the right to re-enter their homeland. . . .

The new regime exhibited democracy in form, but with a stiff dose of personal power and inefficient bureaucracy. Fortunately most of the personal power was used in the public interest and within the framework of the laws as far as possible. . . .

The main contribution of Ataturk to the prosperity, progress, and survival of the Turkish nation is not confined to the sweeping reforms most widely publicized abroad. More fully, it consists of his liquidation of all tendencies toward . . . imperialism, militarism, and extreme nationalism in Turkey, preaching the doctrine that all imperialism is a liability, . . . that the Turks should be busy for hundreds of years solely in developing their own homeland . . . and that anything diverting attention from this task would be a national danger for Turkey. . . .

The remarkable feature of the whole thing is the fact that this respect for decency and this hatred of militarism were sponsored by one of the most successful and brilliant military masters in history. The world situation offered to Ataturk many occasions when he might have used his genius for personal adventure and glory, but he abstained from all that, preferring to create good-neighbor relations with Russia, Greece, Yugoslavia, Romania, Bulgaria, and the Middle Eastern Islamic neighbors.

His main fear was that he might become the blind dictator, a slave of flattery and conceit. . . .

In respect to the continuity of the regime which he established in Turkey, there was considerable hesitancy in many minds, both inside and outside of the country. The following questions persistently occurred to those interested in the welfare of Turkey: Was not the whole thing a product solely of Ataturk's personal influence? Could it be expected to survive him? Would there not be a conflict for the succession between the leading figures in public life?

Ismet Inonu, Ataturk's closest co-worker and his prime minister for twelve years, was considered the fittest man to succeed to the presidency. . . . So everything stayed under harmonious, friendly control. The death of the first president of the Turkish Republic did not interfere at all with the continuity and stability of the regime.

The Philosophy of the Revolution

Be a lion at home
and a fox abroad.
—Persian proverb

⋙INTRODUCTION: Unlike the reforms in Turkey, which were essentially an internal struggle against the corruption of the decaying, imperialistic Ottoman Empire, the revolution in Egypt had as its primary goal full independence from British involvement in Egyptian affairs and control of the Suez Canal. Many Egyptian nationalists believed that internal reforms could not take place until the British were ousted from Egypt. A popular revolution in 1919, after a promising start, failed to bring about lasting reforms, and internal corruption in the Egyptian Government worsened in the 1930s and 1940s. It was in this atmosphere of disappointment and bitterness that the famous Egyptian leader Gamal Abdel Nasser grew up.

As a young schoolboy in Cairo, Nasser was on the streets protesting his government's restrictions on its citizens, and it was during these early years that he became an ardent Arab nationalist. Nasser was most concerned about British influence over Egyptian politics, British control of the Suez Canal and the establishment of a Western-backed country, Israel, in the heart of the Arab lands. After the revolution of 1952, which toppled the corrupt government of King Farouk, Nasser emerged as the voice of the people of Egypt. He instituted land reforms and managed to remove the British from the Suez Canal in 1956. His subsequent attempts to bring about Arab unity, through the short-lived Egyptian-Syrian union of 1958-61 and his sponsorship of many Pan-Arab conferences, reflected his belief in the need for Arab solidarity in the face of other world power blocs.

In the following excerpt from his book *Egypt's Liberation: The Philosophy of the Revolution,* Nasser discusses his theory that Egypt is inextricably bound to the Arab world, to the African continent and to the Islamic world. In Nasser's view, Egypt cannot forget these ties in developing a nationalistic policy of its own. It is interesting to note that in this piece, written in 1955, Nasser mentions the possibility of using Arab oil as a weapon in world power politics, which was finally undertaken in 1973.[6]🖎

A ROLE IN SEARCH OF A HERO

[I remember] a famous tale by a great Italian poet, Luigi Pirandello—"Six Characters in Search of an Author." The pages of history are full of heroes who created for themselves roles of glorious valor which they played at decisive moments. Likewise the pages of history are also full of heroic and glorious roles which never found heroes to perform them. For some reason it seems to me that within the Arab circle there is a role, wandering aimlessly in search of a hero. . . .

Here, let me hasten to say that this role is not one of leadership. . . . It is a role such as to spark [the] tremendous power latent in the area surrounding us . . . with the aim of creating a great strength which will then undertake a positive part in the building of the future of mankind.

THE FIRST CIRCLE

There can be no doubt that the Arab circle is the most important, and the one with which we are most closely linked. For its peoples are intertwined with us by history. We have suffered together, we have gone through the same crises, and when we fell beneath the hooves of the invaders' steeds, they were with us under the same hooves.

We are also bound in this circle by a common religion. The center of Islamic learning has always moved within the orbit of its several capital cities—first Mecca, then shifting to . . . Damascus, next to Baghdad, and finally to Cairo.

Lastly, the fact that the Arab states are contiguous has joined them together in a geographical framework made solid by all these historical, material and spiritual factors . . . .

[When we speak of our latent power] we make the wrong definition of strength. It is not strength to shout at the top of the lungs: real strength lies in acting positively with all the effective means at our command. When I try to analyze the elements of our strength, there are three main sources which should first be taken into account.

The first of these sources is that we are a community of neighboring peoples linked by all the material and moral ties possible, and that we have characteristics and abilities and a civilization which have given rise to three holy religions—factors which cannot be ignored in the effort to build a secure and peaceful world. So much for the first source.

As for the second source of strength, it is our land itself and its position on the map—that important, strategic position which embraces the crossroads of the world, the thoroughfare of its traders and the passageway of its armies.

There remains the third source: oil—a sinew of material civilization without which all its machines would cease to function. The great factories, producing every kind of goods; all the instruments of land, sea and air communication; all the weapons of war, from the mechanical bird above the clouds to the submarine beneath the waves—without oil, all would turn back to naked metal, covered with rust, incapable of motion or use.

Here I would like to pause for a moment to deal with the subject of oil. . . .

I read recently an article published by the University of Chicago on the world oil situation. It would be a good thing if every Arab could read it, grasp its implication and see the great significance revealed by its statistics.

The article points out, for example, that in the Arab countries the effort to extract oil requires comparatively little capital. . . . According to the article, it all adds up to the fact that the cost of producing a barrel of oil in North America is 78 cents, in South America, 48 cents, but in the Arab countries the cost is only 10 cents.

The article further says that the center of world oil production has shifted from the United States, where oil wells are going dry, where the cost of land is going up and the wages of workers have risen, to the Arab area, where the fields are still virgin, where vast tracts of land continue to cost almost nothing and where labor is comparatively cheap. . . .

It is a fact, too, that the average daily production per well is 11 barrels in the United States, 230 barrels in Venezuela and 4,000 barrels in the Arab area. Have I made

Rarely has a leader been regarded with such reverence as Gamal Abdel Nasser of Egypt. Hundreds of thousands of Egyptians attended his funeral in October 1970. (Wide World Photos)

clear how great is the importance of this element of strength? I hope so.

So we are strong. Strong not in the loudness of our voices when we wail or shout for help, but rather . . . from the ties binding us together, making our land a single region from which no part can withdraw, and of which no part, like an isolated island, can be defended without defense of the whole.

THE INTERIOR OF THE DARK CONTINENT

So much for the first circle in which we must turn, and in which we must act with all our ability—the Arab circle.

If we consider next the second circle—the continent of Africa—I may say without exaggeration that we cannot, under any circumstances, however much we might desire it, remain aloof from the terrible and sanguinary conflict going on there today between five million whites and 200 million Africans. We cannot do so for an important and obvious reason: we are in Africa. The peoples of Africa will continue to look to us, who guard their northern gate, and who constitute their link with the outside world. . . .

There remains another important reason. It is that the Nile is the life artery of our country, bringing water from the heart of the continent.

As a final reason, the boundaries of our beloved brother, the Sudan, extend far into the depths of Africa, bringing into continuity the politically sensitive regions in that area . . . .

We shall not, in any circumstance, be able to stand idly by in the face of what is going on [in Africa today] in the false belief that it will not affect or concern us. . . .

ISLAMIC PARLIAMENT

There remains the third circle, which circumscribes continents and oceans, and which is the domain of our brothers in faith, who, wherever under the sun they may be, turn as we do in the direction of Mecca, and whose devout lips speak the same prayers. . . .

When I consider the 80 million Muslims in Indonesia, and the 50 million in China, and the millions in Malaya, Siam and Burma, and the nearly 10 million in Pakistan, and the more than 100 million in the Middle East, and the 40 million in the Soviet Union, together with the other millions in far-flung parts of the world—when I consider these hundreds of millions united by a single creed, I emerge with a sense of tremendous possibilities which we might realize through the cooperation of all these Muslims, a cooperation going not beyond the bounds of their natural loyalty to their own countries, but nonetheless enabling them and their brothers in faith to wield power wisely and without limit.

And now I go back to that wandering mission in search of a hero to play it. Here is the role. Here are the lines, and here is the stage. We alone, by virtue of our place, can perform the role.

After the Revolution:
Algerian Self-Government

❧INTRODUCTION: The Algerian revolution was successfully completed in 1962. After eight years of bitter guerrilla warfare and mass demonstrations, the French finally turned the reins of the government over to the Algerians. As would be expected, the task of running a country after so much disruption and destruction was tremendous, especially as the Algerians lacked trained manpower as a result of the French colonial policy of educating only enough Algerians to fill the low-level civil service posts.

Ahmed Ben Bella, the revolutionary we met in an earlier selection, escaped to Egypt after his arrest, where he helped to organize shipments of weapons to rebels in Algeria. Later he became the first leader of independent Algeria and faced the task of inspiring the masses of people, who were used to being kept in their place and led by others, to work for themselves. One way of doing this was to strive for visible accomplishments, things people could see and talk about and take courage from. Once inspired, they would regain their hope for the future and their determination to build a new and strong nation. At the same time, people had to be made to realize how difficult change is, so that they would not expect to achieve success instantly and without hard work and dedication.

In the following selection, Ben Bella describes some of his first steps toward rebuilding his country after a century of colonization by the French and years of bloody revolution.[7]❧

The situation in Algeria, after seven years of war, was appalling. The country had been bled dry, and everything was dislocated. The [French extremists who most actively resisted Algerian independence] had blown up schools with plastic bombs, burnt down the library of Algiers University, and destroyed tons of administrative files. Thousands of teachers had abandoned their posts. . . . The massive exodus of nine-tenths of the French population of Algeria in the summer of 1962 had brought a collapse of the economic structure. Out of ten million Algerians, there were two million unemployed, including over two hundred and fifty thousand in the town of Algiers alone. Urban unemployment had been aggravated by an influx of starving people from the country districts. . . .

The problem of this army of urban unemployed was well nigh insoluble: there was not, and there would not be for a very long time, enough industry to absorb them. It was therefore necessary to try and convince them that they must return to the land. Before all else, we had to reorganize the agricultural sector, both to provide the unemployed with work and to ensure the country's food supplies. "Operation Ploughing," was therefore our first battle.

The operation was launched on the 15th September, and after a month and a half it suffered a grave setback. We had made a serious mistake, and the situation was critical. The socialist countries had promised to send us tractors, and the press and radio had already announced their arrival. In the minds of the *fellaheen* [peasants] this meant that other people were coming to do the ploughing for them: consequently, nobody did any more work. Nobody in the local administration took even the smallest initiative; everyone was waiting for the tractors.

I decided to adopt radical methods. I summoned a meeting of the [agricultural leaders] in Algiers. . . . I explained to them that we had just got to roll up our shirt-sleeves and start ploughing with anything which was available. . . .

Whenever a breakdown was reported to me, I would rush off to the site and investigate: if the need arose, I would penalize the incompetent administrator, without going through the formality of advising my Minister of the Interior. I requisitioned seed, ploughs, and tractors on the spot. These were unorthodox methods which were censured by some people, who could only shout "Dictatorship!" But which was preferable, to respect the formalities and lose the battle of "Operation Ploughing," or to disregard them and win it?

In the end, we won it. The ploughing and sowing were finished within our time limit; in addition, the rains were favorable, and in 1963 we had a magnificent harvest. . . .

Underdeveloped countries are, indeed, extremely vulnerable. Most of them exist solely by the production of some one kind of agricultural raw material: in Cuba, for instance, it is sugar. In certain African countries it is coffee; it is wine in Algeria, jute in Pakistan, and cotton in Egypt. Now, the price of these raw materials is fixed, not in the capital city where they are sold, but in the capitals of the West, where they are bought. It follows that the underdeveloped countries are always dependent, . . . always exploited, and the disparity between their standard of living and that of the great industrial countries, far from becoming smaller with the passage of time, is merely aggravated. The great nations can ease their consciences by allowing two, three, or many more political parties: it is flattering to them and creates a good impression. . . . But we are still an impoverished and illiterate people, . . . and we are not strong enough to allow ourselves to play such a sophisticated game. In our country, it could only lead to confusion, division, and anarchy; or even worse, to the surreptitious and unwarrantable interference by a foreign power in the fight for votes. We needed a single party which could unite and lead all the country's different elements: a party which could act, and act quickly, to make up for lost time in the reorganization of the social and economic structure from top to bottom. . . .

The sight of swarms of thin and ragged children on their knees at the feet of healthy adults, removing the filth from

their boots, had always seemed to me symbolic of the
humiliation of the "natives" in underdeveloped countries
. . . .

I know exactly what the answer . . . would have been from
a theoretical socialist: the only practical solution to the
problem of the shoeshine boys is an economic one. Abolish
unemployment, and the exploitation of children will cease
automatically. Suppress the cause, and the effect will disappear. That is the orthodox answer which, though
economically correct, is not acceptable in terms of human
beings. It would take years to eradicate the cause, and
meanwhile the shoeshine boys would be abandoned to filth
and disease, illiteracy, and humiliation. . . .

I therefore resigned myself to doing that which all good
economists condemn: I decided to attack the effect rather
than the cause. . . . We decided to assemble the shoeshine
boys in the Salle Ibn Khaldoun and, after explaining our
plan to them, to distribute them among different rehabilita-
tion centers. The operation was carried out amid the
delirious enthusiasm of the Algerian people, and was a very
great success. . . . There can be no question of tolerating
the renewal of such a degrading profession in free Algeria.
Arrogant and lazy people will have to do as I do: buy a
brush, and clean their own shoes.

The framework of our welfare campaign also included
the provision of homes for old men . . . for women, and a
home for elderly couples at Sidi-Moussa. At the time when
my government was formed, there were hundreds and
hundreds of old men and women sleeping under the arcades of Algiers. I was working until very late at night at
that time, and before going to bed between one and two
in the morning, I used always to be driven round the town
to get some fresh air. Human shapes lay stretched out
everywhere, motionless, and wrapped in rags. In the
shadows of the arcades they looked like corpses of people
who had dropped dead in the struggle for life, and night
after night my heart ached to see them in such numbers.
It was a happy day for me when, after having opened the

Ahmed Ben Bella, the first President of independent Algeria, liked to get out of his office and visit the people. Here Ben Bella and Nasser visit a nationalized farm taken over from the French. (In the Middle East, it is considered perfectly natural for good friends of the same sex to hold hands.) (Wide World Photos)

various centers which I have mentioned, the order went out to collect these poor wretches and settle them in the homes which awaited them.

We carried out these operations because, quite simply, they satisfied one of the deeply felt longings of the Algerian people; but we were fully aware that the essential problem still remained to be solved. Our people had just emerged from a hundred and thirty years of darkness and neglect; they needed to have visible and tangible proof that the Algerian authorities were really working for their good. They expected affection and care from the first Algerian government of Algeria. . . .

I had never appreciated this state of mind so fully as when I was going my rounds by car. I was driving through a small village one day when I found the *fellaheen* [peasants] building a mosque, so I decided to stop, and I got out of the car. I was recognized at once and immediately surrounded by village people. We had started talking when an old man came up to me and said: "Ahmed! At last you have come! But you have been too long coming to see·us—why have you been such a long time? You have been President for months now, and we have been waiting and waiting for you." I said to him: "My father, Algeria is a big country, and there are over a thousand large villages. Even if I visited three a day every day of the year, and did nothing else, it would take me over a year. So just think what a long time it would take me to visit twenty thousand small villages such as yours." "Yes, yes," said the old man, "you are right, Ahmed. Nevertheless, we have been waiting and waiting." And the crowd around him agreed with what he had said.

It was because I could feel the pulse of the people that I knew that immediate action was needed to stop abuse. It was necessary to use somewhat unorthodox, or quite simply revolutionary, methods. The price of meat and vegetables suddenly started to soar during January and February 1963, at the time of Ramadan [the Islamic month of fasting]. I instituted an inquiry and discovered that these cruel and abusive rises in price were the work of the market middlemen. . . .

The war, Revolution, and Independence had passed these gentlemen by without leaving a mark on them. Having lent money to the farmers to finance the planting of certain vegetables, they were in control of the crops, which were thus already mortgaged to them. This enabled them to sit at their telephones and gamble (on a certainty) on the rising prices. They would telephone to the growers, saying: "Do not bring any tomatoes today." Then there would be a tomato shortage, the price would rise, and when it had reached the desired level, the middlemen would once more open the flood-gates.

They achieved the same results by an even simpler procedure, that of "stocking." Instead of distributing a certain vegetable in the market, they would keep back stocks of it.

One day, I went down to the market myself, summoned the middlemen and said to them: "I am told that there are no more onions in the market. But I have just seen quantities of them in your stores." "Mr. President," they said, smiling politely, "We cannot touch those, they are for stocking." "For stocking?" I asked. "What does that mean?" "It means, Mr. President, that they are sold." Perfectly correct bills were at once produced, signed by nonexistent men. "Very good," I said, "everything is in order." They smiled [at] each other as they watched me leaving.

But the next day the smiles disappeared when I returned at the head of a crowd of two thousand children. I showed them the famous "stocks" of onions, and said to them: "Get going! Today, everything is free. Now is the moment to replenish the larders of your families." Then the children flung themselves on the stocks of onions: wherever they had passed, there was no longer an onion to be seen. As I left, I said to these gentlemen: "I'll be back tomorrow with four thousand children." But it was not necessary; they had realized that the splendid game of "stocking" could no longer be played in the new Algeria. . . .

[There was a] paradoxical and intolerable situation which was general in Algeria at that time. Political power was in the hands of the Algerians; but economic power, including the land itself, was still in the hands of Europeans. They were still in possession of their vast estates and they continued to exploit the *fellah* [peasant], as in the past. It was clear that this state of affairs was contrary to even the most elementary ideas of justice. As long as Algerian soil was still in the hands of the big landowners, whether French or Algerian, the words "Independence" and "Revolution" made no sense. . . .

In March 1963, my government promulgated the decree nationalizing the majority of the big landed properties. Some of the *colons* [French settlers], at the time of the Evian agreements [between France and Algeria, which led to Algerian independence] had sabotaged their machinery, burned their harvests, and destroyed their stocks before leaving the country. As there was now some anxiety that the big estates might be sabotaged by their dispossessed owners, it was decided to take possession of them before the decree was made public. The [liberation army] in a remarkably secret and well-organized manner, marched on the big estates very early one morning and occupied them, calling upon their owners to leave. This is how [the wealthy Frenchman] Borgeaud's famous [estate] was nationalized. . . .

There was an outburst of joy throughout the whole country, and I must confess that I had never felt so happy in all my life. The land had come back to the people who cultivated it and Algeria had taken a decisive step on the road to socialism. . . . I was told that Borgeaud, whose name symbolized French colonialism to the Algerian people, was "very surprised" by the blow which had struck him. He immediately left for France, where, presumably, every comfort awaited him. I visited [his estate] after his departure. The house was so astonishing, and so typical, that I decided that not a stick of furniture, not a book, not an ornament was to be moved. My intention is to preserve Borgeaud's house just as he left it, and to turn it into a museum where future generations of Algerians will be able to see how the great feudal lords lived, in the days when we were their serfs.

There was great danger that the richest of the Algerians would replace the French propertied classes and constitute [a] class which would continue to keep the masses in a state of poverty. After the Evian agreements, a certain number of properties, both in the towns and in the country, had passed from the hands of Europeans into those of Algerian businessmen. These properties had been bought at low prices, and the Algerians had then proceeded to cash in on them with a greed which fairly equaled that of their predecessors. During the months which followed the decrees of Mareb, my government was called on to nationalize not only farms, but hotels, restaurants, cafés, and business concerns which had belonged to Algerians for a short time only.

We had never at any moment envisaged turning these nationalized properties into state-controlled concerns. It was up to the workers to elect their own managerial staff and direct their own undertakings. In the forum, democracy was no longer a formal political game, dominated by the money power, but had taken its place where it ought to be: at the foundations, on the actual working-sites, in the solid relationship between [labor and management], and in the equitable distribution of profits. From now on, the state could only intervene in the process in the capacity of counselor. . . .

Oil in the Middle East

ໄ►INTRODUCTION: In addition to revolutionary political activity, dramatic economic change has come to much of the Middle East. Discoveries of vast quantities of oil and natural gas have brought sudden wealth to several countries of the area. Nowhere was the effect of this bonanza more dramatic than in Kuwait.

Until the time of Iraq's invasion of Kuwait in August of 1990, the Kuwaitis had created the most successful economy in the Middle East, turning oil revenues into profitable investments worldwide. A country about the size of New Jersey with a population of just over two million, Kuwait in 1988 had a per capita Gross National Product of $13,680, compared to the U.S.'s $19,780.

Kuwait's wealth enabled it to buy technical expertise to attack its problems and meet the basic needs of its people. Instead of being overwhelmed by its riches, Kuwait set up a welfare state that was the envy of the world. All Kuwaiti citizens received free medical care and free education through college. They paid no taxes and no water or telephone bills. Basic foods were subsidized to keep prices down, and every Kuwaiti who could not find private employment was guaranteed a government job. Anyone who wished to buy a house was assured of a twenty-five-year bank loan.

Fortunately for the Kuwaitis, they have been planning for years for the days when their 90 billion barrels of oil reserves would run dry, so the Gulf War of 1991 was not as devastating economically as it might have been. The Kuwaitis had established the Kuwait Investment Company which lent money and invested in projects all over the world. For example, the KIC had constructed an office building, hotel and parking garage in

Atlanta, Georgia. Kuwait also established a development bank to help less fortunate Middle Eastern countries.

At the time of the Iraqi invasion, Kuwait had so many successful investments abroad that its investment income had surpassed its oil revenues. Thus, despite the devastating effects of the Gulf War, when Kuwait as a country was almost totally destroyed and its oil wells set on fire, Kuwait's investment income (plus the war reparations which Iraq will have to pay) will insure a prosperous future in which Kuwait will be able to rebuild its country.

Kuwait's rags-to-riches story is typical of the changes taking place in other small, oil-rich Middle Eastern states, such as Qatar and the United Arab Emirates— and to a lesser extent in larger states, such as Saudi Arabia and Libya.

The following selection consists of two parts. The first [8], written during Kuwait's early days of prosperity in the 1960s, gives a sense of the early transformation of a desert economy into a modern technological one, including the effects that the discovery of oil had on education and culture. The second part [9] presents information about oil throughout the Middle East, clarifying both the importance of oil for the region and the striking differences in income between the oil-rich states and the majority of countries that have little or no oil.🙂

[Three decades] ago very few people had ever heard of Kuwait. [Now, because of its great oil wealth, almost everyone has.] The present ruler . . . has been in on the whole great oil adventure, for when it began he was the [country's] finance minister, a minister with a very [small budget]. Now [forty] years after the first well began to gush, Kuwait has become [one of] the richest [countries] in the world. . . .

It is easy enough to earn money, but to make sensible use of it is [difficult]. The Sheik of the Bahrein Islands has the same difficulty. He, too, is overwhelmed with money and is trying to invest it in what will prove of permanent benefit to his people. His people, however, . . . want big shiny American cars today, or tomorrow at the very latest
. . . .

The poor man is more aware of his poverty when he can

see what his more favored countrymen are able to afford.
[Not so very long] ago the differences between the classes
were not so striking or so obvious. Camels and donkeys
were the only means of transport, and in the shops of the
bazaar there were only necessities to tempt people. If you
were thirsty you drank tepid brackish water or coffee,
whether you were Sheik or beggar. Nowadays, the shops in
the bazaar and the big new ones outside have all sorts of
luxuries to arouse your desires. You earn more money than
before, but on the other hand prices rise very time you
have a little extra. . . .

In the old days those who could write confined their art
to inscribing the wisdom of the Koran on parchment, but
now posters with photographs of elegant men proclaim
from every shop in the bazaar that you are not properly
dressed without a Parker 51. . . .

Those who cannot afford a car . . . save up and buy a
bicycle. There are no more fantastic ones in the world than
those that dash about the narrow streets of Kuwait, a constant danger to all traffic. The transition from camel to
automobile and bicycle has come too swiftly for the people
to be able to adjust. . . .

The bicyclists fondle their new animals. They deck them
out like camels, hanging saddle bags of Persian carpet over
the bar, . . . and the . . . handlebars are beautified with lovely golden fringes. The whole frame is covered with bands
of colored Scotch tape. . . . I have examined some parked
bicycles which had thirty-six reflectors gleaming in the sun-
light all the way from one mudguard to the other. . . .

I saw young Bedouins with black locks reaching to their
shoulders and dressed in all the voluminous garb of the
desert, who with that wore brown suede shoes and Swiss
watches which showed the date and wound themselves up
automatically. . . .

Dreams of a new Arab Empire are again being dreamed,
but before these desert countries can get anywhere they
must have water and knowledge, especially water to make
the desert blossom. Kuwait has great plans for tapping the

Shattel-Arab, the broad river of the combined waters of the Euphrates and Tigris from the mouth of which water is now shipped in barrels and tanks to Kuwait. Someday in the future, however, it will be brought in pipes overland. . . . With the help of that water they will cultivate the golden desert. Irrigation channels will crisscross the desert, and Kuwait will become a new Eden flowing with milk and honey.

There is much to be done at home, however. . . . They have now solved the problem of drinking water, for, after centuries of making do with sunk wells, which only yielded muddy, brackish water, they have used some of the oil money to build the largest distilling plant in the world. This sucks in sea water through thick pipes, boils it, traps the steam and cools it into crystal-clear drinking water free of all microbes.

The plant has a capacity of a million gallons a day, enough to provide the entire town with all the water it needs and that of a quality it has never known before. . . .

The distilling plant, of course, can be expanded. In fact, they reckon that one day it will be producing five times the present quantity. After that you will not hear any more the cry of the water seller in the streets, offering Shattel-Arab water from a goat skin draped across a donkey's back, or poured into old [gasoline cans]. There is no doubt that this distilled [water], good as sterile water, is going to make a tremendous improvement in the town's health. Typhus, dysentery, and intestinal parasites, which you get from water and milk, are [greatly] on the decline; the Kuwaitis are waging war against the myriads of flies which carry trachoma [an eye disease] from person to person.

Kuwait's hospital service has come into being as swiftly as all the other things. [In the 1950s] they built a hospital of 250 beds. [Now] there are [many hospitals of more than] 750 beds. . . . Clinics for outpatients have been started in the town, and they treat some 60,000 patients a month . . . . A sanatorium for . . . tubercular patients [has been built]. There are . . . school doctors with assistants and nurses and a miniature army of specially trained women who spend all their time treating the . . . trachoma patients. There are motorized clinics that drive round to the desert towns and visit Bedouin camps to see if any help is needed, but now they are thinking of replacing these by permanent clinics and medical stores in . . . villages round about in the desert. . . .

Enlightenment is what is needed most . It is not enough [in the modern world] just to be able to read the Koran and write your own name; . . . and so Kuwait is building schools with much of the oil money.

Sheik Yussuf ben-Isur built the first . . . school, where boys could learn more than to read the Koran. There was no state [treasury] in those days, so when he got the idea, Sheik Yussuf went to the merchants and pearl dealers of Kuwait and spoke to them so persuasively of the advantages of having children who knew more than the older generations that they nodded agreement and clubbed together to contribute a certain sum. They decided in their wisdom that half of the amount was to be used to build a school, and the other half to buy or build boats which would go out in the summer and fish for pearls at the banks, and the proceeds from the pearls they got were to be the school's revenue. The school was started in 1922 and proved a success. Progressive Egypt provided the teachers.

Five years later another school was started. Instruction was given in religion, arithmetic, Arabic, and business practice and when prospecting for oil began in 1936, science and geography were added to the curriculum. In 1941 there were four schools, and the war had put a temporary stop to prospecting. It was discovered that the revenue from the pearl boats no longer covered the cost of the schools, so the merchants voluntarily paid an income tax of one-half percent. . . .

Today Kuwait has [over 100] schools, a technical school, a business college, and a purely religious Islamic institute. In addition, there are the private schools the oil company runs for its own officials and workers. These include a Technical Training Center where Kuwaitis learn the skilled trades needed in the operations of the oil company. [The Kuwait Oil Company], in fact, is a state within a state; it has its own hospitals and clinics.

Today [a young Kuwaiti] learns arithmetic and belongs to the Boy Scouts. They have great excitement tracking in the desert, fox tails hang in the troop hall, and everybody [kneels down on] his bare knees on [the Sabbath], which is Friday. . . . [A Kuwaiti boy] plays with toy [trucks] and jet [planes] as children do everywhere, but when it comes to drawing he lets his imagination run riot in colorful pictures of foaming waterfalls, wide rivers, and great lakes fringed with virgin forest. That is his fairy-tale world, the world which he has heard of but never seen, a wonderful world where you can find shade beneath green trees and be lavish with fresh water.

Kuwait has three superschools built with oil money and designed by English architects. Each has cost £1,000,000 [about $1.5 million]. There are no schools in Europe to compare with them, and probably not in the USA is there anything so magnificent and lavish. I went over one when it was inspected by Sheik Abdullah al-Jabir, who has charge of all the schools in Kuwait. . . .

The Sheik pointed out the wonders of the place to me with justifiable pride, yet I believe that what he liked best of all was the model of a *baghala* [a sailing vessel] in the handicraft room. He studied it closely, and it was obvious that he knew the name of every sheet and block.

Kuwait's educational system calls for the serving of 14,000 free meals every day in the various schools in the town. These are supplied from a central kitchen, which must be one of the largest in the world. The food is distributed in thermos container cars, and even on holidays the schools' dining rooms are opened so that the children can come and have their lunch there, as on ordinary days.

Today the poorest Bedouin can send his boy straight from his tent, unwashed and with lice in his hair, to one of these palaces, and there, without its costing him a penny, his son will be washed, clothed, and stuffed with knowledge.

Modern Kuwait is dominated by its oil industry. Note the Arabic numerals (125)
on the oil truck, showing the origin of modern Western numerals. (Embassy of
Kuwait, Washington, D.C.)

In Kuwait itself, there is only the oil industry to absorb
the production of the good schools. There are [few] possibilities for industry, as all other raw materials have to be
imported and commerce has no local products to trade in.

So, what will happen if the goose stops laying its golden
eggs, if the wells run dry? Someday they must, and whether
that will be in ten years or a hundred no one can tell. Or
suppose the scientists discover that it no longer pays to take
all the trouble with oil, because it is much easier to get
power, light, and heating from the sea, the sun's rays, the
air, or some still undiscovered source of energy? It is not
impossible. What would happen to the hospitals and the
schools and the free meals and the running of the water
distillery, if the . . . wells . . . run dry? I asked Sheik Abdullah that question, and he had his answer.

By the time the oil ceases to flow, or its place is taken by
something else, said the Sheik, the people of Kuwait will

have worked up to a cultural level which will raise them high above other peoples of the Middle East. They will be the Phoenicians of the Persian Gulf, who will trade in foreign lands with the products of other peoples. Kuwait will [let] others do the heavy work and only deal . . . in finished products. . . .

You can hear very much the same thing from the Sheiks of other oil lands of the Middle East, Bahrein, Saudi Arabia, Iraq . . . All those countries, into which millions pour from oil royalties without their having to do anything but use them in the best possible way, are dreaming of training their young people to be capable of deeds which will put their country at the head of the Arab world.

꘎POSTSCRIPT: As important as oil is to some Middle Eastern countries, it does not play a major role in the economic life of most nations of the region. The popular image, based partly on fact and partly on exaggeration, is that the Middle East is awash with oil. Factually, it is true that more than half of the earth's oil reserves are located in the Middle East, but it is a greatly misleading exaggeration to think that all countries of the region are as oil-rich as Kuwait and a handful of other small nations. In reality, only a minority of Middle Eastern countries have a substantial quantity of oil. The majority have very little oil or none at all, as the table on the next page shows.

Notice that none of the 20 Middle Eastern countries have a higher per capita GNP than the United States. Moreover, only six—Saudi Arabia, Kuwait, United Arab Emirates, Qatar, Bharain and Israel—have a per capita GNP higher than $6,000 per year. These countries have a combined population of only 36 million, or roughly 10 percent of the 345 million people in the Middle East. In other words, the overwhelming majority of the people in the Middle East are not well off.

Oil income, then, can be seen as a desperately needed source of capital for development efforts in the Middle East. For several decades the price of oil was artificially low, costing no more than $1 or $2 per barrel. The cost of a gallon of gas at the pump in the U.S. in those days was about 25

OIL IN THE MIDDLE EAST, BY COUNTRY

Country	Recoverable oil (2000 in billions of barrels)	Population (2000 in millions)	Per Capital GNP (1998 in US$)
Saudi Arabia	263.5	21.6	6,910
Iraq	112.5	23.1	—
U.A.E.	97.8	2.8	17,870
Kuwait	96.5	2.2	—
Iran	89.7	67.4	1,650
Libya	29.5	5.1	—
Algeria	9.2	31.5	1,550
Egypt	2.9	68.3	1,290
Oman	5.3	2.4	—
Yemen	4.0	17.0	280
Qatar	3.7	0.6	—
Syria	2.5	16.5	1,020
Tunisia	0.3	9.6	2,060
Turkey	0.3	65.3	3,160
Bharain	0.1	0.7	7,640
Jordan	0.0	5.1	1,150
Morocco	0.0	28.8	1,240
Israel	0.0	6.2	16,180
Lebanon	0.0	42.2	3,560
U.S.	21.8	275.6	29,240

Source: Oil figures from *Oil and Gas Journal*, January 1, 2000; population and GNP figures from Population Reference Bureau, *2000 World Population Data Sheet.*

cents. Then, in the early 1970s, the oil-producing countries became better organized and began to use OPEC (Organization of Petroleum Exporting Countries) as a cartel. OPEC met regularly to set the price of oil, which began to rise and reflect the real demand for oil in the world. The table on p. 211 shows the recent history of oil prices.

From a high of $37 per barrel of imported oil in 1981 (more than $40 on the open market) oil prices fell gradually and then precipitously in 1986, hovering around $18 a barrel for over a decade. Then in 1998 the price fell to $12, lower than it had been in 25 years. The decline of oil prices in the 1980s and 90s was largely a result of the so-called "oil glut," a surplus of oil caused by reduced demand, which in turn was a result of global economic recession and, more importantly and lastingly, conservation measures taken by oil consumers.

Crude Oil Prices in the U.S.
(Dollars per Barrel)

Year	Domestic	Imported
1978	10.61	14.57
1979	14.27	21.67
1980	24.23	33.89
1981	34.33	37.05
1982	31.22	33.55
1983	28.87	29.30
1984	28.53	28.88
1985	26.66	26.99
1986	14.82	14.00
1987	17.76	18.13
1988	14.74	14.56
1989	17.87	18.08
1990	22.59	21.76
1991	19.33	18.70
1992	18.63	18.20
1993	16.67	16.14
1994	15.67	15.51
1995	17.33	17.14
1996	20.77	20.64
1997	19.61	18.53
1998	13.18	12.04
1999	17.90	17.26
2000	29.06	27.69

Source: U.S. Energy Information Administration, *Petroleum Marketing Annual 2000.*

The production of smaller, more fuel-efficient cars, greater emphasis on home insulation and lower thermostat settings, and the use of alternative sources of energy, such as the sun, water, wind and nuclear power, have combined to reduce demand for oil substantially and thus greatly reduce oil income in the Middle East.

As the chart on p. 212 shows, oil income in the Middle East reached an all-time high of $300 billion in 1980 and then dropped to as low as $60 billion in 1986, leveling off at about $100 billion a year throughout the 1990s. Because of reduced income, many oil-producing countries in the Middle East had to cut back on their development efforts during the 1980s and 90s. Saudi Arabia, for example, which had been devel-

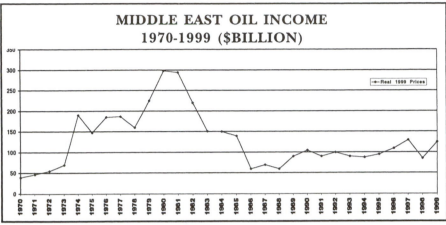

Note: The income figures shown in this chart represent the combined earnings of all members of the Organization of Arab Petroleum Exporting Countries, including Algeria, Bahrain, Egypt, Iraq, Kuwait, Libya, Qatar, Saudi Arabia, Syria, Tunisia and the United Arab Emirates.

Source: Organization of Arab Petroleum Exporting Countries, *Secretary General's Annual Report 1999.*

oping an $18 billion industrial city called Jubail, had to call a halt to all new construction projects there in 1983. At the same time, Qatar and the United Arab Emirates were forced to trim government payrolls by 20 percent. As the chart on p. 213 shows, these three countries are among the wealthiest in the Middle East. Their cutbacks will still leave their citi-

WORLD OIL DEMAND, SELECTED COUNTRIES
(Millions of Barrels per Day)

	United States	Canada	Japan	France	Italy	Germany	United Kingdom
1970	14.7	1.5	3.8	1.9	1.7	2.6	2.1
1975	16.3	1.8	4.6	2.3	1.9	2.7	1.9
1980	17.1	1.9	5.0	2.3	1.9	2.7	1.7
1985	15.7	1.5	4.4	1.8	1.7	2.3	1.6
1990	17.0	1.7	5.1	1.8	1.9	2.4	1.8
1995	17.7	1.8	5.7	1.9	2.0	2.9	1.8
1998	18.9	1.9	5.5	2.0	2.1	2.9	1.8
1999	19.5	1.9	5.6	2.0	2.0	2.8	1.7
2000	19.7	2.0	5.5	2.0	1.9	2.8	1.7

Source: U.S. Energy Information Administration, *International Petroleum Monthly,* July 2001.

OPEC COUNTRY SHARES OF OIL INCOME US$ PER CAPITA, 1998 AND 1999

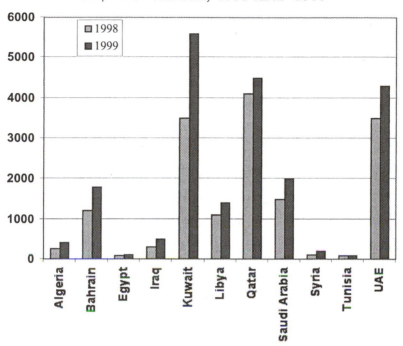

Source: Organization of Arab Petroleum Exporting Countries *Secretary General's Annual Report 1999.*

zens relatively well off, but lesser endowed countries will feel the pinch of reduced development funds.

Recently, especially in 2000 and 2001, the price of oil has recovered and even spiked upwards in response to increased demand and the limiting of supply by OPEC. How long this will last nobody knows. Conservation measures have been uneven in the industrial world, as the chart of "World Oil Demand" shows on p. 212. Some countries, such as France, have actually reduced demand for oil since 1980, while others, such as Canada, Italy, Germany and the United Kingdom, have maintained their 1980 levels. The U.S. stands out as an exception to this trend, increasing its annual demand for oil about 15 percent over its 1980 level. A rapidly growing economy in the 1990s and a relaxation of conservation measures combined to increase U.S. demand for oil. In 2000 half of all motor vehicles sold in the U.S. were either trucks or sports utility vehicles.

In the long run, conservation measures that reduce the consumption of oil will benefit both consumers and producers. Oil, as a non-renewable natural resource, will run out eventually. Conservation measures which lower consumption will extend the lifetime of the oil supply, giving consumers more time to develop alternative sources of energy and producers more time to develop new sources of income. In the meantime, much of the world will depend on Middle East oil for energy and the Middle East will depend on oil income for development investments.

Islamic Feminism

৯INTRODUCTION: It is difficult to generalize about the status of women in the Middle East. The stereotype is that of women forced to wear a veil, dispirited and totally subjugated to men. This stereotype has rarely corresponded with reality. It overlooks the fact that even in the most traditional of Middle Eastern countries women have always had extensive power and influence in something of great importance to them, the management of their families.

In the Middle East of today, the position of women ranges from completely traditional, in countries such as Afghanistan and Saudi Arabia, to very modern, in countries such as Egypt, Iraq and Morocco. While in Afghanistan, the old Taliban leadership had banned women from working, in Egypt 50 percent of Egypt's Television Corporation employees are women and in Morocco 20 percent of the judges are women, a figure higher than in the U.S. And while in Saudi Arabia women are not allowed to drive cars, in Iraq the General Federation of Iraqi Women has a million and a half members with 222 subbranches throughout the country. It is thus difficult to generalize about the status of women in the Middle East. One needs to talk about specific countries and specific social classes within these countries.

The following excerpt is from Elizabeth Warnock Fernea's book, *In Search of Islamic Feminism*. After visiting nine Islamic countries to assess the status of women, Fernea concludes that feminism in the Middle East is necessarily made up of somewhat different ingredients than in the U.S. As an Iraqi woman leader puts it, "We see feminism in America as dividing men and women—separating women from the family." As a result, the General Federation of Iraqi Women supports such things as maternity leave and child care which address the needs of both men and women in terms of work and the family.

In addition, feminism in Islamic countries tends to grow out of religious belief; there is really no secular feminism. Indeed, Islamic feminists believe that the Koran already supports gender equality. Thus, when discrimination against women is detected, Islamic feminists tend to interpret this as either (1) a misinterpretation of the Koran or (2) a case of class inequality, where a woman's inability to succeed is caused by poverty or a lack of education; her right to succeed, however, is already established.

In the following selection, the author describes her meeting in Morocco with the leaders of a women's movement who, by collecting one million signatures, brought about a revision in family law and also inspired the election of the first two women to parliament. [10]❧

[A] family discussion raged about the quality of men's and women's lives in Morocco. I use the word "rage" to reflect the spirit of the discussion, which was intense and spirited. Every member of the family was telling me how to write my book.

"You must first explain about the changes in the family law," said Fatiha.

"And interview some judges, to get their point of view," said her husband. "Because they are the ones who will implement the changes in the law."

"Oh, yes," I answered. "That's one of the principal issues I want to write about . . ."

"And," she added, "when you write that, don't forget to mention the work of Leila Abouzeid."

The entire family focused on Leila, who smiled, pleased. Clearly her family was very proud of her contributions on this crucial issue. It was King Hassan II himself who appointed her to the special commission formed in 1992

Palestinian women, demonstrating here after Friday prayers, have played a central Role in the Intifada and have also been leaders in various anti-war movements in the Middle East. (Jerusalem Press Service)

to evaluate *mudawana*, or Moroccan family law. The commission's mandate was to judge whether the current law fulfilled the spirit of the Qu'ran [Koran] or not, and to measure its effects on women, men, children, and the family. It was also empowered to make recommendations. The group's work was finished, the recommendations had been forwarded to a committee of religious scholars (all men), and the King's proclamation of reforms had been recently published and analyzed in the media.

"And is it a beneficial document for women, the King's new proclamation, I mean?"

"In the past, as you know, madame, family law was administered by qadis, religious judges. Everyone knows that in the past these qadis tended to discriminate against women. Well"—he opened his hands toward us, almost apologetically—"they thought the modern world was full of sin and it was women's fault because they didn't stay at home like they're supposed to . . ."

"But how can they stay at home?" broke in Soad. "How ridiculous. They have to go out and work."

"Yes, yes, Soad, I'm trying to explain to madame the mentality of these qadis, that's all." Abdul Hadi paused again. "Well, of course women have to go out and work, that's the name of the game these days. What I am trying to say now is that qadis really can't discriminate against women anymore, at least in terms of divorce proceedings, because of the careful wording of the new law."

Zakaria smiled at his father proudly.

"I agree with you, my dear," returned Fatiha, "in general, that is. . . ."

Laughter interrupted her, a relief from the intensity of the conversation. Legal reforms changing women's position affected the everyday functioning of the family, that basic cornerstone of Moroccan society, indeed of all Islamic societies. What the King had done, and what the qadis will do with the new *mudawana*, would have reverberations in everyone's life for years to come—men, women, children. . . ."

"Leila," [Abdul Hadi] said, "we will arrange for B.J. to talk to a judge in the Court of Appeals, the highest court of appeals. Then she can ask those who are actually involved in these cases."

Morocco's national courthouse stood in the center of downtown Rabat. It was set in a small fenced garden, far back from Boulevard Muhammad V. . . .

"These are the judge's private chambers," explained Leila. "No one is allowed up here except the judges and their clerks—and now—us! . . ."

[We] knocked on the judge's door and were admitted by her clerk, a young woman in a brown print djellaba and head scarf.

"Please." She invited us to sit down. "Madame the Judge is in a meeting. She will be with you soon. . . ."

I turned my attention instead to the row of coat hooks mounted on a strip of varnished wood by the door. There was a black top coat, and next to it what was obviously Madame's judgely robe. . . .

"But don't they wear hats? Or wigs?" I asked Leila.

"Oh, judges don't wear hats here or wigs or turbans like the qadis. We're just like you in the United States," said Madame Assisa Oaulalou, who had come in, shut the door carefully, introduced us to her clerk Fatima, apologized for being late, and drawn up a chair to sit not at her desk, but more casually, between Leila and myself.

"In the Supreme Court, though," she added, "the men wear Moroccan dress, including a red tarbush or fez."

All this was pronounced in soft but exceedingly clear French. . . .

Madame Oaulalou turned to me, listening to Leila describe my purposes. . . .

Madame Oaulalou had been a judge in the High Court of Appeals for a year, she said, but before that, she had worked as assistant to the president in the lower courts, which dealt with crises, with urgent lawsuits.

"Are you the only woman judge?" I asked.

Madame Oualalou giggled. "Oh, no, madame. There are many women judges in Morocco."

My eyes widened. "But, but . . ." I stuttered. "There are no women judges at all in Egypt."

She smiled in a kindly way. "Yes, I know, but that is Egypt. There are many Muslim countries where women are not allowed to act as judges. We are not one of them. One must look carefully at the history and experience of each country by itself . . ."

I nodded humbly. "And not make generalizations about Muslim women." I finished her sentence.

"Exactly." She smiled at me, turned to Leila, said something in Moroccan Arabic which I found difficult to catch. Leila replied. Again I didn't understand.

"You have your book with you, B.J.," Leila said in English. "You might show it to her now."

Madame the Judge looked at the cover of *Women and Family in the Middle East: New Voices of Change,* a collection of articles by Western and Middle Eastern scholars, which I edited in 1985.

"This is Morocco on the cover," she noted. "Look at the variety of women's lives, even in this picture. I have to tell myself to take each case before me on its own merits first, *then* begin to look for general patterns. . ."

"My youngest daughter is a lawyer," I began. "She would be interested in knowing the percentage of women judges in Morocco."

Madame Oualalou considered. "At least twenty percent!" she replied.

I was once more surprised. "I think that figure is higher than in the United States."

"Yes," agreed Madame Oualalou. "When I was in the United States some years ago, I found that people did not want to believe me. So please write about it, madame, and stress how many judges we have who are women. God knows we have worked hard to reach this level. . . ."

I had the feeling we had overstayed our time, but Madame the Judge insisted we must stay for coffee. She relaxed and talked about her education and her work: she was a specialist in cases involving grievous harm.

"It is my duty to decide who is responsible for inflicting that harm—who is legally responsible."

"And you enjoy your work?"

"Oh yes," she answered. "But my responsibilities are very heavy. I work at home as well as here. I have no children, you see, so my time is less taken up than it would be otherwise. And here judges have more authority than in the United States. We listen to witnesses, we make definitive judgments in serious situations."

We finished our coffee and rose. Madame did not stop us. But as she took my hand, she said, "May I ask you a favor?"

"Of course."

"You can put in your book that Moroccan women are coming along, but there is much work to do."

I nodded.

"But also, can you say this in a pleasant way? If women here in Morocco are not trained or do not all hold responsible positions like mine, it is not because of their biological differences from men."

I am puzzled again. "It's not?"

"No, it's because of their social position in the society. It's because of class. We have to keep struggling against that."

On Boulevard Muhammad V, Leila and I tried to cross, but the traffic was against us. Bicycles, taxis, and cars were struggling to move around this circle in front of the railway station, the hub of the wheel from which . . . many streets fanned out into the neighborhoods of the city. Everyone was on the way home for the two-hour lunch. . . .

After a substantial meal, the main meal of the day, the family would take a short siesta. Then, in late afternoon, the traffic would converge once more on this principal hub, as shopkeepers, students, lawyers, teachers, and judges like Madame Assia Oualalou returned to their offices, to work until dark, when the sounding of the call to prayer throughout the city announced that the sun had set on another day and that God is great.

"Now, B.J.," said Leila, "before we go any further with these talks—the *mudawana*, the Parliament ladies, and so on, we have to meet Latifa. Without her none of this change would have taken place."

"Who is she?"

"A dynamic young woman. You will see. I will phone her this afternoon."

We were lunching in town, with [friends]. Roast chicken in a small, dim, but agreeable restaurant . . . I told them what Madame the Judge had said, that women's status in Morocco was basically a matter of [social] class. . . . Clearly, I had to rethink some of my own preconceptions about the place of women in modern Moroccan society.

The American feminist movement is based on the central idea that socialization, not biology, determines the roles which men and women will play throughout their

A woman, Anan Ashrawi (left), headed the Palestinian delegation to a Mideast peace conference. She is a major spokesperson for the Palestinian cause. (AP/Wide World Photos)

lives. Socialization is responsible for the way both men and women are treated in society . . . Women's roles, according to this theory, are constructed: they are not the result of biological differences between males and females. It is socialization that determines who gets power. Therefore, feminists believe, to assure justice and equality of power between men and women, one must work to change the ways in which children are socialized: at school, in the home, in the religious institutions, in the workplace. . . .

Socialization, then, is seen in the West as they key to female progress. Not biology. And as I began to ponder the issue of barriers to women's progress and how my Middle Eastern friends perceived those barriers, I began to wonder whether in Morocco, *class*, the position of the woman in the social structure of Moroccan society, did not operate in much the same way as . . . socialization did in our own country. Was it class formation that kept women back? That was what Madame Assia Oaulalou had said, a woman who occupied an important position in Morocco as a judge in the High Court of Appeals. Class. Not biological differences. . . . Hadn't Leila said that all the women of that committee were members of the upper class or upper middle class? Didn't that contribute to their power in society?

Class, the idea of social class, wherein people are rated not on their intrinsic moral behavior or native talents but on their position in the social hierarchy, is a distasteful subject to most Americans. We tell ourselves that we are a classless society, that it does not matter where we come from, what our origins may be. What matters is present behavior, hard work, and achievement. . . .

"Not *sometimes*. *Always* we must struggle to make people listen, even if they don't want to," [Latifa said].

Well, I thought . . . this was indeed the woman who launched the campaign to change the *mudawana*.

"How did you do it, really?" I asked.

She did not even wait for me to identify what "it" was. Because she knew that all over Morocco she was given credit—and blame—for "it." What she did, she told me in rapid-fire detail, was to collect one million signatures on a petition to the King himself, asking him to consider reforms in family law, the laws crucial to women's lives, the laws regulating marriage, divorce, inheritance, child custody, and polygamy.

"But," she added, . . ."I did not do it alone. We did it together, the members of the union, and their brothers and sisters and cousins and mothers and fathers and grandfathers and grandmothers. Everyone knew that the law was not working. Everyone wanted to change it—not just women alone!" . . .

"I did forget one thing," she said, and . . . launched into a nonstop account of how the one million signatures not only jump-started the King's commission to reform family law, but served as a wake-up call to the political parties, which were then reorganizing for the 1993 elections.

"How did it do that?"

Latifa wagged a finger at me. She was a head taller than I and her moving finger, at the level of my forehead, flashed past my eyes as she spoke. . . .

"The political parties saw what was missing in their cadres: women!" Thus, Latifa said, "they added women to the slates of the major political parties. For the first time in Moroccan history, after thirty-seven years of independence, two women are sitting in Parliament."

"One last question. . . ."

"Do you consider yourself a feminist, [Latifa]?"

She laughed. "Of course." Looking at Leila, she added, "And even if I didn't consider myself one, I have been made into one by the fundamentalists and the media, right, Leila?"

"Yes," said Leila. "Tell her, Latifa."

"When the reform commission was suggested by the King, there was an outcry among the fundamentalists. They mobilized in the mosques and wanted to condemn me, me, Latifa Djebabdi, to death. Because I was that awful thing, a feminist."

"How did you feel?" I asked. "How did you react? . . ."

"I felt terrible," she said. "But I felt I could not show it. I am a Muslim too, you know. I knew they were demonizing me for their own ends, because we had one million people behind this association . . . And my family and my husband stood behind me. . . ."

"Do you think the fundamentalists would have attacked us if we were one of those other little women's organizations with nice, well-meaning educated elite ladies in it? No, they attacked us because they saw that we were powerful. We have seventeen offices in Morocco and one in Paris."

"They are religious Muslims and saw you as against Islam?" I questioned.

Latifa dismissed this with a toss of her head.

"Religion! They are not interested in religion. They are interested in power."

"But they didn't put you in jail or . . ."

"No," said Leila, taking up the tale. "The King inter-
vened. He had not forgotten the problems in Algeria with
religious fundamentalists. He basically told them to stop,
that we were a country where free discussion was allowed,
and they must be quiet and let the commission do its
work. And they did."

"The business of calling people feminists is just playing with words," said Latifa. "It has a bad association [here]
with the West—free sex, drugs, all that. The religious fundamentalists are not against that. They want us to see the
West as corrupt. What they are really against is women
asserting their rightful place in Islamic society."

We were at the door now. "Islamic feminism?"

Latifa tried that one on. "Well, if you like, madame. Frankly,
I prefer something like Islamic women's movement. . . ."

"So what did you think, B.J.?"

"Impressive woman!"

"Yes," said Leila, "but don't do what they do in America,
B.J., and give one person all the credit. She works hard, but
she has hundreds of people who work with her and help
her. . . . The union is a real association, not an organization founded by foreign women's groups or foundations or
any group that has 'ism after their names."

The Arab-Israeli Conflict

❧INTRODUCTION: During the Arab-Israeli war of 1973, the Arabs were able to use their oil as a political weapon. By cutting back oil supplies to the West, they attempted to make certain that Western powers would listen to their demand that Israel be forced to abandon the Arab land it had occupied during the Arab-Israeli wars of 1967 and 1973.

What were these wars about? What is the source of the conflict between the Arabs and Israelis? These questions are very difficult to answer; almost every "fact" is disputed by one side or the other. The basic dispute relates to who owns the land of Israel (formerly Palestine). Since the Jews were expelled from Palestine by the Romans 2,000 years ago, they have been a homeless people and have prayed for eventual return to their land. But during the millennia of the Jews' Diaspora (scattering), the land was inhabited by Palestinian Arabs, although it never has been an official Arab state.

From the early sixteenth century until 1947, Palestine was under Turkish or British rule. As a result of the persecution of Jews in Europe in the late nineteenth and early twentieth centuries, the Zionist movement, the objective of which was to bring about a return of the Jewish people to Palestine, began to grow. This movement was resisted by the Arabs who felt that the land belonged to them. During World War I, the Arabs, with British aid, drove the Turks off the Arab land they possessed only to find that France and Britain had secretly agreed to divide this land once the Turks had been driven out. This private arrangement was made official through the League of Nations mandate system, by which Britain gained control of Palestine. In 1917, Britain issued the Balfour Declaration, a document ratified by the League of Nations, which stated that the Jews had a right to a "homeland" in Palestine as long as the rights of the existing population were not affected.

At the time of this declaration, the population of Palestine was largely Arab, but with the increased persecution of Jews in Europe and the rise of Hitler, Jewish immigration to Palestine vastly increased. The Arabs demanded that Jewish immigration be limited, and the British put a quota on the number of immigrants. World War II, however, created a large number of Jewish refugees who had no place to go, and Britain's continued refusal to increase the number of immigrants elicited great criticism in the West. By the end of the war in 1945, it was clear that something had to be done, and in 1947 the United Nations voted to partition Palestine into Arab and Jewish sections. This plan was accepted by the Zionists but rejected by the surrounding Arab states, which, as they had warned they would do, promptly attacked the new state.

This first war in 1948 was won by Israel and resulted in an increase in the size of the Jewish state. Continued hostility between the two sides led to follow-up wars in 1956, 1967 and 1973. Israel won decisively in 1956 and 1967, and the two sides fought to a stalemate in 1973.

The chief issue at stake today is the future of the 1.7 million Palestinian refugees who have been made homeless by the various wars. The Arab states have agreed to recognize the existence of Israel if Israel returns the land it conquered in 1967 and either allows the Palestinian refugees to return to their lands in Israel or compensates them for their losses. It is possible that a Palestinian state will be set up on the West Bank of the Jordan and in the Gaza strip between Israel and Egypt.

The selection that follows presents a hypothetical debate on the major points in the Arab-Israeli conflict between an Israeli (David) and an Arab (Daud, which means David in Arabic).[11]

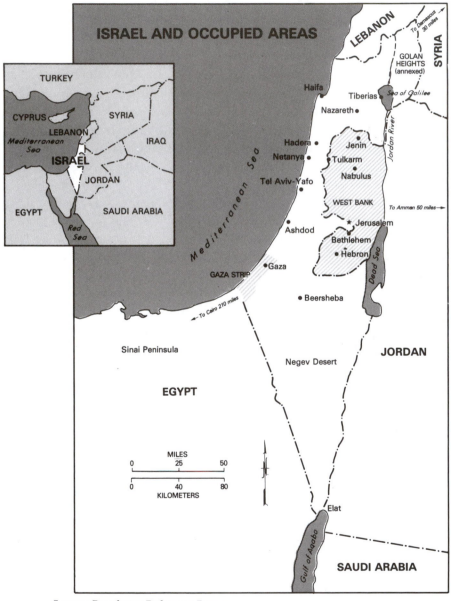

SOURCE: Population Reference Bureau

DAUD: Well, looking back on the Arab-Israeli conflict, it all seems inevitable, doesn't it? Like it had to happen.

DAVID: Yes, I guess it does. We were two oppressed peoples with nationalistic feelings coming into conflict over the same land.

DAUD: But there are still some things I'm not clear about. For instance, the beginnings of Zionism. Where did this idea come from? Why did the movement spring up after so many years?

DAVID: Well, for many reasons, but mostly because the Jews in Eastern Europe were victims of pogroms—the systematic beating and murder of Jews in their ghettos.

DAUD: But pogroms had happened before, and no one had left Europe.

DAVID: They had happened, but not so frequently and violently. It became clear that without our own country we would never be allowed to live our own lives.

DAUD: But why my country? My people, the Palestinians, were living there!

DAVID: The Jews came to Palestine because it is the promised land for the Jewish people; it is our ancient homeland, for which we have prayed for almost two thousand years. In our prayers, for all this time, we have said, "Next year in Jerusalem."

DAUD: Wait a minute. The Jews may have lived in Palestine in the past, but they left. We Palestinian Arabs have lived in Palestine since that time. How can people who have been gone for almost two thousand years return and expect the people who live there now to move aside and make way for them?

DAVID: First of all, we moved away because we were forced to. Second, many of the Arabs living in the Israeli section of Palestine came there during the 1920s and 30s and 40s. They were new arrivals just like the Jews. And finally, no one was asking you to move aside. You could have stayed. All we wanted was a place to settle.

There was room for both of us. We accepted the terms Britain gave us in the Balfour Declaration of 1917. This didn't declare a Jewish state but a home for the Jewish people, and we accepted that. After the slaughter of six million Jews by the Nazis and the incredible Jewish refugee problem caused by World War II, it became apparent that more than a Jewish home was needed; that a Jewish state was needed.

DAUD: And that's just the point! We Palestinian Arabs were also living there and wanted our own state.

DAVID: I don't know what you mean by a Palestinian Arab. Palestine was part of Turkey for hundreds of years until after World War I, when the League of Nations put it under British control under the mandate system. It was never a state in any formal sense.

DAUD: You know what I mean. I am an Arab. I lived in Palestine until I was thrown out by European Jews who had never seen Palestine or the Middle East in their lives, people who spoke German or Russian or Polish.

DAVID: The Jews didn't throw you out; you left. But let's get some history straight. The Palestine that was designated a "homeland" for the Jews was originally four times the size of Israel today. But the British, in violation of the League of Nations mandate, turned over three-quarters of it to the Arabs. This was your "homeland." Why weren't you satisfied with that?

DAUD: You're referring to what eventually became Jordan. Well, we don't want to simply live in Jordan. We want a state of our own. Israel is sitting on land that was worked by my father, my grandfather and my great-grandfather. In fact, at the time of your Balfour Declaration in 1917, 90 percent of Palestine's population was Arab and only 10 percent was Jewish.

DAVID: That's a figure that's trotted out all the time, but it's very misleading. If you look at that small fraction of Palestine where the Jews settled—where they were allowed to settle—you will see that by the end of the

A historic moment: David Ben-Gurion, standing beneath a picture of Theodor Herzl, founder of the Zionist movement, proclaims Israel's independence after the 1948 war with the Arabs. (United Press International)

nineteenth century Jews were actually the largest religious group in the area. Most of the permanent Arab population lived outside the Jewish settled areas. But my point is simply that Jews have always lived in Palestine. Many Jews never left. They have, in a sense, held the land for us in our scattering—our Diaspora—until our return.

DAUD: How can land worked by my relatives and ancestors for centuries belong to a people scattered all over the world?

DAVID: Some of your ancestors worked some of the land for centuries, but as I just mentioned, in the Jew-

ish settlement areas of Palestine there were as many Jews
as Arabs who had lived there for centuries. In fact, as
more and more Jews settled in these areas, more and
more Arabs followed them to take advantage of the
progress the Jews were bringing with them. Besides, you
talk as if the land of Palestine were completely occupied
when we arrived. Much of it wasn't. We have drained
swamps and made the desert green. We have taken land
that was never cultivated or occupied before and put it
to good use. The land that was occupied or owned we
bought and at outrageous prices.

DAUD: You bought some of it; you bought the land that
was not taken in the 1948 war and the land that was not
appropriated by your government when my people fled
during that war. But when all this land became Jewish land,
the Arabs were evicted to make room for Jewish labor.

DAVID: Well, that's what we came for—to work our own
land. We were a desperate people with no land of our own
who legally acquired whatever lands we settled on. Anyway, there were Jewish landlords who hired Arab labor.

DAUD: And you wouldn't have been able to hire anybody unless you were bankrolled by Westerners. This is
another reason we have never been able to accept you.
You can't deny that you are here because of the power
of the Western countries; indeed, you are a part of the
West, a potential tool of the Western colonial powers.
You think like Westerners and have come here on Western money and were voted into existence by a United
Nations dominated by Western countries, especially the
United States. Israel is a Western arrow in the heart of
the Arab nation. In fact, we Arabs have been the innocent victims of Christian anti-Semitism in Europe and
America. The Christians in the West have worked out
their guilt feelings for the way the Jews were treated by
giving you our land.

DAVID: You may have a point about Christians' guilt
feelings about the Jews—in fact, many of them probably
wanted to get rid of us, and they didn't care where we

went. But it was the Jews who wanted to go to Palestine, their holy land.

DAUD: You as a people wanted to go to Palestine after World War II only because the United States wouldn't admit as many of you as wanted to settle there!

DAVID: That's only partially true. There are many Jews who are not Zionists, who personally do not want to live in Palestine, although they support the state of Israel. They might live in America but agree with Herzl, the founder of Zionism, that the solution to the mistreatment of Jews in Europe and around the world had to be the establishment of a Jewish nation—a return to their holy land. In fact, the whole world, as represented by the United Nations, believed in this goal and voted to establish the state of Israel.

DAUD: The whole world my eye! The whole Western world you mean—the Western world that dominated the United Nations at that time. The Arabs never agreed to have a Jewish state. We told you we would attack if such a state were formed, and we did, as soon as Israel was declared a state by the United Nations in 1947. The war has continued off and on ever since.

DAVID: Yes, you attacked, and you lost. You lost more land than you would have lost if you had just accepted the U.N. partition. First you refused to accept the U.N. declaration, and then you refused to accept the verdict of war.

DAUD: How could we accept what was unjust and wrong? In 1917, the year of the Balfour Declaration, Palestine was clearly an Arab country. But the Zionist movement in Europe created constant immigration. You ask us to be law-abiding and accept the original decision of the United Nations. Well, you Jews weren't so law-abiding. During the years 1939 to 1943, against British law, you smuggled 20,000 immigrants into Palestine.

DAVID: Wait a minute. The most recent evidence shows there were more "illegal" Arab immigrants than Jewish ones. The British applied a double standard, overlooking the flood of Arabs and severely restricting the number of Jews who could come in. In fact, some scholars feel that it was the Arabs who displaced the Jews in pre-Israel Palestine, not the reverse. But let's forget that. The point is, we were both refugee populations; we needed a place to go. If you had accepted the U.N. partition plan, there would have been room for all of us.

DAUD: Accepted it! What if someone wanted half your house and when you protested said, "Oh, don't worry, there'll be room for both of us!" You forget that we Arabs were also a persecuted people. Since 1516, we have been ruled by outsiders, first by the Turks and then by the British and French. But the people who betrayed us the most were the British. In 1914, the British came to us and encouraged us to fight against the Turks by promising us our independence. So for four years we fought the Turks, and with British help we won. But all this time, the British and French had been plotting. With their secret Sykes-Picot Treaty they divided up the Arab lands. So after World War I we had a new ruler—the British. And with our independence at stake again in 1947, you expected us just to agree quietly when the United Nations, without our permission, divided our land in half!

DAVID: But you never had been independent! There never was a Palestinian Arab state and the United Nations was giving you one.

DAUD: You mean half a one. You can't deny that the Arabs living in Palestine were a settled people and, therefore, a nation.

DAVID: Some Palestinians were settled, some weren't. As for nationhood, I'm not sure what you mean by that. You didn't have a nation-state, but you were a people with a shared past, I'll admit that. But that's a pretty theoretical point. Practically speaking, if you had just stayed in Palestine instead of fleeing, you could have kept all you had and benefited from the Western technology the European Jews brought with them. Your standard of living would have gone up. Why, look at how much better off the Arabs in Israel are today compared to pre-Israel days.

DAUD: How could we have stayed in Palestine? In 1947, after the United Nations declared Israel a state, the surrounding Arab states attacked to prevent our land from being partitioned. With a war going on we fled for our lives! In fact, you wanted us to leave to make room for Jewish immigrants! As for your economic arguments, what is money compared with freedom and independence and the right to run one's own country?

DAVID: You could have stayed! In fact, many Palestinians did stay and are now full Israeli citizens who vote and send members to Parliament, and live in a democracy such as doesn't exist in the Arab world. The Palestinian refugees today are mostly those who foolishly followed leaders who told them to flee, who told them that they would soon be able to return to the land under Arab rule. Once these Palestinians chose to flee, they forfeited their right to their land in the new state. The responsibility for their loss lies with them and their leaders.

DAUD: That's not true. Did you ever hear of Deir Yaseen—the village where 250 men, women, and children were murdered by your terrorist groups, the Irgun Zvai Leumi and the Stern Gang? That's why people fled—for fear of atrocities—and it was just what you wanted. And these gangs were led by your former Prime Ministers Menachem Begin and Yitzhak Shamir.

DAVID: Oh, you're always trotting out Deir Yaseen. Yes, it did happen, and it was a tragedy perpetrated by one of our splinter groups. But it was the only time it happened. Thousands of your people stayed and were perfectly safe, and live as Israeli citizens today.

DAUD: And hundreds of thousands—600,000 or more, in fact—fled and are today living in refugee camps provided by the United Nations. As a matter of fact, they now number over 1.7 million because of births in the years of their exile.

DAVID: So whose fault is this? If you took care of your refugees as we have taken care of ours, there would be no problem. Remember, for every Palestinian refugee there was a Jewish refugee from an Arab country, fleeing the ghettos, the persecution, the second-class status that Jews were always relegated to in Arab countries. In 1948, there were 850,000 Jews living in Arab states; today there are only about 29,000. We took in all of these people. In the same way, the Palestinian refugees could have been settled long ago in any one of twelve or more Arab countries. But the Arabs have kept the Palestinians in those horrid camps as political pawns rather than take them in as brothers. You are simply using these poor people as cannon fodder to attack the sovereignty and the security of Israel.

DAUD: What makes you think the Palestinians want to live in Egypt or Kuwait or Morocco? Their home is in Palestine, not in other Arab countries. Would an American settle in England or Scotland just because they speak English there? The Palestinians want to live in their own homeland, not someone else's. As for the refugees, your state was set up to take in refugees. The Arab countries were not created for this purpose. They respect the right of the Palestinian people to have their own country. Besides, the United Nations has stated by a majority vote countless times that the Palestinian refugees should be repatriated to Palestine or compensated for their losses.

DAVID: So now you listen to the United Nations. In 1947, you refused to accept its decision. In any case, we cannot take in over a million Palestinians. They would be a fifth column—a people constantly plotting against us—and we would become a minority in our own state.

DAUD: Well, you are guilty of the same double standard with regard to the United Nations. You accepted the partition of 1947, but you haven't listened since. We accept the United Nations now because it has become truly representative of the world and is not dominated by the West as it once was. You have always identified with the West and

Palestinian refugees in Jordan line up for food. Refugees from the 1948 and 1967 wars live in refugee camps supported by the United Nations in Jordan, Syria and Lebanon. (Arab Information Center, Washington, D.C.)

not the Middle East, to the point that in 1956 you conspired with Britain and France to attack Egypt. As soon as Nasser kicked the British out, there you were, jointly attacking the liberator of the Egyptian people.

DAVID: Do you expect us to stick our heads in the sand? Egypt attacked us in 1948, at our birth, and by 1956 Egyptian inspired guerrilla attacks on our land were making it impossible for the people on our borders to live in peace. We had to react.

DAUD: Yes, so you reacted by taking over more of our land with Western help, Western arms, and the information of Western spies. We have always known that you were an expansionist state. We have heard your Zionist leaders talking of an Israel stretching from the Nile to the Euphrates. You have annexed the Golan Heights, which is Syrian property, and are attempting to settle 100,000 people onto the West Bank, a place we Palestinians hope will be our home one day.

DAVID: Where do you get this? We are not an expansionist state. All we want is to live in peace. But we are forced to deal with the dangers on all sides of us. When you are being attacked by guerrillas and terrorists, you must weed them out. This means war, and if some Arab states lose some land, well, that is their own fault for harboring the terrorists. If you don't want war and don't want to lose land, then why don't you make peace?

DAUD: There you are again, talking about peace now that you have what you want—somebody else's land.

DAVID: Why can't you be realistic and accept things the way they are? You tried to turn the clock back in '67 when Nasser forced the U.N. units to leave the Egyptian-Israel border and closed the Gulf of Aqaba to Israeli shipping, and where did it get you? A disastrous war that you lost in six days! The clock can't be turned back. Israel exists. Why don't you accept it?

DAUD: President Nasser had every right to do what he did. Israel had never allowed U.N. troops on its soil, and Egypt legally had the right, as the United Nations agreed, to ask that U.N. troops leave its soil. As for the Gulf of Aqaba, you had taken it illegally, in an act of war in 1956, and had no right to be there. So, in 1967, you, along with your Western allies and spies, again took advantage of our unpreparedness and attacked. Once again you expanded, taking the Sinai a second time, the Syrian Golan Heights, and East Jerusalem, including some of our most holy Moslem places of worship.

DAVID: And why did we take these things? Because we were provoked by murderous Arab guerrillas and Arab armies hemming us in on all sides. What did you want us to do, wait until we were swallowed alive? Your leaders have always threatened to push us into the sea. For years, the Syrians had been firing rockets on our settlements from the Golan Heights. That is why we have now annexed this land. Our children in that area spent half their lives in bomb shelters. From the Heights, the Syrians could see everything and fire on everything. And as for East Jerusalem, that is the most holy of places for Jews, the location of the Wailing Wall, built of the stones of Solomon's temple.

For you Moslems, Mecca is your most holy city, whereas Jerusalem is at best third. For us, Jerusalem has been in our hearts for the almost two thousand years of our exile. Furthermore, while East Jerusalem was in Moslem hands, no Jews were allowed to visit the Wailing Wall. Now that all of Jerusalem is in Jewish hands, the holy shrines of all religions are open to all.

DAUD: No matter how you phrase it, it stills adds up to one thing—expansion. The more room you have, the more Jews can emigrate to Israel. We know your goal is to get three million Russian Jews to come to Israel. Where are you going to put them? In Arab houses and on Arab land conquered in your various wars! And on the land you occupied in the '67 war, what have you done but build more and more settlements?

DAVID: There is plenty of room in Israel; we have the whole Negev desert yet to inhabit. We Israelis have made the desert bloom again, and there is therefore no problem of space. Yes, we have built some kibbutzim (communal settlements) on the occupied lands, but this only serves as an incentive for you Arabs to come to peace terms with us. Then you will get most of your lands back, but not all, for we must always have secure borders. We cannot have the Syrians rocketing our settlements or the Egyptians playing military games on our borders. We also cannot let Palestinian terrorists brought up in those refugee camps slip into Israel and murder innocent citizens.

DAUD: Since when have you Israelis been so concerned with the lives of civilians? For one ambush killing of three people or for the ten Israelis killed in Munich at the Olympics, you murder hundreds in raids on refugee camps in Jordan, Syria, and Lebanon. You think nothing of bombing villages with your American Phantom jets and your napalm. But you learned in 1973 that we Arabs can be tough as well. With all your American arms and American intelligence, you were just sitting on our occupied lands waiting for them to become yours as time passed. Not only was your government building settlements on Arab land, not only were you pumping Egyptian oil out of the Sinai, but you passed a law making it legal for private parties to buy land in the Occupied Territories. That was the last straw. So Egypt successfully attacked in the Sinai and showed you we Arabs can fight too. You will never be allowed to live in peace on occupied Arab lands.

DAVID: Well, in point of fact, the 1973 war was a stalemate, and it was that only because you attacked on our holy day, Yom Kippur, when we were unprepared! And you complain about us killing civilians. We only rarely and accidentally kill civilians while going after Palestinian terrorists. And since the Lebanese government couldn't control these terrorists, we lost our patience and had to invade Lebanon in 1982 to do the job for them.

DAUD: You should hang your head in shame over that invasion! You not only killed hundreds of Lebanese civilians and left hundreds more homeless, you stood by and watched while the Christian Lebanese, the Phalangists, murdered hundreds of innocent Palestinians in the Sabra and Shatila refugee camps. Even your own government admitted its guilt and fired your defense minister, Ariel Sharon.

DAVID: Well, at least we admit it when we make an error. Since when has your PLO (Palestine Liberation Organization) chief Yasser Arafat ever admitted an error? We invaded Lebanon to cut him and his terrorists down to size, and we accomplished our mission! His forces had to leave Beirut, and he had to leave the country for Tunisia.

DAUD: All you have accomplished is to help destroy Lebanon! Everyone is at everyone's throat, the Palestinians, the Lebanese Moslems, the Christians, and the Druze. It is a tragedy you have created!

DAVID: Well, it is not as if Lebanon was not warned what

would happen if they didn't control the terrorist attacks on our villages from Lebanese territory. There are no more attacks now. And as for the fighting between Lebanese groups, that was going on long before we invaded!

DAUD: All this proves to me is that you want more land and will use any excuse to get it. You have no respect for established boundaries in the Middle East! You think nothing of moving into the West Bank (Jordanian territory) or the Golan Heights (Syrian territory) or Lebanon. You have even bombed an Iraqi nuclear plant because you didn't like their having nuclear power!

DAVID: Well, we did these things because we had to in order to survive. We have learned the hard way that if we do not keep an upper hand, then our people get attacked. The Syrians and Lebanese refused to control the Palestinian terrorists so we had to do it for them.

DAUD: I wish you could get it into your head that all Palestinians are not terrorists. The ultimate aim of the PLO was the development of a secular state in Palestine, open to all Middle Eastern peoples and religions. This was and is a just cause. Now, since 1988, the PLO has recognized Israel's right to exist and is willing to accept a two-state solution.

DAVID: You speak of the PLO's just cause. What cause can justify the killing of innocent Israeli mothers and children, of non-political Israeli athletes in Munich at the Olympics? What cause justifies these acts? The answer is no cause. These are the acts of madmen, of inhuman madmen! And you ask us to trust the PLO now!

DAUD: You Israelis have a short memory. Not long ago it was you who were the prize terrorists and killers. When the Stern Gang murdered or the Irgun Zvai Leumi murdered—your terrorist groups that preyed on the British and the Palestinian Arabs—you called them patriots. Again, I do not condone the radical elements among the Palestinians, but we are a desperate, displaced people as you Israelis once were, who have spent our lives in refugee camps. And we look across into a rich Israel and know that we or our parents once lived there.

DAVID: If it's rich, which it isn't, it's because we made it that way by hard work. It wasn't always the way it is now. Nothing justifies the killing of innocent children.

DAUD: So you ask us to give up and accept being displaced forever. That is something you claim you never did in your 2,000-year exile. Perhaps you have unwittingly created a new Diaspora. And now with the "Intifada" (see "The Intifada: An Uprising for a Nation," pp. 287-306)—the rock-throwing and civil disobedience of the Palestinians in the territories occupied after the 1967 war and in Israel—you have a new reminder that we Palestinians have our own culture and customs and refuse to live quietly as second-class citizens. So now you have two antagonistic groups of Palestinians—those outside Israel in the Diaspora created by the 1948 war, and those living in the Occupied Territories. The only way you can satisfy us is to give us our own land on the West Bank and Gaza, but if you continue to build Jewish settlements in the West Bank where you already have settled 70,000 Jewish settlers against the wishes of the United Nations, then the last hope for peace will be gone.

DAVID: Well, perhaps you are right. Perhaps we both need to be more compromising in order to get some sort of settlement. After all, we are both desperate peoples who have trouble seeing the world from the other's point of view. The one sure thing is that this conflict is and has been tearing the Middle East apart. And in such a situation neither of our people is getting the rest and peace it deserves. We can't enjoy our state while we are being attacked from within and without, and you can't rest until you have a place of your own. So we both have to compromise.

The Life of Joseph Baratz

PART I

᪣INTRODUCTION: Throughout their long exile, the Jewish people have always faced some degree of persecution, ranging
from prohibitions against owning land to laws governing all
aspects of their behavior, but anti-Semitism grew especially violent at the end of the nineteenth century in Russia and Eastern
Europe, at a time when nationalist movements were strong in
Europe. The Jews became a convenient scapegoat, for as a
minority they were easily preyed upon. False rumors would
spread about what Jews did to Christian children or how they
controlled the economy, and mobs would descend on the Jewish communities killing, destroying and looting. In Russia, this
kind of mob violence was called a pogrom.

As a result of the pogroms, the Jewish people despaired that
they would ever be accepted in the various countries in which
they lived. This feeling was expressed in a book by Theodor
Herzl in which he outlined a plan for the establishment of a
Jewish state. With Herzl as its head, the Zionist movement in
Europe took form, and small numbers of Jews began to emigrate to Palestine.

The story of the building of Israel by the *halutzim*, the early
pioneers, is a thrilling one. The first wave of settlers, known
as the first *Aliya*, an "ascent" or return to the holy land, was
a result of increasing repression and violence toward Jews in
Russia and Eastern Europe in the 1880s and 1890s. Further
repression of Jews after the abortive Russian revolution of 1905
led to a second wave of immigration. The thousands of Jews
who went to Palestine during this period were dedicated to

243

the creation of a new life. Some of them could not tolerate the difficult conditions; thus, the early Jewish settlers who stayed were, in effect, the fittest, for they not only had chosen a most difficult way of life but had survived.

The third Aliya to Palestine followed the Balfour Declaration of 1917. Further waves came in 1924, as a result of the repression of Jews in Poland, and in the 1930s and 1940s, in response to the rise of Nazism in Germany.

One of the pioneers was Joseph Baratz, a Russian Jew who grew up in the Ukraine. At the age of thirteen, he experienced his first pogrom, the sacking of the Jewish section of the town of Kishenev, where he and his family lived. A year later, he made up his mind to emigrate to Palestine. The following excerpt, taken from Baratz's autobiography, describes his life in Russia and his decision to leave. [12]

I was born in a Ukrainian village on the shores of the Dniester. . . . We lived in the Jewish quarter and we were a traditional community, very different from our Russian neighbors in looks, manners and customs. The men wore long gabardines [coats] and curling side-whiskers; the married women shaved their heads and put on thick black wigs. Our food was kosher [permitted according to Jewish law]. Our language was Yiddish [a German dialect with some Hebrew and Slavic words spoken by many European Jews]—Hebrew had long been reserved for prayers, and we had little occasion to use Russian. We had our feasts and our traditional songs, music and dances. Our schools were the *heder,* where the usual elementary subjects were taught in Yiddish, and the *Yeshiva,* a Hebrew seminary. . . .

Our conditions were indeed uncertain and hard. Except for a small, wealthy minority we were not allowed to leave the Pale [the Pale of Settlement, the only place Jews were allowed to live in Russia] . . . We were kept out of Russian schools and universities and we were surrounded by legal restrictions and were at the mercy of corrupt officials—so were Russians with full citizenship but to a lesser degree. No Jew, if he could help it, would go to law, because he knew that justice was weighted against him. Worse than any of this was the constant fear of some abominable accusation of ritual crime which was often followed by pogroms.

We . . . were largely cut off from the outer world; segregated by our own traditions and our fears almost as much as by Russian anti-Semitism, we lived timidly in the narrow circle of our small-town interests. . . . Some [Jews] joined Russian political parties . . . but the crushing of the Liberal Revolution of 1905 was followed by pogroms more savage than had yet been known, while a wave of reaction spread all over Russia. Other young people became members of the Zionist Youth Movement [a movement calling for the Jews to have their own homeland].

The World Zionist Organization was formed in 1897, and the Jewish National Fund started raising money for land settlements in 1901. There had been talk of buying Palestine from the Turkish Government, but it had come to nothing; then the British had offered Uganda [an East African country] as an immediate refuge for the Jews of Eastern Europe, and Herzl, a Viennese and the prophet of the movement, had proposed at a Zionist Congress that this offer should be accepted. But we were more traditional than the Western Jews: For us, there could be no question of a "return" anywhere except to the Holy Land. . . .

None of these problems worried me until I was thirteen. We were not well off but we were a happy and united family without great cares. Then in 1903 the quarter of the town in which we lived was sacked [in a pogrom]. We escaped unhurt but afterward I saw the wounded and went to the funeral of those who were killed. Perhaps it was this that turned my thoughts seriously toward Zionism.

I had a friend of my own age. We always went about together so that people called us the "twins." Together we joined the Zionist Youth Movement. We both liked physical work better than reading or writing, so after school we would go to the Zionist library and tidy up the books and scrub the floor. . . .

We were helped by the coming to Kishenev of a great Zionist leader, Joseph Sprintzak. I don't know how old he was in those days, but he made a tremendous impression on us. . . .

With his help we became more active, but we had to meet secretly. There was a tailor who lent us a room in his house; he was a wonderful old man. There we held our secret meetings and we wrote our illegal proclamations: We said that the Jews ought to defend themselves when there were pogroms, and we told them to leave Russia and to go to Palestine. We could have got into a lot of trouble by doing this. After the leaflets were written they still had to be distributed; the tailor had several daughters and they all helped. . . .

When I was about fourteen I began to feel that all this talk about Zionism wasn't really Zionism. I began to want to go to Palestine, and I intended, when I got there, to be a peasant. This was a new idea among us, and I can't exactly explain how it first came to us. In the early days, Palestine had been thought of mainly as a refuge, though much had been written about the new country and the new culture we were to build; now we felt that in order to construct our country we had first to reconstruct ourselves. We had been intellectuals, semi-intellectuals, middlemen for too long. We had to work with our hands and above all we needed a peasantry—that had to be the foundation of it all. . . .

For two years I thought about it and I made up my mind to go, but I was afraid to tell my parents. I had sisters and a half-brother (we were as fond of one another as though we had been full brothers); still, I was my mother's only son. How could I tell her, knowing what it would mean to her? All the same, in the end I told her.

Father went to ask the rabbi; the rabbi said, "No." How could a boy of sixteen undertake such a journey? Besides, in Palestine I might fall among freethinkers and myself drift into irreligious ways.

There was an open struggle between . . . my parents [and me]. They brought every possible pressure to bear on me. Not that my father ever beat me, but he argued and argued with me, and my mother cried. What made it easier in the end was that a friend of ours who was already settled in Palestine came home on a two-month visit and offered to take me with him when he went back and to keep an eye on me. Then my parents gave way, and it was my father who gave me the money for my journey—it was not a great amount, but it was a lot for him.

On my last night my friends gave a party for me. We sang and we danced, but we were sad because my father hadn't come. Then at midnight he came—an old Jew in his black kaftan and with side-whiskers—and he too began to sing and to dance. He sang in Hebrew and the only words of his song were the words of the Passover prayer: "Next year in Jerusalem"; this he sang over and over again, and he danced for about two hours.

Early in the morning, straight from the party, we went to the station. I and the friend with whom I was to travel at last got into the train. My father, my mother, my relations, my friends—all were on the platform. My mother cried, and as the train drew out she called after me: "Joseph, my child, be a good Jew." And I too was crying, and I wished I were staying with my father and my mother.

The Life of Joseph Baratz

PART II

&INTRODUCTION: Many of the early immigrants to Palestine from Europe were strongly influenced by the socialist movement. They hoped to develop in Palestine a just society in which all people would be equal economically, socially and politically—a society without private ownership, in which there would be no employers and employees, but all would be workers and the fruits of their labor would be shared equally. Many Jewish immigrants to Palestine were shocked to find that some of the previous immigrants employed Arab labor and seemed to be in the process of becoming a landed aristocracy with an Arab peasantry. From a socialist point of view, this not only was economically and socially backward but would not bring about the development of the "new Jew" that the Jewish socialists hoped to create. After centuries of landlessness, they felt that the only way the Jews could gain the virtues of being self-sufficient was by getting back to the land and working it with their own hands. Thus a great many early immigrants worked day and night not only to create a new land but to create a new person through work.

A result of this philosophy was the amazingly rapid development of productive agricultural communities, some of them engaged in extremely difficult work, such as draining swamps or irrigating desert land. Although many of the agricultural communities now are completely modernized and have developed small industries in addition to their agriculture, the work ethic still lives, and settlements are still being formed in the hostile Negev desert.[13]&

We went by train to Odessa; there we embarked on a tiny ship. The journey to Jaffa took about nine days. The ship was packed with Christian pilgrims (this was in December, 1906, shortly before Christmas); there were also a few Jewish pilgrims, and a couple of *halutzim,* "pioneers," like myself. . . . The great waves and the rocking of the ship and the groaning and the stench inside the crowded hold were terrible.

At last we anchored outside Jaffa harbor. Arabs in long white shirts came in little rowboats to take us off. The sea was still rough; we looked at the tiny boats and we thought that we would never get there. Some people refused to leave the ship; the Arabs climbed on deck and picked them off and dropped them into the boats. Some of the boats capsized, but in the end we all landed.

Jaffa was a little Arab town; it was the only sizable seaport in those days. We had been told that it had several Jewish inns and that the one to go to was kept by Haim Baruch. It was all strange to us—the flat-topped, cream-washed houses like boxes, the minarets poking above the roofs, and the dusty palm trees, and the dark, loose-robed people in the streets, but it was good to be on dry land, and coming to a Jewish inn was a little like coming home. . . .

We rested [for a while], then I said goodbye to my parents' friend, who was taking the stagecoach to Jerusalem. The rest of us also decided to move on. We were at last in Palestine—in the Land of Israel, as it was called in Hebrew—but Jaffa was a town, and of what possible interest was a town to us? Where should we go?

All our lives we had heard about the Bilu group—the "Biluïm" who had founded Rishon le Zion. Rishon means "first," and Rishon le Zion was one of the very first settlements. The ritual wine we drank at Passover came from the vineyards of Rishon. . . . We wanted to see them, so we set off to Rishon.

It was a distance of about ten miles. As there were no buses and we had no money to take a cab, we went on foot. . . .

Naturally we were excited when we saw them—in a moment we would see a Jewish village . . . we imagined a village like in Russia—hens pecking in the road, children shouting by the river, and not a soul in sight while the sun is high and all the peasants are in the fields.

But what was this? We were in a pretty street of neat brick houses with red tiled roofs; from one of them came the tinkling of a piano. The street was full of people strolling up and down. We couldn't believe our eyes. We asked:

"Who are these?"

"Biluïm"

"And who does the work?"

"Arabs."

"And what do the Jews do?"

"They're managers, supervisors."

It was a great shock to us. I said to myself: "This isn't what I've come for," and I could see that the others were disappointed as well.

All the same, Rishon was a fine place. The people were kind to us. That evening they gave us a meal—fried eggs and bunches of grapes to follow—and allowed us to sleep in a vineyard. But the next morning we left and walked on to Rehovoth, another settlement.

There I found a friend from Kishenev who was a farm laborer. He put me up in his room, where there were already four or five others, and he got his employer to hire me. The next morning I went out to work. At last I was on the land. . . .

The first day I went to work I didn't know how I would get through it. Our tools were primitive—there were hardly any spades and, of course, no tractors—we used hoes mostly. My hands felt as if they were on fire. But we soon got used to it and grew muscles and horny palms.

It was a great happiness for me to be on the land, and the people among whom we lived were interesting. . . . Nearly all the settlers, old and new, were Russians, but they all spoke Hebrew, though Yiddish and Russian were also often heard. They read books in many languages.

I made friends with Zvi, a boy of about my age. We both joined the "Young Workers"—the right-wing Labor

A chief goal of many of the early Zionist immigrants to Palestine was to get back to the land. Here some halutzim *(pioneers) work in tobacco fields near Jerusalem in 1927. They were part of the fourth Aliya to Palestine.* (United Press International)

Party which had grown out of the Zionist Youth Movement we had belonged to in Kishenev. . . .

I was not to stay in Rehovoth long—almost before I had begun I was removed from the agricultural work I loved. One night, after I had been there for about three months, I had gone to bed early and was already asleep; suddenly Zvi came in and shook me awake. A message had come from our party headquarters that young *halutzim* were needed for work in Jerusalem and two of us had been chosen. We were not at all pleased but it didn't occur to us to refuse. We were sure that the people who ran our party would never have asked us to do this if it were not for the good of the country, and it was this, after all, that we were here for. So the next morning we set out. Once again we went on foot . . .

There were Moslems and Christians and Jews living in Jerusalem; the Jews were Yemenites, who looked almost like Arabs. . . .

Soon we discovered what we had been called for. The New City was beginning to be built on the outskirts of the Old. . . . Now our two parties had decided to call for *halutzim* to take part in all this building. Of course, we had no experience of this kind—we told them so, but all they said to us was: "Go and learn." . . . We were told that we were not only to rebuild Jerusalem, but to renew the spirit of these young Jews; it made sense to us. The words of the Passover prayer in Palestine are not "Next year in Jerusalem" but "Next year in Jerusalem rebuilt." For the pilgrims the rebuilding was that of the heavenly rather than of the material city—the rebuilding of righteousness; for us it was both, so we did as we were told and stayed, though our hearts were still in farming.

Once again we had to learn an unfamiliar task. We had no money for our keep while we were doing it, so it was arranged that we should get a subsidy raised by a group in Odessa called The Friends of Zion. . . .

Those first weeks in Jerusalem were terrible. I had been given a hut among some olive trees; every night I would creep under the trees and cry—I was afraid that I would not hold out and I was lonely and my fingers ached; by day I pretended to be cheerful—I was a pioneer, I was ashamed—but at night I couldn't sleep, I missed my father and my mother, and I came out and sat under the trees and cried.

Our subsidy hardly paid for our food, and even when we began to earn a little we still went hungry. So after a time, three of my friends and I decided to get together and to live as a little community. After that things went much better for all of us—the money stretched farther and we cheered one another up. . . .

[At last we were able to leave Jerusalem and go to a settlement named Zi Khron.] Here we were in the middle of the conflict between the old settlers and the newcomers. It was going on in many settlements and it caused much hardship to the *halutzim* who could not get work. The real question was whether Jewish labor was to be employed at all, and we were not thinking only of ourselves; how were the many thousands who needed refuge to come in at all unless there were a market for their labor? To many of the farmers our ideas of becoming new and better through work made so much nonsense. But [what would be gained] so long as the Jews in Palestine were like proud colonials who needed lots of Arab wage-earners to work their places? . . .

[In those days] we were always dancing. You would hardly think it possible after the day's work we'd done. We would come into the dining room dead tired, and eat our meal quickly, and then sit with our elbows on the table, resting, not talking much at first. Outside it was dark, but the dining room was bright with kerosene lamps or the feast-day candles. Then a discussion would start and others would join in. And then somebody would begin to play the harmonica or the guitar, or to sing, and other people joined in the chorus and clapped [to] the beat. All at once our tiredness went from us and we got up and danced. In a moment there would be a ring of us, our hands linked, barefoot or in our heavy boots, stamping out the steps of the *hora*, two steps clockwise and one step back, slowly at first, then getting faster and faster, whirling round and round. Or we would go outside and dance on the roads and in the vineyards. All over the village and the plantations the young people would laugh and sing and dance. If it was a Friday we would sometimes dance all night.

That was how I [met] Miriam, the sister of the friend I had worked with in Athlit. She was seriously ill when she arrived and she stayed some days in bed. Then one evening, when we were dancing the *hora* in the dining room, there she was beside me; we looked at one another and laughed. Round and round we twirled to the singing and the clapping; when we were quite breathless the ring broke up and we sat down together.

Miriam looked [thin and pale]. Dr. Joffe came and scolded her for being up. She waved her hands at him:

"Aie, what's the good of spoiling a fever! Much better sweat it out," and in a few moments she was dancing again.

Evening after evening we danced together. Miriam didn't stay long in Zi Khron, but afterward, whenever she could get a lift in a cart, she came on the Sabbath. . . . One evening several of us were walking in the vineyard. I remember I had a bunch of grapes in my hand; I held it out to [Miriam] and I asked: "Where are you now?" She laughed and she said: "In Hapzibah." It means "I love you," and it is the name of a little settlement. I stopped, and all at once I saw her and it seemed as if my heart melted. I said "Hapzibah," and she too said "Hapzibah" again, and we walked on. . . .

All that year the *halutzim* in [our area] were restless. We were happy enough working on the land, but we knew [with] more and more certainty that the ways of the old settlements were not for us. This was not the way we hoped to settle the country—this old way with Jews on top and Arabs working for them; anyway, we thought that there shouldn't be employers and employed at all. There should be a good life. But how was it to be achieved? What was the best way for us to help each other?

The way of life we dreamed of did not yet exist, but more and more of us were attracted to work in Galilee. . . .

But it was more than a year before I went to Galilee. . . .

That September, on the eve of the New Year, Miriam and I announced our engagement and gave a party. We had hardly anything to eat and none of us had any money, except a few Turkish [coins] Miriam had brought with her. She spent them all on bread, rice, lentils and oil and we had a princely feast. Everybody was happy and we danced without a break till sunrise. . . .

In the meantime, there had been a new development . . . . Dr. Ruppin, who was at the head of the Palestine Office of the National Fund [contributions from Europe to aid the establishment of Zionist settlements in Palestine], was a man of great imagination and courage. . . . He decided that a tract of land should be handed over to [some] *halutzim* to develop on their own responsibility. Such an experiment could not be tried out on a big scale [so] 750 acres [were] offered to the *halutzim.*

The group who took it on were among the best workers in the country, but they didn't mean to settle [there]: They would try it out for a year, then if the experiment were a success they would hand [it] over to a permanent group. . . . Toward the end of the year . . . we were approached by Dr. Ruppin. We held a discussion about it. [The land] was being offered to us; it was ours for the taking. We were very happy. . . .

By this time we were ready; we were trained, we knew each other, and we had worked out our ideas as far as we could without trying them out on our own land. At the bottom of them was a view of life we held in common. . . .

There [in the Diaspora] we had been cut off from nature, from our roots, and everything had been distorted by the need for security—even the family had become a little fortress. We had had to buy security with money and make money with whatever are the money-making faculties of the brain; we had lived on our brains and we hadn't used them properly because we had been cut off from the growing, natural side of life. That was why we had become so dry, so barren.

We [Jews] had had to use our brains to buy; now we would use our hands to give, and in our communities we would do away with money altogether. We would have among us neither masters nor paid servants, but we would give ourselves freely to the soil and to one another's needs. Thus nobody would have to be ambitious or to worry for himself or his family; the community would protect him, there would always be all the others to help him out. . . .

The Life of Joseph Baratz

PART III

&**INTRODUCTION:** As we have seen, many Jewish immigrants believed in the value of getting back to the land and setting up a society in which all people would be equal. These immigrants settled in agricultural communities and, having no model on which to build, began to develop them by trial and error. Today the most common types of agricultural settlements are the *kibbutz* and the *moshav*. The chief difference between the two is that there is more private property in the *moshav* than there is in the *kibbutz*, in which almost everything, including the land, is communally owned.

To join a kibbutz, a person must go through a trial period of a year before formally applying for membership. If one is accepted as a member, one joins a group of people who collectively decides the individual nature of their particular kibbutz. Decisions are made in group meetings. The work of the kibbutz is done by various committees, the membership of which generally rotates. There is a work committee that decides which jobs people are to do on the kibbutz. All property on the kibbutz, including even clothes in some kibbutzim, is owned collectively. Except for a small amount of pocket money for personal items, everything a person needs is given by the kibbutz. In many kibbutzim, children do not stay with their parents but live in a Children's House where all their needs are taken care of. After their parents are finished with the day's work in the fields, their children visit them for a

couple of hours before they return to the Children's House
for dinner and the night. In some kibbutzim, the sexes are
not segregated until the middle teens; all children use the
same bathrooms and shower rooms and sleep in the same
rooms. To the degree possible, all people are treated in exactly
the same way.

In the following selection, Joseph Baratz describes the growth
of the first kibbutz in Israel, Degania, of which he was a founding member. It is interesting to note how the kibbutz evolved
naturally, and how important decisions were made as they came
up rather than by any prearranged plan. [14]

Our village lies in the valley close to where the Jordan
flows out of the Sea of Galilee. The hills of Galilee are
on one side of us and the mountains of Syria and [Jor-
dan] are on the other and in the distance we can see the
snow cap of Mount Hermon.

In winter the fields are green, then yellow with corn
and barley, and in spring there are wild cyclamens everywhere and poppies and cornflowers and many other wild
flowers. Degania, the name we gave our village, means
"cornflower. . ."

Today, when you come down the new road from the
hills, you can see the lake and the Jordan [River] and
the valley with its groves, gardens and fields, and many
fishponds; the whole valley is beautiful and fresh with
water. But when we came . . . this road did not yet exist;
there were no trees, only burned grass and a few shrubs.

We arrived in summer. It was very hot down there, two
hundred meters below sea level. The air buzzed with mos-
quitoes and it lay heavy and close between the hills. The
flat valley was like a hot plate, the heat pressed on it.
Everything was burned brown. The river was a trickle.
But when the rains came, it flooded the land; and when
the waters withdrew, they left swamps and mud. For months
on end we were cut off by mud. It sucked the boots off
your feet and no cart could get through it, and the swamps
bred fevers.

There was water all around us, but to get it to the fields and the houses you had to bring it up in pails or barrels. We used mules—two big [cans] to each mule—then barrels on carts. Later on we had an Arab water wheel—the mules turned it—and still later we had a steam engine. Today it's all quite different. The water is pumped by electricity and runs through pipes, but this only came about after forty-three years. The malaria has been fought down. We planted eucalyptus trees to drain the swamps, and as more fields came under cultivation this itself helped to drain the land. . . .

In 1911 we were twelve, ten men and two women. The reason for this number was that six men were to do the ploughing, two to act as watchmen [against Bedouin robbers], one [to serve] as secretary-accountant, and one to be in reserve; the two women would do the housekeeping . . .

In spite of its hardships, that first year was wonderful and full of joy for us. There seemed to be no limit to the work we could get through; what the body couldn't do the spirit made up for. But it was very hard indeed. Nearly everybody had malaria and there were cases of yellow fever. It was the climate that made us suffer most. It was so bad that at first we used to say: "We shall never be able to raise children in this valley, we must move to higher ground," and we thought of building our village on the top of a high hill and of going down to our fields in the valley every day.

In the beginning we had only grain crops. We tilled them with primitive tools. We had no farm animals except six pairs of mules and two horses. . . . Nowadays we plough with tractors, but for a long time we ploughed with mules.

The ploughs and the harvesters and the seed had all been given us by the Palestine Office. We had a contract with it: It provided the land and stocked it, and, in return, we paid it 50 per cent of our net profits; the rest we kept, and in addition we got fifty francs [$1.50] a month a head as wages."

All the men in the *kvutza* [small group or community; also used for age group] worked happily from the beginning, but at first the women were not happy. The reason—there were only two of them—was that we still thought women could only cook and wash. We men went out before dawn, six of us with our mules and ploughs, and we stayed out until after dark; then we would come home and wash and have our meal, and then we would sit for hours talking about our work, telling each other about our animals, how the soil was getting black, and later how the green was showing. We were so enthusiastic, there was never any end to it. The women listened and were jealous; their work was quite different and the conditions for it were very hard. There were neither stoves nor kerosene—not to speak of electricity as there is now. They cooked in the open over a wood fire on two stones placed upright. . . .

One day they came to us. "Listen to us," they said. "We came to this country with the one idea in our heads—to work and to live with nature. But what now? You men are happy, you like your work, but we are worse off than our mothers were in their small towns. What do yourselves think of it? Should we continue in this way, with this difference between your lot and ours?"

We couldn't understand them. Our fathers had been breadwinners and our mothers had cooked. "How else can it be?" we asked. "Should a woman plough? Or should the men cook? What would other people think of us? We should be ashamed before everybody."

But in the end the women won. Gradually we understood and we changed. Now we know that women can do farm work, that they can even plough, and they can even fight. Not their words but their actions have proved it to us. . . .

When our first child, Gideon, was born—he was the first baby in the *kvutza*—everybody fussed about him and nobody knew what to do with him. Our women didn't know how to look after babies. There was nobody whose advice Miriam could ask; the other women were still younger than she was. She found her own methods.

After the child was born she was dangerously ill and both of them had to spend some time in hospital. But when she came back she began to work as before, and wherever she went she took the baby with her. She took him to the vegetable plots and to the kitchen and to the poultry run. If she were in the cowshed she put him down on the straw and the cow licked him. The whole of Degania cried over the baby. They cried because they thought he would die of dirt, or they cried because the baby cried. . . .

But the child grew up to be strong and healthy. Now he is a father himself, a big, sturdy, handsome man. He has married a South African girl and lives in Tel Aviv, working on the mobilization of labor [for] the Negev [desert].

Miriam . . . was nearly killing herself, working as hard as ever and looking after him as well and sometimes getting up in the middle of the night to wash his things, and going back to sleep again for a little. . . .

We saw it couldn't go on like this. . . . By the time there were four children in the colony we decided that something must be done.

It was a difficult problem. How were the women both to work and to look after their children? . . . Somebody proposed that the colony should hire a nurse. But Joseph Bussell said, ". . . All the women, whether single or married, should take part in looking after them; then the mothers could do other work as well. And the cost of the education of the children must be borne by the community as a whole."

So we didn't hire a nurse, but we chose one girl to look after the lot of them, and we put aside a house where they could spend the day while the mothers were at work. And so this system developed and [has since been] adopted in all the *kvutzoth* [communities], with the difference that in most of them the children sleep in the Children's House, but with us they stay at night in their parents' quarters. . . .

Gideon was a real pioneer among babies. As he grew bigger there was no kindergarten and no school in the *kvutza* to send him to, so we sent him to Ain Harod, a big *kvutza* in the Emek which had its own school; but when he finished that school there was again a problem. He was a gifted boy with an interest in mechanics. Should he go to the Technical School in Haifa? At first Miriam and I were in favor of it. But a meeting was held and it was decided not to send him. Everybody came to the meeting and everybody discussed the question; the arguments on both sides were carefully weighed. Shouldn't the boy be given every opportunity of learning, and wasn't the Technical College the best training school? But then education wasn't only learning. Gideon was a country child; in Haifa he would be subjected to the influences of the town. He intended to stay on the land, and we could employ him on our own machines—we were getting them just then. As for training him, we had people among us who had been trained as mechanics; they could teach him.

Miriam and I felt no disappointment over this decision; on the contrary, coming out of the meeting we were very happy. It had been a good meeting. Everybody had felt deeply concerned over Gideon; everybody wanted the best for him. . . . There was no conflict between personal interests and communal interests—they were the same. I am not saying that it is always and invariably like this, but for the most part Miriam and I have found it so.

Today we have seven children and eight grandchildren, and Degania is swarming with youngsters of all ages. Fifty of the second generation are full members of the *kvutza*, a hundred are below eighteen, which is the membership age. Our fears that the children would suffer from the life or the climate were proved wrong. The children are fine. The swamps had been dried; the climate has changed. It is hot, but the children like it.

They run barefoot in summer when the earth is like fire, and it doesn't worry them, because this is where they have been born and bred. . . .

In 1930 we put up a big new school for our children and the children of the valley. We were given a donation for it by Miss Henrietta Szold. She was a great American Zionist; she had founded the huge American women's Zionist organization Hadassa—it ran our most important medical service—and when Hitler came [to power in Germany] she started the "Youth Aliyab," an organization which rescued tens of thousands of children from Europe and brought them up in Palestine. . . .

Of course [the children today] are brought up very differently from the way we were brought up ourselves. To begin with, they are real country children; they look as if they had the country in their bones. They know the ways of the land almost without being told. They swim like fish in the lake and in the river and they are excellent with animals. . . . They have much more freedom than we had in our schools. . . . The school has its vegetable plots and its orchard and its flower garden, and the children help to grow them, and they also help in the kitchen and with the housework, and wait at table, boys and girls alike. The school is meant to train them for the land, but they get a good secondary education— they learn the Bible and literature and all kinds of things. When they are about twelve or thirteen, they start helping with seasonal work, and in their holidays they work with their parents. They are magnificent workers—it seems to come naturally to them—but not if you give them something to do just to keep them busy: They have to feel it's really useful. In the middle school they spend two-thirds of their time at lessons and a third at work, and in their last year it's the other way round.

When they finish their course they can go on to the agricultural or the technical high school in our valley. There are two other high schools for kibbutz children in the Emek—all four have been set up by the Association of Kibbutzim. . . .

Nowadays if anybody has a special bent for something he may be sent away to the university or a training college or an art school (though we haven't so far any artists among our children). In the early years it was much more difficult—we couldn't afford it easily and there were many fewer scholarships. . . . But it is still only done if the kibbutz really thinks it worthwhile. . . .

Of our seven children, four—Yona, Batya, Michal and Eli—are members of Degania; they work in different branches of farming, and Batya and Eli have, like their mother, specialized in dairy work. Of the three others, Devorah and her husband are on the land, though not in a kibbutz; Amos with his family is in Herzlia, where he works for a film company; [and] Gideon is in Tel Aviv, with his South African wife, who prefers living in town. . . .

We are a great mixture in Degania nowadays. People have come from everywhere—Germans, Rumanians, Poles, Persians, Moroccans, Iraqis; some have come as adults, others as children to be trained and have stayed on—though the idea of these training groups is that they should go out and found new settlements.

As you know, in the beginning we were all Russians—so were nearly all the early *kvutzoth*, as the Second Immigration also came from Russia. Later kibbutzim have been founded by Germans, Rumanians, groups from other parts of Europe, and people from England, South Africa, Canada, and the United States. Recently *halutzim* have come even from such faraway places as Australia, New Zealand, and South America. It is natural that the members of the founding group should be mostly from the same country, and to some extent their nationality gives its character to the *kvutza*—although, when it comes to the children born in the settlements, you can hardly tell them one from another. . . .

Of our original founders' group, only six are left in Degania—Miriam and myself, Tankhum and his wife, Haya, and the two brothers, Haim and Yaakov Berkowitz. . . .

A typical settlement in Israel. Although technically it is not a kibbutz, it is similar in many ways to the kind of kibbutzim Joseph Baratz writes about. The chief difference is the extent to which private ownership is allowed. (United Press International)

Many of the people who were with us at the beginning have died. Others have left us for personal reasons, or because they found our particular way of life too difficult, or because, after trying it out, they came to the conclusion that they preferred to build a different kind of settlement. They have done no less for the pioneer movement or for the country than we have, but their role [has been] different.

Just after World War I, there was a lot of argument about the *kvutzoth*; it was going on all over the country. Some people thought that everybody could live in this way; others [thought] that it was only suitable for a few people; still others disapproved of it altogether, saying that it interfered with the freedom of the individual and discouraged him from taking initiative. And there were those who said, "The *kvutza* is a form of life which is wonderful in itself but my heart desires a more private existence. . . ."

You would hardly recognize Degania for the place we came to almost half a century ago, and it is very different today from those early years, when we had nothing but grain crops or when we first started on our mixed farming. There were no agricultural research stations in those days and the experts knew little about the country, so we had to fumble our way along; we tried this and that and made mistakes, and we sweated blood over them, but the farm grew—the crops and the dairy and the vegetables and the poultry.

The whole balance of our farming is different from what we had expected. The dairy has become enormous, and so is the poultry farm—the chicken runs are like a snowstorm with these huge white Leghorns, and the incubators are like a factory. Tnuva, the marketing cooperative, which has its branches all over the country, markets the whole of our produce for us. . . .

Our main crops are wheat, barley, vegetables, bananas, grapes, grapefruit, olives and alfalfa. The alfalfa shot up astonishingly after irrigation was introduced—eight crops a year! We feed our cattle on it and we sell the rest. The bananas and the grapefruit have done well ever since we started planting them—we sold about 76,000 kilograms of bananas last year—but it took a lot of trouble to discover the right sort of olives. We grow apples, too, and recently we have started date palms. There is very little we can't grow in our valley if we put our minds to it. . . . But it is a curious thing, I find it easier to talk about the past than the present, and sometimes I even look back to those days with a kind of envy. Of course, everything has improved in a hundred ways. But there was something very good about that time. There was something very good about the way we lived and worked. Not that the young people nowadays work less hard than we did. You should just see them in the Negev—you should see what they're doing to their land, and it's a real desert if ever there was one—as naked as your palm. But now everything is more organized; there is a well-planned task and a great organized army of labor. When we came, we were the first and we were alone and the future was unmapped; there was something limitless about it. And then there was the spirit of that first tiny group; that comradeship I think is something that can never quite be equaled. . . .

Living conditions have changed too. We were very austere in the beginning—perhaps even too austere. Not that we could afford to be otherwise, but we also believed in it. A great advantage of the kibbutz life is that it is suitable for pioneering, but the pioneering spirit tends to be austere. Single people lived in dormitories, families had a room, but there was the bare minimum of space and furniture. The whole life of the kibbutz was in the dining room—this was our only meeting place; that was where we ate, and rested, and held discussions, and read and wrote, and sang and danced. There was no social life anywhere except in the dining room, with its bare board walls and its narrow tables and benches, and its kerosene lamps; even when we put up a permanent building in cement, for a long time it was still much the same. The food was poor and monotonous, and the clothes were whatever cost least to buy or make, the same for everyone, so that when they came from the laundry they were interchanged. There was no sanitation except outdoor closets, and the washing arrangements were two huts with showers, one for women and one for men. Actually, this was only changed last year.

But now you should see our rooms—there are chairs and cupboards and window curtains; each room is allowed a kettle and a spirit lamp and its own small portion of tea and biscuits, so that people even entertain in their rooms! The women don't make up, but when you see them in their pretty holiday best you would hardly know they are peasant women.

Of course, it isn't anything to complain of, and by other standards it would even perhaps seem funny that at sixty-four, after forty-five years' work, we should live in one room and have seven pounds a year pocket money if the kibbutz can afford it, and nothing put by for a rainy day, and that we should complain of too much luxury. Not that I do complain, but some people think it is too much. I don't think there is too much in Degania, though perhaps there is in some other settlements. . . .

So the *kvutza* has done well by us. [It] watches over its people—no one is alone, neglected, allowed to go under or be soured by his struggle for his living. And nobody feels he is alone, and that helps him to behave decently. Suppose that I quarrel with someone here, do him some injury, some harm. I know a hundred pairs of eyes see it—that makes me think twice. In town, if you behave badly to someone or he behaves badly to you, you needn't meet that person again; you can avoid him; you needn't settle things squarely with him, humanly. Of course, there is always the law to punish you if you go too far, but that's impersonal. Nobody can force me to be good. I ought to be good because I feel the need for it inside me and for the sake of the community—the *kvutza* constantly gives one that feeling.

Of course, things are not always smooth. There are petty differences, jealousies like everywhere else, but in the atmosphere of the *kvutza* they don't get out of hand. And as time passes the *kvutza* influences people and gives them discipline from within. . . .

Miriam and I have never had a moment of disillusionment with the life of the *kvutza*. There have been hardships—plenty—but never a moment of doubt or disappointment. Not that I think it is necessary for everyone to live in this way; I don't think it is good for everyone; I believe that there are many for whom it isn't good and who shouldn't even try it; but we ourselves have always found it good.

Nor is it necessary for every Jew to live in Israel, nor for everyone to work on the land. But we have found it very good to work on our land. The land has been very good to us. We have had a difficult life, and there are still many problems and difficulties. The land is still waiting to receive the many thousands who need a refuge, or who may one day need a refuge, or whose hearts are in exile from it. It is waiting to feed and to comfort them and to give them the peace and the certainty that we have received. And until they have received it we cannot rest. There are still deserts in our country to be made fruitful, barren acres to dig and to water, and the brains of our scientists and our strength, and the strength of our young men, must be given to this hard task. And the people who come in from all the corners of the world, after all the barren and restless centuries, must learn what the land will ask of them and what the land [will] give them. And we ourselves must be watchful to keep alive our spirit and to be ready for whatever is asked of us.

We know that the land responds to work and to selflessness. It does not give itself in the same way to greedy hands or to rapacious hearts; but to us who, for all our sins and errors, have asked of it nothing but to feed and shelter the hungry and homeless multitudes, it has given itself gratefully. It has rewarded us. We who came to this barren soil of swamp and desert, to this climate that was moody and dangerous, see around us the green valley teeming with life, with children, with rich harvests, and beyond the hills, throughout the whole country, our children are carrying on our work. When we planted our trees we said, "Our grandchildren shall not be hungry." But we ourselves are indeed most happy; few people can have seen such fruit of their labors.

Israel: The Forging
of a Nation

☙INTRODUCTION: If the pogroms in Eastern Europe led to a trickle of immigrants to Palestine during the first twenty-five years of this century, the rise of Adolph Hitler and the Nazi Party in Germany opened the floodgates in the 1930s and 1940s. Hitler came to power in 1933, blaming Jewish capitalists and Communists for Germany's economic problems and promising a thousand-year rule of pure (Aryan) Germans. To achieve his goal, he launched what has become known as the Holocaust, the attempt to eliminate all Jews and non-Aryan peoples, such as Gypsies. As German armies swept across Europe during World War II, Jews were rounded up and herded into concentration camps to be shot, gassed or worked to death as part of Hitler's so-called "final solution." Before this genocide came to a halt with the defeat of Germany in the war, a total of six million Jews were killed.

Hundreds of thousands of other Jews in Europe became refugees. As a result, the pressure to create a Jewish state intensified and in 1947 the United Nations voted Israel into existence. The following selection describes the complex process of populating Israel and maintaining the Jewish character of the state. [15]☙

Israel is a nation of immigrants *par excellence.* It has grown faster through immigration than any other country in

Refugees from Europe stayed in settlement camps when first arriving in Israel.
(Embassy of Israel, Washington, D.C.)

human history. In 1948, at the time of independence, Israel had a population of less than 1 million; by 2001 it had a population of 6.4 million, made up largely of immigrants and the children of immigrants. In 1950, the Israeli Knesset (the parliament) passed the Law of Return, granting every Jew in the world the right to emigrate to Israel, to become a citizen and to receive state support during settlement. Since then, more than 3 million Jews have migrated to Israel.

Because Israel was founded as a "homeland" for Jews, it is often perceived as having a homogeneous population, but Israel's founders and settlers come from more than seventy countries, speak almost one hundred languages and represent a variety of cultures, races and traditions. While the majority of Israelis are Jewish by religion, they are quite diversified in other respects. (Even in religious terms the Jews of Israel are divided, with about 15 percent being ultra-Orthodox, 50 percent secular or non-observant and the rest somewhere in between.)

Moreover, about 20 percent of Israel's population—more than 1.3 million people—consists of Arabs, mostly Moslems (15 percent) but including some Christians (2.1 percent) and Druze (2 percent).

POPULATING ISRAEL

In 1880, there were only about 25,000 Jews living in Palestine. From 1882 to 1939, various waves of immigrants (Aliyas) added another 430,000. By 1947, a year before Israel's independence, there were approximately 630,000 Jews and 660,000 Arabs in the area of Palestine that was to become Israel, sometimes referred to as Western Palestine. When Britain announced the creation of Israel, four Arab states—Egypt, Jordan, Lebanon and Syria—attacked the new country to prevent its establishment. Israel won

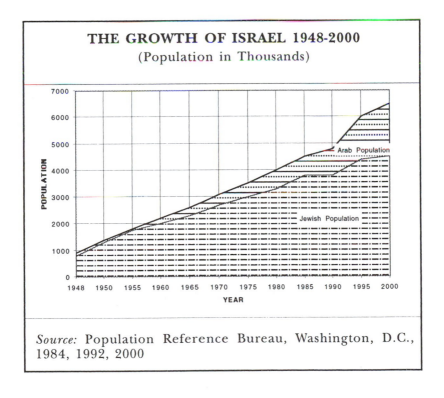

THE GROWTH OF ISRAEL 1948-2000
(Population in Thousands)

Source: Population Reference Bureau, Washington, D.C., 1984, 1992, 2000

the War of Independence but in the process more than 500,000 Arabs fled and settled in nearby Middle East countries, many in refugee camps. These displaced Palestinians, now numbering over 2.5 million, are the central issue in the Palestinians' claim for their own "homeland" and independent state, the same arrangement granted to Jews in 1947.

With the departure of the Palestinians, the population balance of Western Palestine shifted dramatically, so that by May 1948, when Israel achieved statehood, there were 650,000 Jews and 156,000 Arabs living in the country. At that point, the Jewish immigration flood broke loose. Jewish refugees from World War II in Europe, Jews living in North Africa and the Middle East anxious to escape the persecutions they experienced there, and Jews held in Cyprus by the British who prevented them from immigrating earlier—all of these groups poured into Israel. Within three years, almost 700,000 Jewish immigrants arrived, more than doubling the existing Jewish population and far exceeding the 500,000 Arabs who had fled.

Since the early years of independence, when as many as 234,000 immigrants arrived in one year, the number of immigrants has fluctuated between 5,000 and 65,000 per year during the 1960s, 70s and 80s. In the early 1980s, the number averaged about 15,000 per year, roughly the same number that left Israel, adding very little to the population through immigration. At that time, the only likely source of population growth was natural increase because the pool of potential immigrants in the Diaspora had dwindled. In the 1980s, only the Soviet Union with about three million Jews and the United States with six million were potential sources of new immigrants. But the Soviet Union severely restricted emigration and American Jews showed little inclination to emigrate to Israel in large numbers. Between 1948 and 1967 only 20,000 Americans settled in Israel, about 1,000 per year. Since 1968, however, the number has increased slightly, fluctuating between 2,000 and 5,000 per year.

In 1989, the immigration scene changed dramatically. The Soviet Union, which had already begun to loosen its emigration policy because of its own social policy of Glastnos, or openness, began to unravel as an empire. In November of 1989, the Berlin Wall fell; then the satellite states of Eastern Europe broke away from the Soviet Union one after the other; and finally the Soviet Union itself disintegrated. At the beginning of 1990, the *Washington Post* would report: "For much of the 1980s, Israeli leaders watched with alarm as their small country lost more population to emigration than it gained in new immigrants. Now, the new wave of Jewish arrivals that many dreamed of has begun to materialize with startling speed. In October of 1989, 1,460 immigrants arrived from the Soviet Union, the highest monthly figure since the 1970s. In November, the figure soared to 3,000, and in December 3,600 were registered. Overall, immigration rose from 4,400 in 1988 to nearly 25,000 in 1989—the highest annual figures since 1973." [16]

Soviet Jews kiss the ground on their arrival in Israel, rejoicing over their "return" to the Holy Land (Wide World Photo)

But the swell of 1989 would become a tidal wave in 1990 when more than 200,000 Soviet Jews flooded into Israel, inundating social services, housing facilities and the job market. The difficulties faced by immigrants in Israel combined with freer and presumably safer conditions for Jews in the former Soviet republics led to a sharp decline in immigration in 1991. Only 167,000 immigrants arrived, compared to the 400,000 that had been predicted. Still, by 2000, one million Soviet Jews had migrated to Israel. When combined with previous immigrants from the Soviet Union, the Russians constitute the largest single group by area of origin in the country, about ten percent of the Jewish population of Israel.

To provide housing and settlement subsidies for this influx of immigrants, the Israeli government requested a $10 billion loan guarantee from the United States; it also stepped up the construction of Jewish settlements in the Occupied Territories. Israeli Prime Minister Yitzhak Shamir saw the newly arrived Soviets as likely candidates for West Bank and Gaza settlement, furthering his cause of "creating the fact" of a Jewish presence in the Occupied Territories. Among right-wing Israelis, the argument goes, if enough Jews settle in the Occupied Territories, the *fact* of their presence will undercut the Palestinian claim to rights in these Territories.

American President George Bush rejected the Israeli request for the $10 billion loan guarantee until the Israelis brought to a halt the new construction in the Occupied Territories. Prime Minister Shamir rejected this condition— in fact, he added 5,000 additional units to the 1992 construction plan—and an impass between the U.S. and Israel developed, to be bridged only with a change of government in Israel and the election of the Labor Party leader Yitzhak Rabin as prime minister. In June 1992, Rabin pledged to curb settlements in the Occupied Territories and the loan guarantee was approved. During the previous year, however, settlements in the Territories increased by 25 percent, actually outpacing the government's ability to entice settlers. By the middle of 1999, there were about 170,000 Israeli settlers living in 160 settlements in the Occupied Territories: the West Bank, Gaza Strip, the Golan Heights and East Jerusalem.

IMMIGRATION PLURALISM

Questions of settlement, employment, education and integration into Israeli society have accompanied every wave of immigration into the country. And different waves have brought different problems, needs and opportunities, for the waves themselves have brought different groups of people at different stages of Israel's development. During the first five Aliyas, between 1882 and 1939 and until approximately 1950, most of the immigrants to Israel came from Europe—Austria, Germany, Poland, Romania and Russia. As we have seen in previous selections, the early pioneers were highly idealistic and committed to democratic socialism. They were also generally young, technically skilled and well educated. These Western (Ashkenazi) Jews set the tone for the new nation of Israel, and until fairly recently they have dominated the politics of the country. They still set the standards in science, technology and education for Israel. For this reason, the Arab countries see Israel as a Western nation, closely allied with the United States, following Western values and customs and enjoying a standard of living more akin to that of Europe than the Middle East. Israel's per capita Gross National Income in 1999, for example, was $18,070, closer to the U.K.'s $22,220 than Jordan's $3,880.

As similar as the Ashkenazi, or Western, Jews were in background and culture, there were important differences based on their country of origin. One of the most important differences was language. Although Yiddish was spoken by many of the Ashkenazis, it was not spoken by the majority of them. In fact, when all immigrant groups to Israel are taken into account, almost 100 different languages are represented. Thus one of the first decisions the Zionists had to make was to choose a national language for Israel.

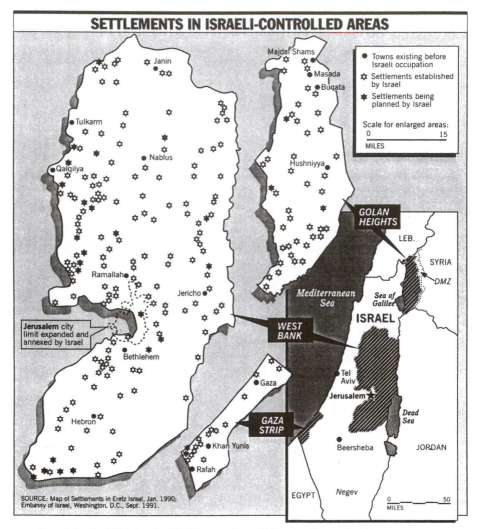

SETTLEMENTS IN ISRAELI-CONTROLLED AREAS

Majdal Shams
Janin
Masada
Buqata

● Towns existing before
Israeli occupation
✿ Settlements established
by Israel
✶ Settlements being
planned by Israel

Scale for enlarged areas:
0   15
MILES

Tulkarm

Nablus
Hushniyya
Qalqilya

GOLAN
HEIGHTS

LEB.

SYRIA
DMZ

Ramallah
Mediterranean
Sea
Sea of
Galilee

Jericho
WEST
BANK
ISRAEL

Jerusalem city
limit expanded and
annexed by Israel

Bethlehem
Tel
Aviv
Jerusalem

Gaza
Dead
Sea

GAZA
STRIP

Hebron
Beersheba
JORDAN

Khan Yunis

Rafah

SOURCE: Map of Settlements in Eretz Israel, Jan. 1990;
Embassy of Israel, Washington, D.C., Sept. 1991.

EGYPT   Negev
0   50
MILES

Copyright © 1991 by the Washington Post. (Map by Dave Cook)

They decided on the biblical language of Hebrew. In the
early days of Zionism, as with Latin, Hebrew was a "dead"
language and was used only in religious ceremonies. But
the early immigrants, who vowed to speak only Hebrew in
the Holy Land, revived Hebrew as a spoken language, and
it is now the official language of Israel. People who do not

speak Hebrew can take a course in it at immigration centers on their arrival in the country.

As immigrants streamed into Israel, especially during the "flood" period of 1948-51, other problems developed. Food and other basic supplies became scarce and had to be rationed, leading to the creation of a black market. Unemployment was rampant, as was inflation, and the lack of housing required the building of special settlements. To make matters worse, Israel had to spend enormous sums of money to defend itself against hostile Arab neighbors.

In time most of the problems surrounding the settlement of new immigrants were solved, but other problems emerged, notably the social and economic disparities that separated the Western Jews from the Eastern, or Sephardic, Jews. While the early settlers were largely from Europe, the majority of the later immigrants, especially after 1950, came from North Africa and Asia, from countries like Yemen, Algeria, Turkey, Libya and Iraq. In 1950-51, 100,000 immigrants arrived from Iraq alone. Since independence in 1948, almost one million Jews from Middle East countries have immigrated to Israel, dramatically changing the social, political and economic life of the country. In 1948, the Jewish population of Israel was 85 percent of European origin; by 1984, it was 60 percent of Afro-Asian origin, a transformation sometimes referred to as "Orientalization."

With the influx of Soviet immigrants in the 1990s, however, the balance has begun to shift back in the other direction, a "correction" that many Ashkenazis welcome.

Jews Living in Middle East Nations, 1998

Algeria	0-100
Egypt	0-100
Iran	25,000
Iraq	120
Israel	4,847,000
Jordan	0
Lebanon	0
Morocco	7,500
Saudi Arabia	0
Syria	250
Tunisia	2,000
Turkey	25,000
Yemen	800

"Thousands of well-educated, talented Soviets have been integrated into Israel's professional class and are revitalizing areas, such as classical music, medicine and math teaching. Most of the 8,000 physicians who flocked to the country in 1991 have been licensed to practice, and 17 new orchestras have been formed from immigrant musicians."[17] However, 40 to 50 percent of the Soviet immigrants are unemployed, many live in one-room shelters, and stories abound of Ph.D.s sweeping floors and doctors hawking drygoods. A pattern of high hopes and unanticipated problems continues to visit the lives of immigrants to Israel, as it always has.

Nowhere is this pattern more striking than with the Falashas, or so-called black Jews of Ethiopia, who claim descent from those who migrated from Jerusalem with Menelik, the son of Solomon and the Queen of Sheba. (Some scholars dispute this claim and believe the Falashas learned their Judaism from Jews in Egypt or those migrating from Saudi Arabia.) Theories aside, in every respect—racially, culturally, educationally, historically,

Afro-Asian Jews now constitute the majority in Israel, bringing a shift to the right politically. (Embassy of Israel, Washington, D.C.)

even religiously—these Ethiopians differ sharply from Europeanized Israelis; yet for decades these same Israelis negotiated with the Ethiopian government to allow the Falashas to emigrate to Israel. Finally, out of desperation in 1984, the Israeli air force secretly flew 7,000 Falashas out of Ethiopia to Israel. And in May 1991, with the concurrence of the Ethiopian government, Israel brought 14,200 more Falashas in a dramatic thirty-six-hour airlift called Operation Solomon. There are now about 50,000 Ethiopians living in Israel.

The persistence of the Israeli government in freeing the Falashas and the exuberant welcome offered to them by the Israeli people stand as a dramatic testimonial to the role that Israel plays as a "homeland" for all Jews, regardless of origin or circumstances. At the same time, however, the Falashas are having problems adjusting to life in Israel. They do not know the language; they cannot find work (indeed, they do not have the education or skills needed to qualify for most jobs); they live in mobile homes that they claim are hot in summer and cold in winter; they feel isolated because these homes are grouped in settlements for Falashas only; and they feel deprived of their own religious leaders, who at home performed marriages and other rituals but are not recognized by the rabbinical authorities in Israel. In short, Ethiopians feel discriminated against in a country that did everything possible to welcome them.

ORIGINS AND POLITICS

Arabic-speaking Sephardic Jews experienced some of these same problems when they emigrated to Israel. Compared to the Westernized Ashkenazi, they arrived with less education, lower level technical skills and non-European customs and traditions. Moreover, they were often denied the right to bring their wealth out of the Arab countries where they had lived. The net result was that Sephardic Jews were poorly equipped to compete in a highly Westernized Israeli society. On average, Oriental

Jews earn less than Jews from Europe and America, and they make up only 40 percent of academic high school enrollments and less than 30 percent of university students while constituting a majority of the population. (Israeli Arabs are even less successful educationally and tend to earn less, on average, than Eastern Jews.)

Not surprisingly, many European Jews tended to look down on these immigrants from Asia and Africa, exhibiting an attitude of superiority similar to what many Europeans and Americans feel toward less industrialized nations. As the number of Oriental Jews increased in Israel, friction between the two groups developed, despite attempts to create equal opportunities for everyone. The Sephardim charged that the best housing was saved for immigrants from Russia and Europe while they were left in substandard housing. In immigration centers, too, they argued, Western values tended to predominate and Eastern values were frowned upon. To reduce conflict, the Israeli government has found it best to plan for people from the same area of origin to live together. New settlements, then, often will have Moroccan immigrants living in one village, Tunisians in another and Ethiopians in yet another, but all villages are linked to a central town. Urban housing schemes also keep ethnic groups separated.

Despite government programs to assist Eastern Jews, a socio-economic gap between the two Jewish Groups remains, and is reflected in Israeli politics. From its inception in 1948 until 1977, Israel was governed by one party, the liberal, Ashkenazi-dominated Labor Party. In 1969, the Sephardic Jews, finding the doors for political advancement closed in the establishment party, began to switch their allegiance to the conservative Likud Party. As their numbers grew so did their influence, and by 1977 they were able, for the first time in Israeli history, to elect a conservative leader—Menachem Begin. As a result, the Sephardim have gained in political power what they have so far failed to gain in economic or social status.

THE CREATION OF ISRAEL
MAJOR EVENTS: 1882-2001 [18]

1882-1903 First wave of modern immigration to Palestine (Aliya); 25,000 Eastern European immigrants arrive.

1897 First Zionist Congress in Basel, Switzerland, organized by Theodor Herzl, formally launches drive for Jewish return to the Land of Israel.

1904-14 Second Aliya; 40,000-55,000 Jewish immigrants arrive from Eastern Europe and Russia.

1917 Great Britain, in Balfour Declaration, supports creation of "National Home" for Jews in Palestine.

1919-23 Third Aliya; 35,000 Jews arrive, mostly from Poland and Russia.

1923 League of Nations establishes British Mandate over Palestine and directs Britain to encourage "close settlement of Jews upon the land."

1924-28 Fourth Aliya; 67,000 immigrants arrive, half of them middle-class, urban Poles.

1929-39 Fifth Aliya; 250,000 Jews, one-quarter of them refugees from Nazi Germany, arrive in Palestine.

1939 Great Britain issues White Paper on Palestine, curbing Jewish immigration and land purchase.

1945-48 Almost 75,000 immigrants arrive, most illegally.

1947 United Nations proposes partition of Palestine into Arab states (Judea and Samaria, or West Bank, and eastern Jerusalem to go to Jordan; Golan Heights to Syria; Gaza Strip to Egypt) and a Jewish state (the remainder).

1948 State of Israel comes into existence (May 14). Total Jewish population is 650,000. War of Independence begins as Egypt, Jordan, Lebanon and Syria invade Israel.

1948-51 Mass immigration; 690,000 Jews arrive from Europe, Asia and North Africa.

1949 First Knesset convenes with David Ben-Gurion as prime minister. Armistice signed with neighboring Arab countries. Jerusalem divided—western half to Israel, eastern half to Jordan.

1950 Knesset passes Law of Return, granting all Jews the right to immigrate to Israel.

1956 Suez Crisis: Egypt nationalizes Suez Canal, closing it to Israeli shipping. Israel invades Gaza Strip and Sinai, then withdraws under U.S. pressure.

1967 Six-Day War (June 6-11): Israel launches a pre-emptive strike against Egypt, Syria and Jordan, gaining control of the Sinai Peninsula, Gaza Strip, Golan Heights and West Bank (including Jerusalem). Jerusalem reunited.

1968 First Israeli settlement in occupied West Bank.

1973 Yom Kippur War: Syria and Egypt attack Israeli forces on Golan Heights and along Suez Canal. After early reversals, Israel closes in on Damascus and crosses Suez Canal.

1977 Likud coalition takes over Knesset under Prime Minister Menachem Begin. Egyptian President Anwar Sadat visits Jerusalem.

1978 Israel invades southern Lebanon to root out Palestinian guerrillas; U.N. buffer zone created. At Camp David with President Jimmy Carter (September 5-17), President Anwar Sadat and Prime Minister Begin agree to conclude peace treaty within three months.

1981 Knesset votes annexation of Golan Heights won from Syria in 1967.

1982 Israel again invades Lebanon to rout Palestine Liberation Organization terrorists and Syrians.

1983 Menachem Begin resigns (September 15), succeeded by Yitzhak Shamir as prime minister. Israeli troops mired in southern third of Lebanon. Number of Jewish settlers in occupied West Bank and Gaza Strip reaches 30,000.

1987 Start of the Palestinian Intifada.

1991 Israel absorbs Iraqi SCUD missile attacks during Persian Gulf War; does not retaliate at the request of the U.S. The international peace conference, involving Israel, the Palestinians, Jordan, Lebanon and Syria opens in Madrid, Spain.

1992 Labor Party defeats Likud; Yitzhak Rabin replaces Yitzhak Shamir as prime minister.

1993 Secret negotiations between the Israelis and Yasser Arafat's Palestinian Liberation Organization (PLO) start in Oslo, Norway resulting in a "Declaration of Principles," an outline for a lasting peace between the Israelis and Palestinians.

1994 In May, as a result of the Oslo agreement, Israel withdraws its troops from Gaza and Jericho on the West Bank, turning over control to the Palestinian Authority. In July Yasser Arafat enters Gaza for the first time since 1967 and makes it the capital of the new Palestinian entity.

1994 As a by-product of the Oslo agreement, Israel and Jordan sign a peace treaty. Israel now has a peace agreement with two of its four neighboring countries.

1995 "Oslo II" is signed in Washington D.C. between the PLO and Israel. It is an implementation plan based on the 1993 Oslo agreement which provides for a series of Israeli withdrawals from most of the West Bank and outlines steps toward a "final settlement."

1995 An Israeli extremist assassinates Israeli Prime Minister Rabin at a peace rally because of his willingness to "trade land for peace."

1996 Benjamin Netanyahu, a Likud member, is elected Prime Minister over the Labor candidate Peres, a colleague of Rabin's. Netanyahu initiates a slowdown of the peace process.

1998 Netanyahu agrees to return 13% more of the West Bank to the Palestinians at the Wye River conference in Maryland. The PLO once again agrees to eliminate passages relating to the destruction of Israel from its charter.

1999 The May 4 deadline for a "final settlement" passes, but negotiations continue between Israel and the PLO. A new deadline is set for September, 2000.

1999 Labor candidate Ehud Barak defeats Netanyahu and becomes Israel's Prime Minister, winning on a peace platform. He immediately declares that a final peace agreement with the Palestinians, Lebanese and Syrians is his highest priority.

2000 In May the Israelis unilaterally withdraw their army from the "security zone" in South Lebanon. The Israeli-Lebanese border returns to where it was in 1982.

2000 In July, the Camp David II "final settlement" talks break down over the status of Jerusalem

2000 In September, Israeli General Ariel Sharon marches to the Western Wall, part of the Temple Mount sacred to both Jews and Muslims, with 1000 armed security guards. The resultant demonstration leads to 10 Palestinian deaths, and quickly expands into a "second Intifada."

2001 In February, Ariel Sharon defeats Ehud Barak to become Israel's Prime Minister.

2002 The Intifada continues and violence intensifies on both sides.

≈POSTSCRIPT: A main difference between the Likud party and the Labor party in Israel is their attitude toward the "Palestinian problem." Israelis who are refugees from Arab countries often join the Likud party and generally take a hard line via–à–vis the Arab world. They demand the annexation of the West Bank and Gaza and have pushed for the continual building of Jewish settlements in these areas.

In contrast to Likud, the Ashkenazi-controlled Labor party has traditionally favored a restriction on settlements, a withdrawal of troops from Southern Lebanon and a negotiated peace settlement with neighboring Arab states and the Palestinians. They are willing to return most of the West Bank and Gaza, as well as the Syrian Golan Heights, in exchange for peace.

After Labor party victories in 1992 and 1999, the Labor party agenda has, to some degree, been actualized. As a result of the Oslo Accords (1993-1995) a partial settlement with the Palestinians has been negotiated and implemented, and the Palestinians now govern Gaza and 40% of the West Bank. In addition, Israel unilaterally withdrew its forces from Lebanon in 2000.

A major reason Israel decided to negotiate with the Palestinians has to do with the changing nature of its population as a result of the occupation of Arab lands taken during the 1967 war. By 1992 there were 1 million Arabs living on the West Bank and .7 million in Gaza. If these lands were annexed, Arabs would constitute 40% of Israel's population. As can be seen in the chart on page 285, because of a higher Arab birth rate, Jews would eventually become a minority in their own country!

There are four elements in the Israeli equation: land, peace, democracy and the Jewish character of the nation. After the start of the Intifada in 1987 (see "The Intifada; an Uprising for a Nation") it became increasingly clear to Israelis that they could not have all four. Keeping Arab land would lead to a situation where enjoying peace, while maintaining democracy and a Jewish state, would become impossible. If the Israeli Arabs and the Arabs in the Occupied territories were allowed democratic freedoms. Jews would soon be in a situation where they could be out-voted. And if Arabs were denied first class citizenship and the right to vote, then Israel would not only cease to be a democracy, it would continue to be in a constant state of war and rebellion. As these truths became evident during the 90's, Israelis concluded that "trading land for peace" was the only strategy that would allow them to retain the

ISRAEL: TWO POSSIBLE FUTURES

Jewish percent of total population

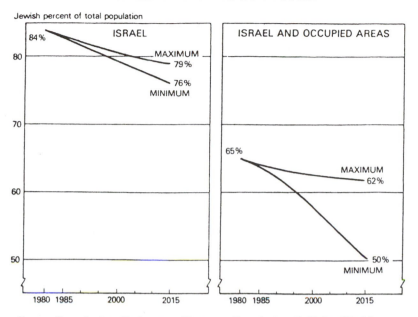

Source: Population Reference Bureau, *Population Bulletin,* Washington, D.C., 1984.

Jewish character of their state while maintaining democracy and achieving peace.

However, from 1996 to 1999, during Benjamin Netanyahu's term as Israeli Prime Minister, the peace process was slowed down considerably. A Likud party leader, Netanyahu launched a series of actions (building a Jewish settlement in an Arab area of Jerusalem, opening an archaeological tunnel under an important mosque, offering to return only an additional 2% of the West Bank) that seemed calculated to anger and discourage the Palestinians. But eventually, under pressure from the Clinton administration and others, along with Arafat's threat to declare unilaterally a Palestinian state by May 4, 1999 if no progress toward peace were made, Netanyahu finally signed the Wye River agreement on October 23, 1998 providing the Palestinians with another 13% of the West Bank in exchange for joint Israeli-Palestinian efforts to combat terrorism. This agreement put the peace process back on track and signified Likud's acceptance of the Interim peace agreement known as Oslo II, as well as a "land for peace" strategy in negotiations.

A further step towards a final peace agreement occurred in May of 1999 when the Israeli Labor party candidate, Ehud Barak, defeated Netanyahu and became Prime Minister. He was elected on a peace platform, and upon taking office immediately declared his highest priority to be conducting peace agreements with the Palestinians, Lebanese and Syrians.

In May of 2000 Barak unilaterally withdrew Israeli forces from a "security zone" in Southern Lebanon. As a result Lebanon is free of Israeli troops for the first time since 1982.

But in July of 2000, hopes for peace in the Middle East took a turn for the worse. At the Camp David II talks, as called for in the Oslo Accords, Israel and the Palestinians tried to come to agreement on the most difficult issues remaining so as to achieve a "final settlement." While progress was made on many issues at Camp David II, the talks ultimately broke down over the issue of Jerusalem, the Israelis wanting sovereignty over most of the city, while the Palestinians demanded full sovereignty over East Jerusalem, especially their holy places on the Temple Mount. An additional unresolved problem area is the Arab "right of return," the right of Palestinians who fled Israel during the 1947 war, and their descendants, to return to what was once Palestine, and is now Israel. The failure of these talks has led to great discouragement on the part of both Israelis and Palestinians.

In September 2000, after a provocative visit with over 1,000 armed security guards by Israeli general Ariel Sharon to the Temple Mount, an area in East Jerusalem sacred to both Jews and Muslims, a series of Palestinian demonstrations erupted leading to a second Intifada, known as the "Al Aqsa Intifada."

In December 2000, Prime Minister Barak resigned from office and called for elections to be held in the Spring of 2001. But with the Al Aqsa intifada raging out of control, the Likud party candidate, Ariel Sharon, known for his tough policies on Arab matters and promising to end the Intifada in 100 days, was elected. Nonetheless, as of this writing in February 2002, the violence continues.⁊

The Intifada: An Uprising
for a Nation

☙INTRODUCTION: In 1882, French historian Ernest Renan wrote a famous essay entitled "What Is a Nation?" Today the essay is still read and the question still asked, especially of ex-colonies that gained their independence in recent decades and of nations like the Soviet Union and Yugoslavia that have disintegrated as unified states even more recently. Imperial powers often created nations where none had existed before, and the local populace, at the time of independence or separation from the union, must face the problem of maintaining the integrity of a state that was created with little concern for language, ethnicity, history or the will of the people.

In raising the question "What is a nation?" Renan examines five factors to see if any one of them, or all five together, is sufficient to bring about the existence of a nation. He first examines race and concludes that many successful nations have more than one race, and that, in any case, there is no racial purity. He secondly examines language, and likewise concludes that many successful nations, such as Switzerland, have citizens who speak a variety of languages. His third category, religion, is also not sufficient, as nations often have several religions existing side by side.

He also rejects his fourth category, community of interests, as being too limited, since there are bound to be many, often conflicting, communities of interest within a nation. Lastly, Renan examines geography. Again he concludes that geography alone is not enough, for some successful nations exist without the benefit of natural boundaries, such as the United

States with Alaska and Hawaii and several island nations around the world consisting of scattered parts.

What is it, then, that makes a nation? Renan feels that "a nation is a living soul, a spiritual principle." Two things, the past and the present, are necessary for this soul to exist. The people of a nation must share a common past. They must have suffered and sacrificed together in the past in order to make the present nation possible, for in the present there must be an active desire to be a nation, a willingness to suffer and sacrifice again, if necessary, to preserve what the people in the past have fought for. Thus it is the will of the people that is needed for nationhood; it is a spirit of determination born of a sense of shared suffering in the past that brings a people together to form a nation.

In this sense, Israel is without question a nation. Indeed, in Renan's sense of nation, where soul and not land or a common language is what makes for nationhood, Israel was a nation long before it became a state in 1948. In a similar way, Arabs in the Middle East talk about "the Arab Nation" held together, to be sure, by language (and to a lesser degree by religion) but mostly by a sense of shared history and suffering.

This concept of nationhood, as distinct from statehood, has become especially important in the last decade of the twentieth century. People within states as diverse as Iraq, India and Canada, and within former states such as the Soviet Union, Yugoslavia and Czechoslovakia, have declared their allegiance to ethnic, religious or linguistic groups and not to secular states. In many instances, these mini-nationalisms have supplanted nation states.

As part of this contemporary movement and consistent with Renan's definition of nationhood, the Palestinians have laid claim to their own nation. While they have never had a state of their own, the Palestinians have developed a distinct identity through several hundred years of colonization (shared suffering) and today see themselves as separate from the people about them: the Israelis, Jordanians, Lebanese, Syrians, Egyptians and others.

Historically, Palestinians have not fared well at the hands of major forces in the Middle East, namely, the Ottoman Turks, the British and the Israelis. As a result of the 1948 and 1967 wars, the Palestinians have been divided among those living in Israel, those in the West Bank, those in Gaza and those in the "Diaspora"—i.e., the countries of the Middle East and beyond.

THE PALESTINIAN PEOPLE				
Country	1986	1990/91	1995	1999
Jordan	1,398,050	1,824,179	2,170,101	2,434,130
West Bank/East Jerusalem	951,520	1,075,531	1,227,545	1,972,283
Gaza	545,100	622,016	726,832	1,112,597
Israel	608,200	730,000	800,755	1,094,350
Lebanon	271,434	331,757	392,315	449,735
Syria	242,474	301,744	357,881	486,826
Remaining Arab States	582,894	445,195	516,724	571,493
Rest of the World	280,846	450,000	500,000	476,782
TOTAL	4,880,518	5,780,422	6,692,153	8,598,196

Source: Palestine Central Bureau of Statistics, 2000.

The table above shows the size and location of various Palestinian groups.

As might be expected, Palestinians living across a wide geographic area, in different countries and under differing economic, social and political circumstances, do not necessarily hold similar views on all issues, including the Arab-Israeli conflict. Developing a Palestinian consciousness has been made difficult by a number of factors. Those living outside Israel are fragmented into many groups, some living as individuals in various Arab countries, others (the majority) living in poverty in refugee camps in Lebanon and Jordan. Those living in Israel or the Occupied Territories have lacked the economic base to promote Palestinian causes or have been suppressed by Israeli authorities—arrested or exiled—if these causes were seen as subversive.

But much of this changed on December 9, 1987, when the Intifada—the Palestinian uprising—began in the Occupied Territories. Since then, Palestinians have come closer together in the common cause of liberating the territories and forming a Palestinian state.

The Intifada (the word means "tremor" or "shaking off" in Arabic) began after a series of isolated or loosely connected events in the Gaza strip, which ignited the bottled up rage of people who have been occupied since 1967. A Jew was murdered in a marketplace in Gaza. The next day an Israeli truck driver made a bad turn and killed four Palestinians from a refugee camp. The Palestinians did not believe it was an accident, and the next morning they threw stones at the Israeli soldiers making the rounds of the refugee camp. A crowd gathered; a flaming bottle was thrown at a soldier; and he shot and killed a seventeen-year-old boy. Then something burst! When the army came for the body for an autopsy and a burial, a crowd of as many as 30,000 refused to give up the body and they held their own funeral. Afterwards an angry crowd attacked the soldiers in the camp with stones and bottles. As

Two Palestinian boys display their toy guns while playing in Gaza City. Children their age engage in stone throwing as part of the Intifada; their older brothers sometimes use automatic weapons or bombs. (AP/Wide World Photos)

word of the uprising spread, towns rose up in rebellion the next day, including refugee camps on the West Bank.

In the initial phase of the uprising, Palestinian women and children were the primary activists, throwing stones and marching in protest; by and large the Intifada was non-violent, although in the first year the Israeli army killed 300, injured thousands and arrested 20,000 Palestinians. A total of eleven Israeli soldiers also died and more than 1,000 were injured in that same year. In the next phase, the violence grew on both sides, including the killing of Palestinians by Palestinians for suspected collaboration. For years, schools and colleges, considered centers of the resistance, were closed in the Occupied Territories, retarding the education of a whole generation of Palestinians.

The following reading consists of interviews conducted by an American journalist, Penny Rosenwasser, in the Occupied Territories in December of 1989. As a Jew, she felt compelled to speak out against anti-Semitism and against the "inhumane and reprehensible" Israeli treatment of Palestinian people, believing that "a secure homeland couldn't be built on the displacement of another people." Rosenwasser continues: "For me, part of Judaism is tikkun olam, or 'repair of the world,' not adding to its ills. So in December 1989 I traveled to Palestine and Israel, burning with a need to witness, to document, to understand, to listen. That first trip I had only myself, my microphone and tape recorder, and many contacts. And a strong will to create an experience that could help me effectively work for change."[19]🔊

QASSEM IZZAT (December 1989)

They are killing us without guns.
—Gazan worker

I met Qassem somewhat by accident. I was stranded in Gaza, hoping to find a Palestinian family in Jabalia Camp with whom I could spend a few nights. Sure enough, Qassem drove me through the dusty mud-rutted "streets" of Jabalia, waving and chatting to many as we passed. Just at dusk we reached Jamal's door, barely in time for Qassem to make it back to his family in Gaza City before the nightly eight p.m. curfew.

But it was in his cramped journalist's office, bedecked with maps and supplied with a stash of dried beans for munching, that he unfolded his story, as shouts rang out from the street below. Held by eyes so intensely open, I felt his silent tension, his soft and heavy heart, his burning spirit.

• *So you said the intifada started here in Jabalia?*

QASSEM: Yes, the intifada started on the ninth of December, 1987, from Jabalia Camp, and then it spread to all of the Gaza Strip, and so continued more than a month just in the Gaza Strip. It was a horrible time, everywhere massive demonstration, thousands of people outside in the streets. The intifada still has daily clashes in the Gaza Strip, people are wounded daily. Now, if today ten are wounded, we say it is quiet. Sometimes 200 are wounded. The hospitals frequently get very crowded, you know. . . .

• *So tell me about the difference between Gaza and the West Bank, in terms of what's happening with the intifada.*

QASSEM: Gaza is a very crowded place, I think the most crowded place in all of the world, and people here are very poor. Two-thirds of the population here are refugees from Palestine since '48.* So these refugees are just living in the camps and they haven't any land, they have nothing. In the West Bank the conditions are different. Most of the people there are citizens or come from the West Bank, so they have better land. They also have some economic advantages, better than in the Gaza Strip. . . .

• *When we were looking at the map and I was looking at the settlements, you said two-thirds I think . . .*

---

* When the Israeli state was formed, many Arabs fled or were driven from their homes, hoping to return soon.

Palestinian children give the V for victory sign. Schools and colleges in the Occupied Territories have been closed for much of the time since the start of the Intifada. (Rick Reinhard)

QASSEM: One-third of the land of the Gaza Strip has been confiscated for military purposes and for settlements.**. This is incredible. This is the most crowded place in all of the world, and they bring 2,000 Israeli settlers to live on one-third of the land, and two-thirds, which is 200 square kilometers, for 700,000 Palestinian people to live on.*** Imagine! You go to Jabilia Camp and you see how it is. One square kilometer, one-and-a-half square kilometers, and 60,000 people living in it. It is easier in New York City; there they have several-story buildings, you know, but here it is forbidden for people to have a second floor. . . .

• *Are the Palestinians in Gaza, especially from the camps, the same culturally as the Palestinians on the West Bank?*

QASSEM: The main thing is they are from the same people, the same culture. . . .

• *When you said you had been detained or imprisoned, what did they do to you?*

QASSEM: I was detained. I was arrested as an administrative detainee.**** I know the main reason is that I am working with a foreign agency. The military government told me, "If you don't stop, we are going to arrest you in six months." In fact when they arrested me, they didn't give any reason. After a time, after my appeal, they wanted to justify their arrest, so they said that I was a leader of the intifada. This is the accusation against any administrative detainee—"leader of the intifada."

• *Harassment?*

QASSEM: Harassment. And you feel insecure for your family, so you are always worried. I am always worried about my son, where he will go. The intifada is happening for these reasons. It's not just for national reasons.

** As of July 1991, it's over 50%
*** Now 1 million Palestinians live in Gaza.
**** Administrative detention, a common practice of the occupation, means that a person can be held for months without a trial or even being charged.

Even if the Palestinians didn't have any national aspirations, the intifada would come from the daily harassment by the authorities.

• *What do you think is going to happen?*

QASSEM: I am a journalist, and I go everywhere, and I see the feelings of the people and how they are thinking. They will not stop the intifada until they have their own independent state. This you can hear from everyone: from kids, from elders, from shebab [the boys], from everyone. But the problem is there are no changes in the Israeli government's mentality. The main thing the intifada did was to give Palestinians a peaceful mind; they want to have their own state next to Israel. Even now, the Israeli and American governments don't accept this lesson, they don't change their policy. . . .

If I'm wounded, who is going to take care of my family? We become numbers, and this is the most horrible thing for a human being—to become like a number. Continuing like this is horrible. It's horrible for the children who are living this life daily.

Now, I can give you an example. My son is four years old . . . . Daily, he asks me: "Speak to me about the jail, papa, how someone is arrested and what he eats in jail." What he hears is people are shooting, people are wounded, people are arrested for throwing stones. This he heard from kids in the neighborhood, from the radio from the TV, from any conversation going on. So the kids are growing up in this condition, and they have this mentality. Imagine how the kids will grow in the future. They are no longer kids. They have lost their childhood. . . .

For two years now, there is education, but in reality there is no education. Children don't learn anything. They learn how to throw stones, they learn how to protect themselves from the soldiers. So that's why I told you that it is better for the Palestinian nation to lose thousands of lives, and then to have their own state. . . .

The problems are solved by negotiations, and Palestinians are willing to do this in order to have their own state. Not to have better houses; they don't need better houses, they don't need better hospitals. They need only freedom, and then they will build what they want. They have the ability. They have the energy. They have the money. They have everything they need to start building. But the main thing they need is their freedom. . . .

• *So what do you think people in the United States should do? What would be your message to them?*

QASSEM: Not to give money to shoot kids. Not to kill people. If they want to give money, give money to help ensure peace. The only state that can pressure Israel is the United States, because they get billions of dollars from the United States . . . .

During the [first] two years of the intifada, 273 people have died in the Gaza Strip. Of those 273, 120 were children, 16 of whom were under six years old. . . . 43,000 Palestinians have been wounded by live ammunition, beatings and tear-gas inhalation in Gaza. 627 women have miscarried from tear-gas inhalation. And this is just what is registered in the hospital. Sometimes people who are wounded or beaten do not go to the hospital. Imagine 43,000 people from a population of 700,000! Among the beaten you find pregnant women, you find kids, you find the elderly. To be beaten up is really more humiliating than to be shot—more suffering, you know.

And about the curfew. What's the meaning of the curfew? The meaning is, it stops life—completely stops life—social life, economic life. Everything is stopped, because you are stuck inside our home and you can't do anything. Every day in the Gaza Strip there is a curfew from eight p.m. to four a.m. So I can't move after eight o'clock. This is daily—from the beginning of the intifada until now. Life is horrible for the people living here. You're awaiting arrest, for soldiers to break into your house to beat you or to beat your family. The mothers worry about their kids. The kids are afraid of the soldiers. . .

When I leave my house in the morning, I never feel I will come back safely. Something will happen to me. For example, fifteen days ago I was with my friend who was working for ABC. He was filming small clashes, and I was in front of him. Suddenly a bullet hit his abdomen. And he is still in the hospital. He was lucky because he is fat. If it had been me, I'd be paralyzed.

Since the intifada started, eighty-eight houses have been completely demolished as well as parts of other houses,

An Israeli border policeman takes aim with a rubber bullet attachment on his assault rifle at Palestinian boys throwing stones in the Anata refugee camp on the outskirts of Jerusalem. He hit the boy in the dark shirt. (AP/Wide World Photos)

leaving 3,000 people homeless. If one member of the family does some activity, the whole family is punished—it's collective punishment. They punish the kids and the families and the mothers. Of course in Gaza, they can't find a house to rent because there is no house to rent. So they have to live in tents. . . .

BEIT SAHOUR: VILLAGE OF DIGNITY
(December 1989)

It's Saturday night just before Christmas in the village of Beit Sahour, a largely Christian town of about 12,000 Palestinians nestled in the hills next to Bethlehem, just outside Jerusalem. All I know about Beit Sahour is its fame for peacefully and persistently resisting taxation by the Israeli authorities. This is one strategy of the Palestinian intifada against the Israeli occupation. In a town like Beit Sahour, I quickly grasp why intifada also means "awakening."

I walk right into an evening's social gathering of several neighboring families. I notice this is a lovely home, but there's an obvious lack of the usual couches and other furniture. My hosts, the family of Issa Tawil, bring out fresh plates of pita bread, hummus, and olives, and uncork a bottle of wine. I unpack my microphone.

• *Can we start by your explaining to me what has been so unusual about Beit Sahour's tax resistance?*

ELLIAS RISHMAWI: Well, Beit Sahour is not the first town to do this. All of the towns of the West bank and Gaza have their own way of expressing their practice of the intifada. In fact, not paying taxes is a trend of existing in all the Palestinian citizen towns. The reason for Beit Sahour's being so famous or special is that 99% of the Beit Sahourians are not paying taxes. They have stuck to their position, and they proved it very strongly and very efficiently during the tax raid against them that was organized by the occupying authorities. The reason for the tax raid was to break the will of the Beit Sahourians, and if things can be measured in the sense of who won and who lost, whose will was at last victorious, I think the Beit Sahourians have won.

• *And you said they took your washing machine?*

EIMAN RISHMAWI: We were subject to two confiscations. First they confiscated my husband's business, his pharmacy, and drug store. Second, they confiscated our house. In fact, the confiscation of our house affected me very much, because when you have chosen every piece in your house, it affects you emotionally. But the confiscations have made me more determined not to pay taxes. They can confiscate our furniture, they can kill us, they can put us in prison. But they can't confiscate our dignity—they can't kill our spirit and our determination.

• *And Issa, when I first came in, you told me you had lost most of your furniture, including the piano you bought for your daughter Muna when her eye was injured in an accident. . . . Muna, how old are you?*

MUNA: I'm thirteen.

• *So tell me about what happened when they came?*

MUNA: When I came home from school, I saw the Israelis. I watched while they took all the sofas and the piano. My mother told them "Take everything but the piano. My daughter plays on it." He said, "Don't tell me what to take. I will say what I will take."

I watched and I couldn't believe it. My friends told me, "Don't be afraid, Muna, don't be afraid, don't cry." But I can't help it. They took everything.

• *So how did you feel?*

MUNA: Sad. Very sad. And now we don't have sofas to sit on. We have to sit on the floor, you know. . . .

• *Well, in terms of adopting this strategy of tax resistance, did you all sit down and have a meeting?*

EIMAN RISHMAWI: From the beginning, when the leaders said "Don't pay the tax," we agreed with them and decided together—all the people in Beit Sahour—not to pay the tax.

MILLANY NASSER: I think one of the articles in the Geneva convention says that an occupying force can only collect taxes which it then reinvests for the people it occupies. The Israelis say they put the money back into the West Bank, but independent reports have said only about 10% of the tax money collected has actually gone to the West Bank for the support of the schools, streets, hospitals, or whatever. They don't, of course, consider the Geneva Convention as applicable to the West Bank, but we do.

EIMAN RISHMAWI: We have a point of view, that you are paying taxes for your elected representative government, but for us, to whom should we pay taxes? To our occupation? What for? We pay taxes for our state, our Palestinian state, but not for our occupier. . . .

ISSA TAWIL: Four months ago when they started to confiscate the belongings of the people of Beit Sahour, they announced that the reason was a shortage in the budget of the West Bank. They said they needed money, and they were obliged to collect the tax from the people. One month later, inside the Knesset, it was announced that there was an excess in the budget of the West Bank of 160 million shekels! [One shekel equals 38¢ in U.S. currency.] So you can see how they are lying.

ELLIAS RISHMAWI: Actually it is considered a very, very fruitful and economical occupation. They have controlled all our resources, they have controlled the tax collection, they have controlled exports and imports to the Palestinian areas.

Now speaking of the resources and services we are getting, we are paying for all types of services, like water supply, electric supply, and telephone. . . .

Imagine this, for water I am paying one dollar per cubic meter, while in an Israeli settlement just five kilometers east of Beit Sahour, they are paying half a dollar per cubic meter. . . .

They make me pay double the price they are paying and they call it democracy. . . .

• *Can you tell me how the siege of Beit Sahour a few months ago took place?*

MILLANY NASSER: Well, it started the nineteenth of September [1989]. The tax cars started coming to Beit Sahour and going to one or two businesses at first, and, of course, immediately all of the other businesses in town closed.

Every day, at the beginning, they went to three or four shops and they emptied out whatever they wanted. They dumped things on the floor, just taking, taking, taking. The word spread around town quickly. They took away the refrigerators and freezers from the grocery stores; they took the machinery from the woodworking shops and from the carpenters, from the people who work in mother-of-pearl and in other small factories—essentially, their means of livelihood.

Some of the machines for heavy work were imbedded in concrete, so they brought cranes and ripped them out of the floors. They ruined them, actually, and every day they threaten they are going to sell them at auction. They threaten and threaten and threaten. If they didn't think they had enough, they went to the houses and they took their furniture. Every day we could see the tax cars coming in with their moving vans in the morning and leaving at two o'clock in the afternoon. For the first few days there was a curfew in Beit Sahour, and during the whole time there was a nightly curfew.

• *What happens when there is a curfew?*

MILLANY NASSER: Well, every day you are confined to your house. That means for twenty-four hours a day you can't leave the house: you can't go on the roof, you can't go in the yard, you can't even be on your balcony. Theoretically this is the case, but practically there are ways to get around it.

• *And if you do that, what do they do?*

MILLANY NASSER: Well, the worst I've seen them do is yell at people and tell them to go back inside the house, but in other towns they have shot people for being on their balconies. You never know; it depends on the soldier. Sometimes they come to the house and beat people up. . . .

• *It's harassment?*

MILLANY NASSER: Yes, harassment.

• *So they're doing all these things, and you're still not paying your taxes?*

MILLANY NASSER: Oh, this is just the beginning. After they saw this didn't work they started putting up road blocks to block off the city, forbidding people to leave and enter. And they didn't allow diapers and vegetables and things that people need in town, like fresh milk, to get in.

ELLIAS RISHMAWI: And soldiers would strip us on the street and ask to see our ID. They would tear up the card and tell us we needed to get a new one by the next day, which cost 130 shekels [about $4.50]. . . .

MILLANY NASSER: Fourteen-year-old boys get six-month sentences for throwing stones. I know a boy fifteen years old who they accused of throwing stones, and he has been in prison for four or five months. He hasn't even been accused in court yet, because the court proceedings have been postponed four times.

ELLIAS RISHMAWI: I was in jail myself and have seen horrible things there. Boys my son's age, ten years old, they brought to the detention. They were kids, children brought to the detention. It is unbelievable what is going on here. You would never believe it unless you saw it with your own eyes.

• *How long were you in prison?*

ELLIAS RISHMAWI: Well, I was in prison twice. Nobody told me why. I was just taken after midnight and was sent to the prison for eighteen days without any questions, without any charges.

- *And what were the conditions like there?*

ELLIAS RISHMAWI: Don't ask me. I'm trying to forget. The totally inhuman conditions. I'm really trying to forget that period of my life. . . . And believe me, this is the most difficult situation we are facing. We are trying our best not only to forget but to forgive those who give us all this suffering, for the sake of the future of this land.

- *So are you all celebrating Christmas this year?*

ISSA TAWIL: Yes, we are going to celebrate Christmas in the church—but half of the youth of Beit Sahour are in prison. It is now nine o'clock in the evening; maybe within one hour, or usually at midnight, they come to arrest people. So maybe you will wake up and find one of us arrested.

MILLANY NASSAR: You can imagine how many children have their fathers in prison right now, their brothers as well. . . .

EIMAN RISHMAWI: The soldiers, they come to our street, to our places. . . . Once they caught a ten year old and beat him severely in front of my kids. We have a point of view, that we are suffering to avoid our kids having to suffer again.

ELLIAS RISHMAWI: Palestinians and Israelis here have their dreams about the land of this area. As Palestinians, I think we have dreamt a lot in the past, and now we've stopped dreaming and started to be a realistic nation. Our attitude is based on our knowledge and acquaintance with the Israelis as a nation in the last twenty-two years under occupation.

I don't think realistically that any Palestinian cannot accept the existence of the Israelis as a nation and as a state. This doesn't mean that we have given up the dreams, but I cannot continue living only on dreams. I can only continue to live on realistic attitudes. Unfortunately, at the time we start to be realistic, the other side starts to be dreamers, and this is our tragedy. I hope they won't wait another forty years to stop dreaming.

* * *

The next day, Muna and her friend Saliba led me from house to house in Beit Sahour, visiting each neighbor and hearing their stories. At every home, upon my arrival, the entire family was summoned whether or not they spoke English; I was greeted with warmth, curiosity, openness, and always a pot of Arabic coffee. When they learned I was Jewish, they were often surprised, but their attitude toward me did not change.

Rabeeh Rishmawi and his brother and their families live a few doors from Issa Tawil's home. Their dwelling was clean and pleasant, though small, and it was clear they had little to spare. Still they cooked me a hearty Palestinian dinner.

• *What happened, Rabeeh Rishmawi, when the soldiers came here?*

RABEEH RISHMAWI: They took me to prison at night, and the next day they came to my shop with many, many soldiers and tax men and took everything in the shop—the big Frigidaire and everything. Then they came to the house and took the television, stereo, washing machine, and the sewing machine my wife used to sew trousers and things like that for the children.

• *How many children?*

RABEEH RISHMAWI: We have five children and one on the way. They took everything that is good in the house.

• *And when they came to take it, what did you say? Did you get angry?*

RABEEH RISHMAWI: No. We said, "Take everything and anything you want. We didn't care because we want them to know we won't pay taxes for them. This is one kind of peace struggle, not a struggle with knives or guns, to show them that we want peace, real peace.

• *So you think it's possible then for Palestinians and Israelis to live together in peace?*

RABEEH RISHMAWI: Yes, it is very simple to live with them because there are many kind people among the Jewish people. But the Israeli government is not good. If they want us to live with them, we can live with them. I speak alone, but there are many, many Palestinian people who speak like this.

• *What keeps you going? I mean this is a very hard situation. How do you keep resisting?*

KALDON RISHMAWI (fourteen years old): Because we want to be free. We want our land. That's it. We're one hand. One voice. And we are walking in one street. The street of freedom.

* * *

Relatives of a Palestinian detainee pose in front of his demolished home. Demolition is a common form of Israeli retaliation for Intifada activities. (Jerusalem Press Service)

By now it was late afternoon on Christmas Eve, and as the church bells pealed, all of Beit Sahour poured out of their doorways and into the streets. Women and girls led our march through the hills together, while the sun set over Bethlehem in the distance. We were on our way to Shepherds' Field for a Christmas Eve mass with Bishop Desmond Tutu from South Africa. Amidst Christmas carols, prayers, and greetings, the mass ended with a plea from an Israeli peace activist.

HILLEL BARDINE: . . . You should know that most Israelis are opposed to the occupation and would like to see it ended. They want real peace with the Palestinians. So why don't we Israelis accept the idea of an independent Palestinian state? Many Israelis do not yet believe that you really are willing to live with us in peace. My friends in Israel need to hear from you that you're prepared to live with us in peace. And I ask the thousands of Palestinians that are here: Will you make your voices heard now? Can we live together in peace?

The crowd responded by roaring: "Yes!"*

* In 1989 [the village of] Beit Sahour was nominated for a Nobel Peace Prize.

The Persian Gulf War

❧INTRODUCTION: The unity of the "Arab Nation" was split asunder on August 2, 1990, when Iraqi military forces invaded neighboring Kuwait, breaking the unwritten law that one Arab state should not violate the sovereignty of another. Moreover, the ensuing war divided the Arab states into opposing camps, with Jordan, Libya and the Palestinians supporting Iraq and Egypt, Syria and Saudi Arabia supporting Kuwait.

In addition, when a coalition was formed to oppose Iraq, headed by the United States and supported by England and France, European troops were invited into Saudi Arabia for the first time, bringing charges from Saddam Hussein, President of Iraq, that King Fahd of Saudi Arabia had desecrated the holy places of Islam, Mecca and Medina by allowing the "infidels" to come in. Coincidentally, Saudi Arabia and the other Arab coalition members found themselves on the same side as Israel, which clearly supported the coalition although it did not participate militarily. Iraq's reaction to this turn of events, as broadcast on Baghdad Radio, was unequivocal and symptomatic of the damage done to Arab unity: "The traitor Fahd should know that the Iraqis will not be after him alone, but will track down every member of his family until the last trace of this evil Jewish family sullying the Arab land and holy places is uprooted."

As might be expected, passions about Saddam Hussein ran high and perceptions and stereotypes varied. To the Arab coalition members, Saddam Hussein was a megalomaniac and a threat to the political stability of the Middle East; to other Arabs, he was a modern-day Saladin, the Moslem military hero

A Kuwaiti military helicopter herds Iraqi prisoners across a stream in south-eastern Kuwait during Operation Desert Storm. (AP/Wide World Photos)

who drove Christian forces out of the Middle East during the Crusades. To many Israelis, Saddam Hussein was a reincarnation of Adoph Hitler out to destroy Israel and the Jewish people; and to Western nations, he was a power-hungry dictator whose quest to control the flow of oil from the Middle East would give him a stranglehold on the world's economy.

The following selection consists of two parts. The first is a chronology of events leading up to the war, the war itself and its aftermath; the second is a hypothetical debate between an American and an Iraqi about the legitimacy of the Gulf War.[20]✍

PERSIAN GULF WAR TIME LINE

July 7, 1990 President of Iraq, Saddam Hussein, makes Revolution Day speech, blasting Kuwait and the United Arab Emirates as stooges for America by keeping oil prices low. He accuses Kuwait of stealing oil from border oil fields.

July 24, 1990 Two Iraqi armored divisions mass on Kuwait border, but Arab diplomats say Iraq has assured

July 25, 1990 April C. Glaspie, U.S. Ambassador to Iraq, tells Saddam Hussein the United States will not take sides in his dispute with Kuwait. The Iraqi leader says border tanks are there only to intimidate Kuwait.

July 25, 1990 Iraqi and Kuwaiti negotiators meet for direct talks in Saudi Arabia.

July 27, 1990 OPEC refuses Iraq's demand to raise oil prices to $25 per barrel, but does decide to raise the cartel's reference price to $21 per barrel by the end of the year.

August 1, 1990 Saudi-mediated talks between Iraq and Kuwait collapse.

August 2, 1990 Iraq invades Kuwait claiming that it is acting to support Kuwaiti revolutionaries in a coup against the ruling Sabah government. The Iraqi army with more than 130,000 troops and 350 tanks takes over Kuwait in a matter of hours.

U.N. condemns Iraqi invasion and demands immediate and unconditional withdrawal of all its forces from Kuwait. U.N. adopts Security Council Resolution 660, calling on Iraq and Kuwait to begin negotiations to resolve their differences. American President George Bush freezes Iraqi and Kuwaiti assets and bans all trade and financial relations with Iraq.

August 3, 1990 The League of Arab States asks Arab heads of state to consider convening an emergency summit meeting to discuss "Iraqi aggression." The League strenuously rejects any foreign intervention in Arab affairs. Americans and Soviets issue joint statement in Moscow condemning Iraq. Iraq says it will withdraw its troops from Kuwait in two days.

August 4, 1990 The European Community imposes an oil embargo on Iraq and Kuwait and agrees to stop selling arms and military equipment to Iraq.

August 6, 1990 Mandatory economic sanctions are

imposed on Iraq per U.N. Security Council Resolution 661 in an effort to end Iraq's occupation of Kuwait. The sanctions require all states to cease trade with Iraq. An exception is made for medical supplies and humanitarian aid, such as foodstuffs. States are also called upon to protect the assets of the legitimate government of Kuwait and not to recognize any regime set up by the occupying power.

Iraq claims the sanctions are "unjust" and "precipitous" and have the objective of starving the Iraqi people. Several hundred Westerners, including twenty-eight Americans, are detained in Kuwait and taken to Baghdad.

August 7, 1990 Bush orders U.S. military aircraft and troops to Saudi Arabia to defend it against possible Iraqi attack in an operation code-named Desert Shield.

August 8, 1990 Iraq announces its annexation of Kuwait.

August 9, 1990 U.N. Security Council declares Iraqi annexation of Kuwait null and void per U.N. Security Council Resolution 662. The Security Council also calls on states, international organizations and specialized agencies not to recognize Iraq's annexation of Kuwait.

August 22, 1990 Bush authorizes first call-up of reserves in two decades.

August 25, 1990 U.N. endorses naval blockade of Gulf per U.N. Security Council Resolution 665, and calls for the use of all possible means to tighten sanctions against Iraq. U.S. states that the authority granted in Resolution 665 was sufficiently broad to use "armed force depending on the circumstances which might require it."

September 23, 1990 Saddam Hussein threatens to attack Saudi oil fields and Israel if Iraq is "strangled" by economic sanctions.

At the end of the Persian Gulf War, American fire fighters worked for more than a year to extinguish more than 200 oil well fires set by retreating Iraqis in Kuwait. (AP/Wide World Photos)

September 25, 1990   U.N. votes to impose more economic sanctions on Iraq (Resolution 670), prohibiting any aircraft to carry any cargo to or from Iraq or Kuwait other than food for humanitarian purposes.

November 8, 1990   Bush orders a new wave of U.S. troops to Persian Gulf to create an "adequate offensive military option should that be necessary."

November 29, 1990   U.N. adopts Security Council Resolution 678, giving Iraq forty-eight days to comply with its demand for withdrawal from Kuwait and sets January 15, 1991, as the deadline. Resolution 678 also authorizes the use of force to remove Iraq from Kuwait.

November 30, 1990   Bush invites Iraqi Foreign Minister Aziz to Washington and offers to send Secretary James Baker to Baghdad before January 15th to meet Saddam to discuss possible peaceful solution to the Gulf Crisis.

January 8, 1991 Bush asks Congress to approve a resolution authorizing the use of "all necessary means" to drive Iraq out of Kuwait.

January 9, 1991 Baker meets with Tariq Aziz for six and a half hours in Geneva, but fails to break the diplomatic impasse as Iraq shows no signs of giving in to international demands. Aziz repeats Iraqi demands for a settlement of the broader Middle East conflict.

January 11, 1991 The United States asks Israel to keep a low profile and stay out of the Persian Gulf conflict.

January 12, 1991 After heated debate, Congress grants Bush the authority to wage war against Iraq. The vote in the Senate is 52-47; the House vote is 250-183.

January 12/13, 1991 Secretary General Perez de Cuellar goes to Baghdad on a two-day peace mission. He meets with Saddam Hussein for three and a half hours, urging him to comply with United Nations resolutions. Talks were "polite but unsuccessful."

January 13, 1991 Israel agrees to absorb an Iraqi first strike rather than launch a preemptive attack against Iraq.

January 16, 1991 Allied air campaign against Iraq begins at seven p.m. Eastern Standard Time (January 17th Baghdad time). Massive air strikes with hundreds of planes and at least 100 Tomahawk missiles move against Baghdad and Iraqi positions in Kuwait. One United States F18 fighter jet and one British Tornado are lost.

January 17, 1991 Allied planes, mostly U.S. and British but including French and Saudi Arabian planes as well, continue to fly day and night sorties over Iraq. Using so-called "smart bombs," these aerial attacks concentrate on military targets and such infrastructural items as bridges.

January 18, 1991 Iraq fires first SCUD missiles at Israel, wounding at least seven people. Most missiles suburban areas of Tel Aviv with minimal damage.

January 26, 1991 Iraq dumps several million barrels of oil into the Persian Gulf from ships and storage facilities. The environmental damage is several times greater than the 1989 Exxon Valdez spill in Alaska.

January 30, 1991 United States and coalition forces declare air supremacy over Iraq. Iraqi forces (some 400 to 600 troops and 40 to 45 tanks) thrust across the border into Saudi Arabia. Coalition forces engage Iraqis at Khafji, Saudi Arabia. Twelve U.S. marines are killed; the Iraqis lose 24 tanks and suffer heavy casualties.

February 15, 1991 Iraq informs United Nations of readiness to deal on basis of Security Council Resolution 660, but Iraqi proposal contains "unacceptable conditions," including withdrawal of Israel from Palestine and other occupied Arab territories and payment of war reparations to Iraq.

February 22, 1991 Iraqi forces set more than 150 oil wells ablaze, sending thick black smoke into the skies above Kuwait and parts of Saudi Arabia. Bush gives Iraq until noon (EST) February 23rd to pull out of Kuwait.

February 23, 1991 Coalition forces launch massive ground attacks into Iraq and Kuwait, using more than 700,000 troops, 2,000 planes and 100 warships against an entrenched forty-three-division Iraqi army of 545,000 troops with 2,500 tanks and 1,500 artillery pieces.

February 25, 1991 Allied forces take more than 14,000 Iraqi prisoners.

February 26, 1991 Less than forty-eight hours after U.S.-led allied forces launch ground offensive, Iraqis issue order to their troops to withdraw from Kuwait, claiming "practical compliance" with U.N. Security Council Resolution 660 under the terms of the Soviet peace proposal.

Iraqi SCUD missile hits U.S. billet in Dhahran, Saudi Arabia, killing twenty-seven and wounding ninety-eight. This is the first successful Iraqi attack on a U.S. target in the war and causes the highest number of casualties.

February 27, 1991   Allies liberate Kuwait City. Iraq informs U.N. that it will comply fully with all twelve Council resolutions and that all of its armed forces had withdrawn from Kuwait. Iraq also promises to release all prisoners of war immediately after the cease-fire.

Coalition forces stop counting the number of surrendering prisoners when the total reaches 30,000. Iraqi casualties are estimated between 60,000 and 100,000 killed. U.S. combat losses since the start of the ground war are 99 killed, 44 missing and 213 wounded, including those killed or wounded in the Dhahran barracks.

February 28, 1991   Coalition forces suspend offensive combat operations. Bush declares unilateral cessation of hostilities at eight a.m. Kuwait time (midnight EST).

March 4, 1991   Iraq accepts all cease-fire terms included in U.N. Security Council Resolution 686.

March 6, 1991   Kuwait government resumes functions of state and directing affairs of the nation from Kuwait.

March 13, 1991   Kuwait complains that only 1,200 of the 33,000 prisoners of war have been released and that Iraq stole more that $100 billion of public property from Kuwait.

March 22, 1991   Embargo on civilian and humanitarian imports to Iraq is lifted by U.N. Sanctions Committee.

April 3, 1991   Permanent cease-fire terms adopted by U.N. per Security Council Resolution 687, a nine-part resolution. Key provisions include the destruction or removal of all Iraqi long-range ballistic missiles and chemical, biological and nuclear weaponry along with an almost total ban on future sales of conventional arms to Iraq. Iraq would also be required to mortgage much of its national income from oil sales to pay for the damage done in Kuwait by its seven-month occupation.

April 11, 1991 Iraq formally accepts conditions of U.N. Resolution 687. Formal cease-fire is effective.

January 1, 1993: Saddam Hussein is still in power two years after the Allied liberation of Kuwait, and finally the last of the more than 200 oil well fires set by the retreating Iraqis in Kuwait has been extinguished.

U.N. officials have inspected Iraqi nuclear plants and found evidence that Iraq was developing a nuclear capability. Iraq tried to prevent U.N. investigators from leaving the country with this information, but by the end of 1992 Iraq had complied with most U.N. requests for information and access to facilities. Armaments have been systematically destroyed.

U.N. sanctions on trade with Iraq have been lifted for all but military commodities and oil. U.N. Resolution 661 still prohibits the importation of oil from Iraq. Iraq is exporting a very small amount of oil to Jordan as repayment of debts incurred before the Persian Gulf War. Two U.N. Resolutions (706 and 712) have been introduced to allow controlled export of oil from Iraq not to exceed $1.6 billion. Profits from Iraqi oil exports would be put into a U.N.-controlled escrow account and used to repay war damage claims from all countries involved. Thirty percent is to be earmarked for compensation of damages, and an additional amount will be used to pay for U.N. special commissions, such as the commission to destroy all Iraqi weapons of mass destruction, the U.N. boundary commission and other U.N. administrative costs incurred as a result of the Persian Gulf War. The remaining $933.7 million will be used to buy food, medical supplies and other humanitarian aid for Iraq. Iraq has not accepted these U.N. proposals.

January 6, 1993 Evidence appears that Saddam Hussein is installing missile batteries in the demilitarized zone of southern Iraq in violation of U.N. resolutions.

January 10, 1993 U.N. issues ultimatum to Iraq to dismantle missile sites within forty-eight hours.

January 13, 1993 Almost two years after the beginning of the Gulf War, the U.S. and other coalition members launch an air strike, with an armada of 110 planes, against missile batteries in southern Iraq.

AMERICA VS. IRAQ: A DEBATE

AMERICAN: I thought you Iraqis had learned your lesson! That you can't just go around starting wars, like you did with Iran in 1980-88 and with Kuwait in 1990. But I guess you haven't learned your lesson after all, as you still continue to resist your penalty for the Kuwait war, the sanctions imposed on you by the U.N. for your invasion. It's been ten years now. How much longer will you continue to be so stubborn?

IRAQI: But it was you who caused all this, by not letting us settle our dispute with Kuwait by ourselves!

AMERICAN: But it was you who took the rash action! Your way of settling was to play the bully and invade Kuwait, trying, of all things, to annex it to Iraq!

IRAQI: Well, we had to. Kuwait was being arrogant and stubborn, and took advantage of us during our war with Iran. If it weren't for us, the Ayatollah Khomeini would be ruling the Persian Gulf states right now! Kuwait, the United Arab Emirates, even Saudi Arabia, should be thankful we fought that war with Iran and kept her pinned within her own borders. The Arab world owes us a debt of gratitude for what we did! But instead, what does Kuwait do but try to take advantage of our weakened state after the war. First, they increased their oil production which brought down the price of oil just when we needed the money to pay off our eight year war effort. Then they began to drill from the Rumayla oil fields which are in dispute between our two countries, and simultaneously refused to negotiate the issue. Lastly, after we had spent $106 billion in defense of the Arab world against Iran, to say nothing of the tens of thousands of young men we lost during the war, Kuwait refused to cancel the $10 billion we owed her!

AMERICAN: So your answer was to invade Kuwait! Even after our American ambassador warned you of the consequences!

IRAQI: Excuse me, she did no such thing. She told us that the U.S. "had no opinion on such an Arab-Arab conflict," that the U.S. would not take sides in the Iraqi dispute with Kuwait. We might even say she led us on, that you wanted Saddam to attack Kuwait so you would have an excuse to attack us!

AMERICAN: She also told you very clearly that the U.S. "can never excuse settlement of disputes by other than peaceful means."

IRAQI: So this gives you the right to mobilize half the world against us! What are you, some kind of policeman for the world? Besides, you don't really care about a little place like Kuwait, only its oil!

AMERICAN: Well, of course we were concerned about the oil. But there is an important principle at stake here as well. You, or any other nation, can't take over another country just because you have the means to, because you have a bigger army!

IRAQI: What you don't understand is that Kuwait was once part of Iraq. For 500 years of the Ottoman Empire we were one country. It was only through British colonialism that a new border was drawn and a nation that had never existed before—Kuwait—was created in 1899.

AMERICAN: But Kuwait had been a separate entity for over ninety years when you invaded, and has been an independent country since 1961.

IRAQI: What is 90 years versus 500?

AMERICAN: This historical discussion is pointless! Neither Iraq nor Kuwait was an independent country under the Ottoman Turks. You have always been part of some empire or other, going back to Genghis Khan!

IRAQI: So . . . in the case of Israel, you do want to re-draw boundaries according to what existed in the past, to give the Jews land they have not held for 2,000 years! But you are going to tell me that is another question! As for Iraq, you American imperialists have just taken over for our old colonizers, the British. You wish to keep us weak and unable to defend our own interests! But we are a free nation, like any other. And we insist on our right to act on our national interests, as you did when

These young Iraqi demonstrators, school children in Baghdad, went to the American, British, Saudi and Egyptian embassies to protest against UN Resolutions, complaining they were running out of milk. (AP/Wide World Photos)

you invaded Grenada. Since Kuwait would not be reasonable, we attacked to take what was rightfully ours!

AMERICAN: Well, the rest of the world didn't see it that way. The U.N., the European community, and the U.S. all protested the invasion. The U.N. passed resolutions calling for an immediate withdrawal to be followed by negotiations, and when you refused placed economic sanctions on your country. Your annexation of Kuwait was declared "null and void." But did you listen to the world? No! You uttered additional threats towards Saudi Arabia!

IRAQI: What did you expect us to do? The economic sanctions were intended to strangle us into submission, and they continue to do so even after ten years. They have, in fact, almost destroyed our country, once the most advanced in the Middle East.

AMERICAN: All you had to do to get out of the mess was to abide by the U.N. resolutions. But instead you refused to negotiate in good faith and tried to tie the Kuwait-Iraq dispute to the resolution of the Arab-Israeli conflict!

IRAQI: Which is reasonable. The root of that conflict is the same as our present one: Western imperialism!

AMERICAN: Well, you had every chance to avoid the inevitable response from the coalition which included Arab countries as well: Egypt, Syria and Saudi Arabia. Since you wouldn't negotiate we had to make you give Kuwait back.

IRAQI: So we reacted with all means at our disposal. We fired a missile at Israel, and attacked Saudi Arabia.

AMERICAN: And you dumped millions of barrels of oil into the Persian Gulf and set fire to 150 Kuwait oil wells!

IRAQI: We were frustrated and felt picked on by the whole world! No one would listen to our legitimate complaints against Kuwait!

AMERICAN: And you paid the price. We attacked and within 48 hours you had the sense to begin withdrawing from Kuwait. And you agreed then to all cease-fire terms which included the planned destruction of all of your long-range missiles, and your chemical, biological and nuclear weaponry, as well as the obligation to pay Kuwait for all war-related damage. To do this you pledged most of your oil income.

IRAQI: Which has bled us to the bone.

AMERICAN: Well, you had to initially cooperate to get a cease fire. But soon thereafter, instead of continuing to cooperate, you began to frustrate the arms inspectors, and now have kicked them out of Iraq entirely. And you have dragged your heels on re-paying Kuwait. In fact, you have barely lived up to the cease fire terms at all!

IRAQI: Because your terms were too harsh and infringed on our national sovereignty. We are a small country. How can we protect ourselves, especially from those religious fanatics in Iran and Afghanistan, unless we have missiles, and other more drastic means of protecting ourselves? All countries have a right to weaponry. And the harsh economic sanctions you have enforced on us have caused one-third of our children to be malnourished. You have ruined our water treatment plants and our food and medical distribution systems! Why should we cooperate with someone who is trying to destroy us?

AMERICAN: You know, you could have avoided all of this by getting rid of Saddam; he is the one not cooperating. He is the one calling the shots in Iraq.

IRAQI: This is just what your plan has been. Squeeze us with the sanctions, offer us impossible terms which we have to reject, and then you think our people will rise up and get rid of Saddam. But we don't give in to such schemes. We will keep our weapons, and we will control the Kurds. In fact, we will starve before we let you control us. We will not be humiliated!

AMERICAN: But it is Saddam who is scheming. If he really cared about the Iraqi people he would have accepted the "oil for food" program in 1992 under U.N. resolutions 706 and 712 when it was first offered. But he knew that if he did that, because he had no intention of complying with the other demands—such as getting rid of your weapons of mass destruction—he would never see the end of economic sanctions. So his strategy was to let conditions get so bad for the Iraqi people—while, by the way, his henchmen were living in luxury—that the world would give in and lift all the sanctions. He thought this way he could get rid of the sanctions while still keeping his weapons. But it hasn't worked out that way, has it?

IRAQI: So then why did he accept the "oil for food" program in 1996?

AMERICAN: Because he finally saw he had no choice. Perhaps he was afraid of an uprising, or a coup, if he didn't do something. To me, the important thing is that $15 billion a month is now being spent to help the hungry and sick after years of neglect caused by Saddam's willingness to let his own people suffer for his political stratagems.

IRAQI: No, you have it backward. It is you who are imposing these sanctions on the innocent Iraqi people, and it is you who are responsible for their misery. Saddam is doing what Iraqis want him to do. He is standing up to the Western imperialists, and protecting our national interests and pride!

AMERICAN: Perhaps this is where our strategy has failed. Maybe economic sanctions cannot work in situations where a dictator who cannot be voted out of office is willing to let his most vulnerable citizens suffer as part of a political strategy.

IRAQI: I am glad to agree your strategy has failed. One by one your sanctions are being ignored. In August of 2000, President Chavez of Venezuela broke the taboo against political visits to Iraq by flying directly into Baghdad. Now we have officially re-opened our airport, and there are daily flights to most Middle Eastern countries and Russia. In addition, we now have domestic flights to Basra and Mosul right through your so-called "no-fly" zones. And it won't be long before Russia and France get Britain to join them in calling for the dropping of all sanctions, and then you will be forced to follow. It looks like Saddam has outlasted you all! He has, after all, won the "mother of all battles" as he called it in 1991!

AMERICAN: Well, my friend, this is easy for you to say. But I wouldn't declare victory just yet. Remember, George Bush, the son of the President who organized the coalition against you in 1990, has placed Iraq on the "axis of evil" along with Iran and North Korea, calling Iraq a terrorist state. The future of Saddam is questionable.

After the War:
The Palestinians and the Kurds

⌘INTRODUCTION: The Persian Gulf War left Saddam Hussein in power but greatly reduced Iraq's military capability and put the country under a series of United Nations sanctions. It restored the government of Kuwait, but even after the oil well fires were extinguished, 60 percent of the country's land was saturated with 150 million barrels of oil, giving off highly toxic gases that could cause cancer and birth defects. The destructive effects and the tragic ironies of this war are numerous, as with all wars, but perhaps the saddest outcome of the Persian Gulf War was the displacement once again of two peoples who have suffered repeatedly for centuries at the hands of superior forces: the Palestinians and the Kurds.

Before the war, about 400,000 Palestinians lived and worked in Kuwait. Today there are fewer than 50,000 left. Most have gone to Jordan where the majority of the 3.3 million population are Palestinians. This massive population transfer has been called "the third uprooting" by Palestinians, after the huge exodus from Israel in 1948 and from the occupied territories in 1967. About half of the Palestinians fled in fear of the invading Iraqi army and the other half in fear of Kuwaiti retribution at the end of the war. Most Kuwaitis believed that Palestinians sympathized with Saddam Hussein and even collaborated with his occupying army in Kuwait.

The Kurds, on the other hand, were arch rivals of Saddam Hussein and had struggled for decades for the right to run their own affairs in Iraq. It has been estimated that over a twenty-year period Saddam Hussein killed more than 200,000

323

Kurds and destroyed 4,500 of their 5,000 villages. He used poison gas in 1988 to kill 4,000 to 5,000 civilians in the town of Halabja. On a tape recording captured after the Gulf War, the Iraqi Defense Minister said: "We have been gassing them escaping. We gas them not once, not twice, but until we get rid of them."

There are twenty million Kurds—about seven million more than the combined populations of Israel, Jordan, Kuwait and Lebanon—living in Iran, Iraq and Turkey, where they have been living for more than 4,000 years, always controlled by others. The Kurds are one of the largest minorities in the world without a land to call their own.

Four million Kurds live in northern Iraq, and in March of 1991 at the end of the Persian Gulf War, they were encouraged by the United States to rise up against the still-reigning Saddam Hussein. They did. But without coalition support from

Kurdish refugees flee Iraq for safety in Iran at the end of the Gulf War. Hundreds of thousands of Kurds left Iraq on foot or in any vehicle they could find. (AP/Wide World Photos)

the air, they were no match for the Iraqi army and air force. Driven from their own towns and villages, more than two million Kurds fled to the mountains. There, cut off from supplies and subjected to a harsh winter, they began to freeze and starve to death before a worldwide TV audience. The United Nations, including the U.S., eventually came to their aid with supplies and then established a "free zone" in Northern Iraq.

One might ask why, if there are twenty million Kurds who wish to live in their own country, there has been no international movement to create a Kurdistan for the Kurds in the way Israel was created for the Jews. The answer is that no one wants a Kurdistan except for the Kurds themselves. Turkey, Iraq and Iran, the countries with major Kurdish populations, are against creating a Kurdistan because it would take territory and people from their own countries, thus diminishing their power and influence in the region. And the major powers are against the creation of a Kurdistan because doing so would destabilize the entire area, possibly leading to land grabs and warfare between the states with Kurdish populations. Indeed, the intention of the U.N. coalition that forced Iran out of Kuwait was to create stability in the region by enforcing adherence to established borders. A major reason Iraq was not invaded at the end of the Gulf War with the purpose of toppling Saddam Hussein was the fear that a weak Iraq would "implode" and Turkey and Iran would be tempted to carve up Iraq with the northern Kurdish part of Iraq going to Turkey and the southern part of Iraq going to Iran. For the purposes of stability in the Middle East, it was determined that a de-fanged Saddam Hussein and a partially weakened Iraq would bring about a balance of power in

the region that would decrease the possibility of war and provide the stability necessary for the steady export of oil from
that important oil-producing region of the world. As the Kurds
have no wealth or natural resources at their disposal, nor any
power or important friends in the world of power politics, they
unfortunately don't count for much.

The following selection, "Common Thread," was written by
a Palestinian professor, who argues that the anguish and the
shared experience of homelessness bind the Kurds and the
Palestinians together.[21]✤

COMMON THREAD

The time: 1948. The place: Tantura, a tiny Palestinian
village on the shore of the Mediterranean, somewhere
between Haifa and Jaffa. The nightmare-memory: I, a
small boy of three, clinging with terror to the tails of my
grandmother's peasant robes, staring into the barrel of
a gun. The agitated soldiers shout their orders: "Sit down.
Hands on heads. Silence." The crowd cowers: old, middle-aged and young, women and children, bewildered,
distraught, hysterical. Silence is enforced by a torrent of
abuse: "Idiots, don't you understand Arabic? We said do
not move."

A woman whispers: "What happened to the men?"
Another: "They rounded them up and took them away."
The first: "Will they kill them?"
The second: "Shut up, do not say things like that, men-
tioning evil brings forth evil." Deadly silence.

A woman: "Will they dump us behind the lines?"
Another: "Who knows?"
A third: "I heard the Jews of Kibbutz Zommarine have
put in a good word for us." Deadly silence again.

A woman: "My man used to tell me resistance was
futile."
Another: "Shut up. This is no time for that."

Vehicles arrive in a storm of sand. The soldiers shout:
"Come on. Move. Get on board."

An old woman pleads: "Please Mister, don't split the
families."

A soldier: "No matter. You are all going to the same place."

The herding becomes more energetic: pushing, shoving and occasional furious use of rifle butts. Some women start crying loudly; the cries become louder and louder until the whole crowd joins in wailing frantically: "We are lost. We are doomed." A few shots in the air fail to restore calm.

The vehicles start moving. I am held tight by my grandmother and look around for my aunts. They are in the same vehicle, Amena, Buthaina and Regina. Years after, I used to say to my grandfather: "Regina! What a funny name for a Palestinian peasant woman." He would gaze into the distance and say dreamily: "Those were the days when you could call your children any name you fancied: Moslem, Christian, Jewish. We wanted to call your other aunt Rachel, but the troubles broke out before she was born and we called her Amena instead." My grandmother would then say: "Old man, why do you keep making up these stories? I never wanted to call her Rachel. I never liked the Jews." He would retort: "But you always preferred to see the Jewish doctor, Rappaport." And she would laugh a short, almost coquettish laugh and say: "Yes, but damn him, he was very good." I close my eyes and bury my head in my grandmother's bosom. The exodus begins.

"Do you really remember all this?" I ask myself. Maybe, maybe not. Maybe I wove it together from the yarns told and retold during long winter nights while we huddled for warmth around the embers burning in an open metal stove, reminiscing about the lost paradise of Palestine, the sad land of oranges. Anyway, what does it matter? The collective memory of my people is made up of many such harrowing nightmares.

Familiar Faces

Another time: 1991. Another place: somewhere in Kurdistan. The nightmare this time traverses a television screen. Thousands upon thousands of hapless Kurds, men, women and children, some bare-foot, some in slip-

pers, clinging to a snow-covered mountain, driven by a
fear which few have known, encountering slow death
while fleeing for their lives. The camera draws nearer.
A man faces it holding his dead infant and cries out
with a broken voice: "Why? Why? Why has the world
abandoned us?"

I choke with pain. The faces are familiar. This man
could easily have been my grandfather, that woman, my
grandmother, the other my aunt. The tormented children's faces are so like those thronging the narrow
alleyways of our refugee camps in Gaza and elsewhere.
And the familiarity does not stop there. The anguish
(why has the world abandoned us?) is one that we Palestinians have been living with for more than four decades.
We have a special relationship with it: we nurse it, feed
it our dreams, give it the best years of our lives and
cherish it to our deathbeds. And if the world were suddenly to take notice of our suffering, we would, I fear,
remain tenaciously devoted to it and ask: "Why has it
taken the world so long?"

Do the Kurds have the same special relationship with
anguish? It would be surprising if they did not. One people (Israel) denies our existence and asks: what
Palestinians? Four peoples (Arab, Iranian, Turks and Syrians) deny theirs and ask: what Kurds?

I am suddenly filled with shame. Comparisons are odi-
ous. What am I doing, using the suffering of the Kurds
to recall my own and my people's? If comparisons are
to be made, I will say that the immediate suffering caused
by the exodus I experienced in 1948 pales in compar-
ison with that inflicted on the Kurds. Measuring human
suffering on a scale is at best indecent.

But why not? Kurdistan-Palestine comparisons may at
least bring home the point that, if we are not careful,
43 years after the Kurdish exodus, the problem of Kurdish refugees will remain, as does that of the
Palestinians.

Shame refuses obstinately to leave me—shame at
belonging to the oppressors, the Arabs. How can a peo-

ple that suffered so much turn into such brutal oppressors? This question, usually asked in relation to the Arab-Israeli conflict, can be equally (justifiably or unjustifiably) asked in relation to the Arab-Kurdish conflict. In both cases I answer that brutality and indecency are not the monopoly of any one people.

A Kurdish refugee carries his daughter through the streets of the Turkish village near one of the refugee camps on the Iraqi border in search of medical aid. (AP/Wide World Photos)

Power Silence

But I note with a heavy heart that very few Arab intellectuals have defended the rights of the Kurds. So I will
write it: "Establishing democratic traditions cannot be confined to calling for democratic forms of government, but
must also extend to acknowledging the existence of non-
Arab peoples in the midst of the Arabs and upholding
their right to self-determination up to and including seces-
sion." This is sorely needed, particularly in relation to
the long-suffering Kurds.

The Arabs of Iraq have entered, perhaps despite the
best wishes of their majority, into a power relation with
the Kurds in which they have been brutal oppressors.
Hence it is the moral duty of all Arab democrats unre-
servedly to defend the rights of the Kurds, including their
right to have a homeland of their own, if they so wish.
The Kurds may decide that it is in their best interests to
be content with autonomy inside a democratic Iraq. But
this is for them to determine, not for Arabs, no matter
how well intentioned. This perhaps is the only basis for
restoring solidarity between the two peoples.

I get a plethora of objections from my Arab friends:
"Why apply standards to us that no other people applies
to itself?" I reply: "Why not? Why shouldn't the Arabs be
a just people even if other peoples are not?" Besides,
most Arabs including these friends justifiably feel morally
outraged when apologists for the Israeli occupation use
similar arguments.

The pain of homelessness that Palestinians suffer daily
should make Arab intellectuals immune to the temptation of denying other people a homeland. But
unfortunately it does not.

Will the world go on considering the Kurds and Palestinians dispensable? Will it continue to regard them as
mere pawns in some global strategic game? Who knows?
What is certain is that, for any one related to the Middle East, the only tenable position to take is to be a
Palestinian Kurd or a Kurdish Palestinian; any other is
woefully inconsistent and unjust.

After the War:
A Chance for Peace

&**INTRODUCTION**: A positive development to come out of the Persian Gulf War was the convening of an international Mideast peace conference to attempt to resolve the decades-long Arab-Israeli dispute over land and security.

Sponsored jointly by the United States and the Soviet Union, the conference was opened by President George Bush and President Mikhail Gorbachev in October 1991 in Madrid, Spain. Subsequently, most sessions convened in Washington D.C. While this conference ultimately stalled, in large part because the Palestinians were not allowed to negotiate for themselves but only through the Jordanian delegation, its ineffectiveness motivated both the Israelis and the Palestinians to try something new: direct, secret talks between the Palestine Liberation Organization (PLO) and representatives of the Israeli government in Oslo, Norway.

The result of these secret talks was the Oslo Accords, the first of which was signed in 1993, whereby Israel recognized the PLO as the sole negotiating body for the Palestinian people, and the PLO formally recognized Israel's right to exist.

Part I of the following selection, "Roots of the Dispute," gives an overview of the history of Palestine as it relates to the Arab-Israeli conflict. Part II presents the major United Nations resolutions affecting all present peace negotiations between the Israelis and Arabs, namely, Resolutions 242 and 338.

Resolution 242 provides the basis for a "land for peace" exchange, that is, in exchange for Israel's withdrawing from territories conquered by war, the Arab states will terminate all claims to additional territory and will acknowledge the sovereignty and political independence of every State in the area. The Oslo Accords were based on this "land for peace" principle.

Resolution 242 also calls for "a just settlement of the refugee problem," a major stumbling block in the Camp David II talks in July 2000, and in later talks at Taba, Egypt in December 2000 and January 2001.[22]❧

ROOTS OF THE DISPUTE

Some of the roots of today's complex Israeli-Palestinian dispute date from biblical times when Rome scattered the Jews of ancient Israel. The land that came to be known as Palestine became inhabited largely by Arabs, although it passed through many hands before becoming part of Turkey's Ottoman Empire.

In 1920, after World War I broke Turkey's grip on Arab lands, Britain assumed a League of Nations mandate over Palestine. The British divided the mandate into two parts, making the territory east of the Jordan River the separate state of Transjordan.

This is the basis of the argument made by some Israelis that Jordan is a Palestinian state created by Britain's partition of the mandate and populated largely by Palestinians who now comprise more than 60 percent of Jordan's 3 million people. According to this argument, those who want a Palestinian state should look to Jordan rather than to the West Bank to realize their aspirations.

From 1920 to World War II, Palestine was a sporadic battleground between the dominant Arab population and a rising tide of Jewish settlers. Then, the Nazi Holocaust gave the Zionist demand for a Jewish homeland an irreversible impetus and led to the 1948 birth of Israel despite the efforts of five Arab states to halt it by taking up arms and invading.

When the fighting ended, Israel held most of what had been Palestine. But Egypt occupied the Gaza Strip, and Jordan was in possession of Arab East Jerusalem and the sizable West Bank. There followed a large-scale new diaspora of Palestinian Arabs, who fled to the West Bank and to other Arab countries.

When Israel took over the West Bank in the 1967 war, its Palestinian population was counted at roughly 1.1 million. Today, the Palestinian population is generally reckoned at between 1.7 million and 1.9 million—a demographic fact that accounts for the tendency of diplomats and the media to refer to the West Bank as Israeli-occupied Arab territory.

Such statements are vehemently disputed by Israel and its supporters who point out that, despite the demographics, the West Bank has been ruled successively by Turkey, Britain, Jordan and, since 1967, Israel, but never by Palestinians. Therefore, this argument goes, there is no clear-cut Palestinian legal claim to sovereignty over the West Bank.

UNITED NATIONS RESOLUTIONS

[Following the Six-Day War of 1967, the Security Council of the United Nations unanimously adopted Resolution 242, and following the Arab-Israeli war of 1973, the Security Council adopted Resolution 338 by a vote of 14-0.]

Resolution 242

The Security Council,

Expressing its continuing concern with the grave situation in the Middle East,

Emphasizing the inadmissibility of the acquisition of territory by war and the need to work for a just and lasting peace in which every State in the area can live in security,

Emphasizing further that all Member States in their acceptance of the Charter of the United Nations have undertaken a commitment to act in accordance with Article 2 of the Charter,

1. *Affirms* that the fulfillment of Charter principles requires the establishment of a just and lasting peace in the Middle East which should include the application of both the following principles:
(i) Withdrawal of Israeli armed forces from territories occupied in the recent conflict;

(ii) Termination of all claims or states of belligerency and respect for and acknowledgement of the sovereignty, territorial integrity and political independence of every State in the area and their right to live in peace within secure and recognized boundaries free from threats or acts of force;

2. *Affirms further* the necessity

(a) For guaranteeing freedom of navigation through international waterways in the area;

(b) For achieving a just settlement of the refugee problem;

(c) For guaranteeing the territorial inviolability and apolitical independence of every State in the area, through measures including the establishment of demilitarized zones;

3. *Requests* the Secretary-General to designate a Special Representative to proceed to the Middle East to establish and maintain contacts with the States concerned in order to promote agreement and assist efforts to achieve a peaceful and accepted settlement in accordance with the provisions and principles in this resolution;

4. *Requests* the Secretary-General to report to the Security Council on the progress of the efforts of the Special Representative as soon as possible.

Resolution 338

The Security Council,

1. *Calls upon* all parties to the present fighting to cease all firing and terminate all military activity immediately, no later than 12 hours after the moment of the adoption of this decision, in the positions they now occupy;

2. *Calls upon* the parties concerned to start immediately after the cease-fire the implementation of Security Council resolution 242 (1967) in all of its parts;

3. *Decides* that, immediately and concurrently with the cease-fire, negotiations shall start between the parties concerned under appropriate auspices aimed at establishing a just and durable peace in the Middle East.

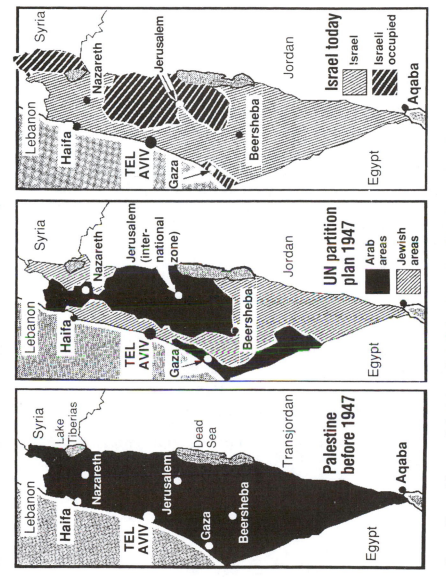

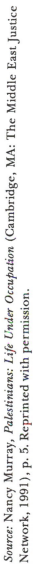

Source: Nancy Murray, *Palestinians: Life Under Occupation* (Cambridge, MA: The Middle East Justice Network, 1991), p. 5. Reprinted with permission.

What Now? After the Camp David II Talks Fail

&INTRODUCTION: Throughout the negotiations between the Palestinians and Israelis, one can see that an ultimate peace agreement is dependent not only on the ability of the negotiators to overcome their mutual distrust and antagonism, but for the Israeli and Palestinian people to experience the benefits of the peace process.

The Israelis need to experience security from violence, and the Palestinians need to experience the relinquishment of Israeli control over their daily lives. But the actions of extremists on both sides have managed to frustrate the peoples' desires. Each Palestinian bomb increases the doubt of the Israeli people that Arafat can be trusted and that the Oslo peace process will truly bring security. And with each Israeli crackdown, the Palestinian people find that the peace process has not brought them the freedom they crave, or with frequent border closures, the economic benefits that peace with Israel is supposed to bring. Thus, a vicious circle has been established. Palestinian frustration, anger and poverty lead to terrorist acts that lead to brutal Israeli crackdowns that lead to increased Palestinian frustration and poverty.

It seems clear in retrospect that President Clinton and Prime Minister Barak miscalculated when they pressured Chairman Arafat into coming to the Camp David II talks in July 2000 before he had had a chance to clear his negotiating position on Jerusalem with the Arab and Muslim world, as well as his own people. The result was no agreement, and anger and disappointment on both sides. As one journalist put it: "When one side believes it is risking its political neck with its generous offer, and the other side thinks it is being strong-armed into concessions its people viscerally reject, you get a stand-off." It is thus not too surprising that such post-Camp David II feelings would lead to some acting out.

But most observers were shocked at the degree of violence and the intensity of the hatred shown after the breakdown of the talks. As one Israeli exclaimed: "What's going on here? It was only two weeks ago that we were buying furniture in Ramallah, gambling in Jericho, importing vegetables from the West Bank and reading about Palestinian plans to build six new duty-free malls. How does all that sit with the outburst of horrible hatred. . . . Where did we make the wrong assumption?"

Perhaps the journalist Deborah Sontag answers this question best when she writes: "For many Palestinians the interim period went on too long and did not change their lives enough. They were still hemmed into refugee camps, and impoverished. They still faced Israeli checkpoints, and (Jewish) settlers still encroached on what they considered their land; nothing essential to them like the return of relatives, the refugees, or the future of Jerusalem had been resolved."

Each side's hatred can be reduced to symbols: the television images of an unarmed, twelve-year-old Palestinian boy and his father being shot dead while huddled against a concrete wall, and a dead Israeli soldier being dumped out of a second story window of a Palestinian police station while his murderer shows his bloody hands. The cries of "Death to Jews" is matched by cries of "Death to Arabs." A Jewish shrine is dismantled; an Arab Mosque is destroyed. As one journalist put it: "What each side sees is the other's core ugliness: the hate-filled Palestinian mob in Israeli eyes, versus the arrogant Israeli military machine in Palestinian eyes."

While general Ariel Sharon's provocative visit to the Temple Mount lit the first fire of the renewed Intifada, known as the Al-Aqsa Intifada, it is also clear that Arafat encouraged his people's rioting. In doing so he undoubtedly had multiple motives including: (a) a safety valve for pent-up Palestinian frustration so that it wouldn't be directed at him; (b) a means of preventing a Hamas

takeover by showing that he too could stand tough; (c) an attempt
to remind Israel of the costs of occupation; (d) an attempt to
advertise the plight of the Palestinian people in the world press;
and (e) an attempt to create circumstances where other media-
tors, more friendly to the Arab cause than the United States, would
be brought into the peace process.

So far the Al-Aqsa Intifada, be it spontaneous or orchestrated,
has only hardened the Israeli position. The result was the election of Ariel Sharon in 2001. The failure of Sharon's hard-line
response to the Al-Aqsa Intifada to bring about a cessation of violence, has brought about great despair and desperation in Israel.
And Sharon's willingness to use Israel's superior military in
response to the Al-Aqsa Intifada has caused great despair and desperation amongst the Palestinians. . . .

But in the long run it is hard to imagine that there is anywhere for the Israelis and Palestinians to go but back to the
peace table. Indeed, some political analysts feel that the Camp
David II talks were a success. In this view it was inevitable that
such difficult issues as the "right of return" of Palestinian
refugees and the status of Jerusalem would not be solved on
the first attempt. The fact that Stage 3 (the last stage) of the
Oslo Accords had been reached, and that all the taboo subjects were openly discussed at the highest levels, was a major
and necessary step towards a "final settlement." But it may be
several years before the two sides feel their way back to serious peace negotiations.

The selection that follows continues the hypothetical debate
started in "The Arab-Israeli Conflict," between David, an
Israeli, and his namesake Daud, a Palestinian.[23]❧

DAVID: Well, you've really done it this time. Barak gave
you the deal of the century, and you turned it down!

DAUD: I agree it was a good offer on most points, but
not on the one that counted most. Barak offered us 95%
of the West Bank, which is fair. But Barak's offer on
Jerusalem was totally inadequate!

DAVID: How can you say that?! For 2,000 years Jews
have ended their Seder each Passover by saying "Next

President Clinton meets with Israeli Prime Minister Ehud Barak, left, and Palestinian leader Yasser Arafat, in July 2000 at Camp David, MD. The Middle East peace talks collapsed in a deadlock over the future of Jerusalem. (AP Photo/Ralph Alswang, White House)

year in Jerusalem," and it has been long-standing Israeli policy that Jerusalem will never be divided again.

DAUD: I find it laughable that Barak is considered flexible while demanding all of Jerusalem, while Arafat is considered inflexible for wanting only half—East Jerusalem—which has always been an Arab city. U.N. resolution 242 states that Israeli armed forces should be withdrawn from territories conquered during the 1967 war. This includes East Jerusalem. You have only controlled it since 1967.

DAVID: Wait a minute. We offered you control over your holy sites in East Jerusalem.

DAUD: Well, thanks for nothing. We already have that to a large degree. We will never accept anything less than full sovereignty over all of East Jerusalem. You will have your capitol in one half, and we'll have ours in the other. Fair is fair.

DAVID: At Camp David II Barak was making offers far beyond what any other Israeli leader had ever offered. He was risking his political future by offering as much as he did. But Arafat wouldn't compromise on Jerusalem to get a deal.

DAUD: Arafat has said—and all Arabs, no indeed all Muslims, agree with him—that Jerusalem is not his to give away, even if he wanted to. In the case of Jerusalem he is negotiating on behalf of a billion Muslims and 2 million Arabs!

DAVID: But no Israeli leader will ever divide Jerusalem.

DAUD: Well, they will have to if they want a peace settlement. After Camp David II President Mubarak of Egypt confirmed to President Clinton that no Arab leader could support Israeli soverignty over East Jerusalem and the Muslim holy sites there. And if Arafat ever agreed to such a thing, he would immediately be assassinated.

DAVID: Just like you Palestinians! When in conflict, resort to violence. Like this second Intifada you started after the breakdown of the Camp David II talks.

DAUD: We started?? Everything was calm after the failure of the Camp David II talks until we were provoked by that murdering general of yours, Ariel Sharon. He is the one who led the Israeli invasion of Lebanon in 1982 and orchestrated, through his alliance with Christian paramilitary groups, the slaughter of 800 Palestinian refugees in their camps. Well, on September 28, 2000 this murderer, hated by all Palestinians, marched to the Western Wall, which is part of our third holiest site in Islam, with over a thousand security personnel! It was like an invasion of the Temple Mount! If this isn't provocation, I don't know what is! Naturally, we demonstrated against this invasion, and within three days you had killed 12 of our demonstrators and wounded over 100! So now another Intifada has started which we will continue until we have our freedom and sovereignty over all of East Jerusalem!

DAVID: Look, Sharon, like any other Jew, has the right to visit the Western Wall which is sacred to us because it is part of our Second Temple. You may remember that when you Arabs controlled East Jerusalem from 1948-1967, we Jews were not allowed to visit the Western Wall. So much for your religious tolerance. And it is for this reason that we can never let Jerusalem be divided again!

DAUD: That we did that was bad. I admit it. But now you and normal Jews can visit the wall any time you like. But when a known murderer, such as Sharon, marches in with a small army—into the courtyard of the Dome of the Rock where Mohammed ascended to heaven—well, he knew there would be protests! He just wanted to be the tough guy.

DAVID: Well, Sharon is like that. He gets in people's faces. But he did it for political reasons; he wanted to become Prime Minister, and it worked! He was elected.

DAUD: So we throw some rocks in protest, and you just gun us down!

DAVID: No Israeli leader can allow mob violence, particularly if it threatens our citizens around our holy sites. And we used great restraint and only used rubber bullets.

DAUD: Oh! Is that why after a couple months of the Intifada there were close to 300 dead Palestinians and fewer than 30 dead Israelis! Is a Palestinian death worth only one-tenth of an Israeli death? And we have suffered over 3,000 injuries as well!

DAVID: Arafat is in charge of controlling his people. If he won't do it, we will.

DAUD: What do you think? That Arafat controls all Palestinians like puppets! Well, he does not! The people are angry. They are sick of Israeli rule, and sick of Israeli foot-dragging on the peace process! And when they are angry, they will riot. No one can stop them from that! And Arafat does not control Hamas, Islamic Jihad or Hezbollah. All he controls is the Palestinian Authority.

DAVID: What kind of leader is Arafat, anyway? If he can't stop the violence, he's no one we should be negotiating with, and if he can, but won't, then we can't trust him! Either way he is a disaster. I myself believe he is behind it all, and is in league with your religious leaders who provoke the people with fiery sermons in the mosques.

DAUD: No, you have it backward. You provoke us through your occupation! We are trying, through the Intifada, to "shake off" the occupation by throwing rocks and burning tires. And in return you shoot us with real bullets, and rocket us from helicopter gunships. And rubber bullets can kill as well!

DAVID: And you shoot innocent mothers with sniper fire, and send suicide bombers to blow up buses full of civilians! You Arabs only understand force, so we are giving you a lesson in it!

DAUD: No. It is you Israelis who only understand force. You have occupied our land through force, and you maintain it by force. So we fight back with what we have. And through guerilla action we got you to leave South Lebanon in the Spring of 2000. And now, through our Al-Aqsa Intifada, we will force you (since you understand nothing about what you have done to us) to finally give us our freedom.

DAVID: You better be careful. Barak is no longer Prime Minister of Israel. Sharon is. And he has a plan. If you don't stop the violence he has planned a series of escalated actions. First, he will bomb your security bases. If that doesn't work he will begin assassinating your terrorist leaders. If that doesn't work, he will attack the Palestinian Authority and remove Arafat. And if that doesn't work, he will either re-occupy Gaza and the West Bank, or he will seal off all Palestinian areas from all Israeli areas. Thus, he is ready with a response for whatever you do.

DAUD: Go ahead! Try to seal us off! You then will find 1 million fifth column Palestinians in Israel itself carrying on the Intifada! And don't forget the rest of the Arab world. You want another Arab-Israeli war? Isn't three enough?

DAVID: You know, things wouldn't have gotten to this point if Arafat had just come to Camp David II ready to compromise.

DAUD: Look, Arafat told Clinton well before Camp David II that he wasn't ready. He knew that Jerusalem would be a major stumbling block, and, as he told Clinton then, he needed a few more weeks to negotiate with his own people and with the entire Muslim world, what minor compromises he might make on Jerusalem. But Clinton and Barak pushed him into coming before he was ready, Clinton because he hoped for a peace agreement while he was still President, and Barak because he needed some successes to fend off Netanyahu and Sharon so he could be re-elected.

DAVID: In that case, it was stupid of Arafat to come to the talks. As Barak has said: "It takes two to tango."

DAUD: I suppose Arafat thought he might get an offer he could accept. But when he didn't get it, he had to say no. Now, because Clinton and Barak jointly blamed Arafat for the failure of the talks, we see whose side the Americans are really on. Clinton, at least, should have understood that Arafat could not give up Jerusalem on his own, and the Americans had the gall to come up with the idea that if you Israelis gave up your claim to the Temple Mount, we should give up our "right of return"! There are 1.2 million Palestinians living now in refugee camps, many still holding keys to the houses they were evicted from in 1947! Arafat cannot sell out those people who have waited so long! So now we Palestinians see that the Americans can never be the neutral, even-handed brokers they claim to be. When push comes to shove, they will always side with the Israelis. Had they listened to Arafat in the first place, the Camp David II talks would have been postponed until he was ready.

DAVID: All this is ancient history now. Barak is gone. Clinton is gone. Sharon is in power, along with President Bush. What you Palestinians need to do now if you want peace is to stop the violence. The Mitchell plan, worked out in the Spring of 2001, calls for a cease fire, a cooling-off period of several weeks, and then a resumption of the peace talks.

DAUD: What a laugh! You know Sharon himself is quoted as saying: "You know my position about peace. It cannot be achieved. The best Israel can hope for is 'non-belligerency, an armed truce.'" You complain about Arafat. But Sharon is the real obstacle!

DAVID: Ha! We know that Arafat is not serious about controlling the violence. His right hand man has been quoted as saying: "This Intifada is strategic. Not for one month, two months. I think it will continue for one year, two years, more than people expect."

DAUD: This is how we show General Sharon that he can't stop the Intifada in 100 days as he pledged during the campaign. He can't do it by force, only by negotiation. He's used fighter jets on our police stations, and invaded a section of Gaza, but the Intifada goes on!

DAVID: You blow up 18 Israeli teen-agers at a disco and expect us to do nothing? Had Arafat, after that atrocity, not agreed to a ceasefire, there would have been an all-out war, and you would lose!

DAUD: We know you have a large-scale military invasion in your plans. But do you think the Arab world would sit still and do nothing? You want another Arab-Israeli war, you'll get it! And if you think Arafat is bad, just get rid of him and you'll get much more hard-line leaders, our version of Sharon!

DAVID: Well, let's stop talking about all-out war and stick to the present. Perhaps the violence we are experiencing now is a necessary step towards peace. You know, a wise professor at Hebrew University pointed out that 'when people shoot and throw stones, that is also part of the process of coming to an agreement. Since there is no military solution, one does not come to the peace process because one has faith in humanity, but because there is no alternative.' He is right, there is no alternative but to work this out. How long this will take, only Yahweh knows.

DAUD: The mayor of Nazareth has said something similar. He said 'the two nations are going to continue living together. The question is how. There will be coexistence. The questions is, what kind of coexistence?' As to how long it will be before there is peace, only Allah can say.

Zionism Comes Full Circle

&INTRODUCTION: As we have seen earlier in "The Life of Joseph Baratz," Zionism is a movement within Judaism that advocates the "return" of the Jewish people to the holy land of Palestine.

During the 1880s and 1890s pogroms against Jews in Europe, especially in Poland and Russia, contributed to the emergence of the Zionist movement, thus, Jews reasoned, if they had their own state they would no longer be a minority population easily discriminated against. Zionists imagined a state that would not only be a refuge for the world's Jewish population but would also allow Jews to "reconstruct" themselves and create a society and culture built upon Jewish values. Thus, the original impulse for the Zionist movement was an "exclusive" one. Jews needed to be safe in their own land, and needed to do all the work in their new country themselves, not hire others—such as Arabs—to do the menial tasks for them.

But as time went on Israel found itself becoming less exclusive and more inclusive. At present, for example, approximately one-fifth of Israel's population is Arab. And it has been estimated that one in three Israelis does not get an education based on Zionist principles. Furthermore, as a result of the signing of the Oslo Accords in 1993, Israel has begun to take the first steps, both politically and economically, towards integration into the non-Jewish Middle East region. These steps towards a more inclusive form of Zionism have been called by some Israelis the "post-Zionist period."

However, as of this writing in September 2001, with the Al-Aqsa Intifada raging out of control, it is difficult to see the path

346

by which Israel can continue its slow integration into the Middle East region. As the violence escalates, more and more Israelis are calling for the sealing off of the Jewish state from Gaza and the parts of the West Bank under the control of the Palestinian Authority. In this view the Oslo Accords, which led to an official Palestinian presence in Gaza and the West Bank, as well as increased economic ties between Israelis and Palestinians, was a grave mistake.

The most extreme version of this view is that Israelis can only trust other Jews, and that the only way to achieve the security all Israelis desire is through a return to the Zionist ideal whereby Jews rely only on themselves in their own homogeneous state. Historically, this view has always been challenged by the secular Israeli left who has argued that there can never be peace in isolation, that security and safety for Jews can only be achieved through genuine peace negotiations and treaties with their Arab neighbors. But now with the Israeli right in power and the violence escalating, a growing number of Israelis are concluding that only through separation from the Arabs can there be peace.

In the selection that follows, Tom Segev, a columnist for the Israeli newspaper *Haaretz*, discusses how the Israeli conception of Zionism, be it inclusive or exclusive, influences not only Israeli society itself but the attitude toward peace negotiations with the Arab world around them. As Segev suggests, if the concept of Zionism is allowed to evolve into a more secular and inclusive view, then peace negotiations along the lines of the Oslo Accords can succeed and will lead to some kind of co-existence and mutual dependence between Israelis and their Arab neighbors. But if "history (is) turned backward" and a more exclusive form of Zionism prevails, then the Oslo Accords will be discarded and Israel will continue to live as a "fortress state." It may well be that peace or endless war depends on the form of Zionism Israel ultimately embraces. [24]❧

Until last September, when the present wave of violence began, Israelis invested the better part of their political and cultural energy in internal matters. The conflict with the Palestinians seemed to be coming under control—there was hope still that peace negotiation was

Israeli Prime Minister Ariel Sharon, speaking here in 2001, is sitting in front of a picture of Theodor Herzl, a founding father of Zionism. (AP Photo/ Robbi Kastro)

progressing, albeit slowly—and many Israelis seemed willing to re-examine fundamental issues of identity, including even the validity of the Zionist ideology itself. Indeed, Israeli society seemed to be going through a transformation, steadily moving toward a so-called post-Zionist, post-national stage of development. That movement now seems to be held off in the face of terrorist violence.

The post-Zionist attitude was made possible by a growing awareness of security and of continuity in this country. It took a hundred years for the Zionist movement to lead only a part of the Jewish people to independence in a part of Palestine. Yet Israel represents one of the most dramatic success stories of the 20th century.

Having developed a national capacity to defend itself, Israel has attained a standard and quality of life that place it alongside several European countries. Most Israelis are becoming better off each year, and despite the widening gap between rich and poor, most Israelis can assume that their children will have better lives than they have had, just as their own lives have been better than those of their parents. There are third- and fourth-generation Israelis; they speak Hebrew with their parents, go to the same schools their parents went to. They have a common way of life, a common sense of humor, common expectations. They don't regard their country as a Zionist miracle anymore.

Within 15 years or so Israel is expected to become the home of the largest Jewish community in the world, meaning that the most significant component of the Zionist dream will be achieved. In the last decade about a million Jews from the former Soviet Union have settled in Israel. Most of them came for economic reasons, not in response to Zionist ideals, and their presence gives force to the post-Zionist trend.

Israel is also becoming more multicultural. Hundreds of thousands of foreign workers, many of them from Africa, are likely to stay permanently and are adding new flavors to Israeli society. The number of ultra-Orthodox Jews, many of whom do not consider themselves political Zionists, is growing, and so is the number of Arabs who live in Israel. According to one estimate, at least one of every three Israeli children today does not get an education based on the Zionist ideology.

It is against this background that Israelis born after the 1967 Six Day War live, particularly in Tel Aviv. They do not live for nationalist ideals or the abstract ideology of Zionism. They live for life itself, as individuals, advocating a somewhat fuzzy blend of Jewish and multicultural values, all in what they believe to be the spirit of America.

Obviously not all Israelis, perhaps not even most, embrace these new trends. And yet more than anything else it was this new post-Zionist attitude that led most Israelis

to support the 1993 Oslo Accords, including the withdrawal from the Palestinian towns occupied in 1967.

Oslo belongs in a slow and often quite painful process
of coming to terms with social and political reality over
the past three decades. Not many years ago Israel refused
to recognize the Palestinian Liberation Organization and
Israeli law forbade even private contacts with the organization. Israel said it would never give up any of the
occupied territories unless in the framework of a final
peace agreement; then it did. Israel once strongly
opposed Palestinian independence; by the 1990s, most
Israelis did not. Like the British, they simply got fed up
with their role as unwanted rulers over territories that
seem not worth the cost and effort of keeping. Ehud
Barak broke an almost sacred taboo when he in effect
offered to share control of Jerusalem with the Palestinians. More Israelis than might be expected supported
these changes.

The recent bombing in Jerusalem, which killed 16 people and wounded more than 100 others, is just one of
the recent catastrophes that may turn post-Zionism into
an illusion. Palestinian terrorism seems to push Israelis
back into the Zionist womb; this may be the Palestinians'
idea of revenge. As the bombs continue to explode in
towns all over Israel, many walls in downtown Jerusalem
have been covered lately with black graffiti slogans saying: "No Arabs—No Terror." Once again it is acceptable
to hate the Palestinians openly.

Many Israelis have fallen back into a siege mentality,
calling for more national unity, in the spirit of the original Zionist struggle. Prime Minister Ariel Sharon has
described the present situation as another round in the
1948 war of independence. The minister of education is
phasing out new history books and replacing them with
older, more "Zionist" ones. Commentators again describe
criticism from the outside, particularly Europe, as anti-
Semitism in disguise. Fewer Israelis than in the past voice
objection to violations of the Palestinians' human rights,
including torture.

It is as if history had turned backward. A statement made about 60 years ago by Bernard Montgomery, the British major general, comes to mind: "The Jew murders the Arab and the Arab murders the Jew. This is what is going on in Palestine now, and it will go on for the next 50 years in all probability." Indeed the same elements of the conflict that led the British to end their 30-year rule in Palestine still determine the situation today, only unlike the British, Israelis and Palestinians have nowhere to go.

Eventually both peoples will have to give up some of their national aspirations. After half a century of statehood, many Israelis had come to acknowledge that premise in the spirit of their new post-Zionist realism. The present wave of violence is testing the fragility of this spirit. Former Prime Minister Benjamin Netanyahu has observed recently that under the influence of Palestinian terror Israel has moved from post-Zionism to "post-post Zionism," meaning a retreat into the past. Regrettably, he may be right.

Declaring War on America

🕮INTRODUCTION: On September 11, 2001 four commercial airliners were hijacked by suicide terrorists: two of the planes destroyed the twin towers of the World Trade Center in New York City; one plane destroyed part of the Pentagon in Washington; and the fourth plane, possibly headed for the Capitol, crashed in Pennsylvania when passengers overtook the hijackers. More than 3,000 people died in these events. This terrorist assault, the most devastating in United States history, marked the first time since the War of 1812 that foreign "troops" had attacked the continental U.S.

The effects of 9/11 were instantaneous and profound, in the U.S. and throughout much of the world. Commentators compared the attack to the Japanese bombing of Pearl Harbor on December 7, 1941, which drew America into World War II, and the Prime Minister of Spain, Jose Maria Aznar, claimed that 9/11 was even more important than the fall of the Berlin Wall in 1989, which marked the end of the Cold War. Some commentators went so far as to say the global battle against terrorism constituted World War III.

The man considered most responsible for the 9/11 attacks against the United States is a Saudi Arabian by the name of Osama bin Laden, the head of Al-Qaeda (al-kaa-EE-da), a worldwide network of terrorists bent on destroying the influence of the West in the Muslim world. Al-Qaeda means "the base."

The son of a wealthy Saudi construction magnate (the 17th of his father's 52 children), Osama bin Laden prepared for the family business by studying economics and management, but he soon came under the influence of Islamic fundamentalists. In 1979, at age 22, he went to Afghanistan to fight with the Mujahideen ("holy warriors") against the Soviet Union. Some 20,000 Muslim extremists from almost 30 countries fought with the Afghans between 1982 and 1992. Known as the "Afghan Arabs," these extremists formed the vanguard of bin Laden's Al-Qaeda organization.

Bin Laden reputedly distinguished himself in battle in Afghanistan and after the defeat of the Soviets in 1989, he returned tQ Saudi Arabia to work in the family construction business, only to find his homeland "invaded" by "infidels," the American troops stationed there after the Gulf War. As one writer puts it: "For the Muslim world, it [the Gulf War] was a traumatic experience in which the sacred all-Muslim unity was [shattered by Arab-Muslim states joining] ranks with the hated West to fight and defeat another Arab-Muslim state. Not surprisingly, the Islamists call this period al-Azma—"the Crisis"—a calamity for Islam and its believers second only to al-Naqba—"the Holocaust"—the establishment of the state of Israel. The Islamists argued that it was clearly demonstrated during the Crisis that regimes as hated and corrupt as Saudi Arabia's and Kuwait's survived only because of the West's commitment to saving its own puppets by all means, including the massive use of force. The only viable strategy for the vanguard of believers was to take on the West, and especially the United States, in order to assert their divine right to establish Islamic societies and governments throughout the Hub of Islam."[1]

Bin Laden left Saudi Arabia for the Sudan in 1991. By 1994 Saudi Arabia had stripped him of his citizenship because of his terrorist activities, and in 1996 the Saudi government was able to bribe the Sudan with money and cheap oil to expel bin Laden, which they did. Bin Laden then returned to Afghanistan for good, living in a cave with his four wives and 15 children and running and financing terrorists training camps for Al-Qaeda. His personal wealth, estimated between $30 million and $300 million, has paid for the training of ter-

1 Jossef Bodansky, *Bin Laden: The Man Who Declared War on America* (Roseville: Prima Publishing, 2001), p. 33.

Osama bin Laden made this videotape in October 2001 after the United States began bombing Afghanistan. He praised God for 9/11 and swore America "will never dream of security" until "the infidel's armies leave the land of Muhammad." (AP Photo/Al Jazeera)

rorists from all over the Muslim world. He has also raised money from wealthy Saudi Arabian sympathizers.

By 1998 Al Qaeda had merged with the Egyptian Islamic Jihad to give bin Laden even more power and reach. In that same year, as part of a broad coalition of Islamic terrorist organizations called the World Islamic Front, he issued a *fatwa*, a holy decree, calling upon all Muslims "to kill the Americans and their allies" in a Jihad, or holy war. The full statement of the *fatwa*, titled "Declaration of the World Islamic Front for Jihad Against the Jews and the Crusaders," follows.[25] ✎

Praise be to God, who revealed the Book, controls the clouds, defeats factionalism, and says in His Book: "But when the forbidden months are past, then fight and slay the pagans wherever ye find them, seize them, beleaguer them, and lie in wait for them in every stratagem (of war)"; and peace be upon our Prophet, Muhammad Bin-'Abdallah, who said: I have been sent with the sword between my hands to ensure that no one but God is wor-shipped, God who put my livelihood under the shadow of my spear and who inflicts humiliation and scorn on those who disobey my orders.

The Arabian Peninsula has never—since God made it flat, created its desert, and encircled it with seas—been stormed by any forces like the crusader armies spreading in it like locusts, eating its riches and wiping out its plantations. All this is happening at a time in which nations are attacking Muslims like people fighting over a plate of food. In the light of the grave situation and the lack of support, we and you are obliged to discuss current events, and we should all agree on how to settle the matter.

No one argues about three facts that are known to everyone; we will list them, in order to remind everyone:

First, for over seven years, the United States has been occupying the lands of Islam in the holiest of places, the Arabian peninsula, plundering its riches, dictating to its rulers, humiliating its people, terrorizing its neighbors, and turning its bases in the Peninsula into a spearhead though which to fight the neighboring Muslim peoples.

If some people have in the past argued about the fact of the occupation, all the people of the Peninsula have now acknowledged it. The best proof of this is the Americans' continuing aggression against the Iraqi people using the Peninsula as a staging post, even though all its rulers are against their territories being used to that end, but they are helpless.

Second, despite the great devastation inflicted on the Iraqi people by the crusader-Zionist alliance, and despite the huge number of those killed, which has exceeded 1 million . . . despite all this, the Americans are once again trying to repeat the horrific massacres, as though they are not content with the protracted blockade imposed after the ferocious war or the fragmentation and devastation.

So here they come to annihilate what is left of this people and to humiliate their Muslim neighbors. Third, if the Americans' aims behind these wars are religious and economic, the aim is also to serve the Jews' petty state and divert attention from its occupation of Jerusalem and murder of Muslims there. The best proof of this is their eagerness to destroy Iraq, the strongest neighboring Arab state, and their endeavor to fragment all the states of the region such as Iraq, Saudi Arabia, Egypt, and Sudan into paper statelets and through their disunion and weakness to guarantee Israel's survival and the continuation of the brutal crusade occupation of the Peninsula.

All these crimes and sins committed by the Americans are a clear declaration of war on God, his messenger, and Muslims. And ulema [official Koranic interpreters] have throughout Islamic history unanimously agreed that the jihad is an individual duty if the enemy destroys the Muslim countries. On that basis, and in compliance with God's order, we issue the following *fatwa* to all Muslims:

The ruling to kill the Americans and their allies—civilians and military—is an individual duty for every Muslim who can do it in any country in which it is possible to do it, in order to liberate the al-Aqsa Mosque and the holy mosque [Mecca] from their grip, and in order for their armies to move out of all the lands of Islam, defeated and unable to threaten any Muslim. This is in accordance with the words of Almighty God, "and fight the pagans all together as they fight you all together," and "fight them until there is no more tumult or oppression, and there prevail justice and faith in God."

This is in addition to the words of Almighty God: "And why should ye not fight in the cause of God and of those who, being weak, are ill-treated (and oppressed)?—women and children, whose cry is: 'Our Lord, rescue us from this town, whose people are oppressors; and raise for us from thee one who will help!'"

We—with God's help—call on every Muslim who believes in God and wishes to be rewarded to comply with God's order to kill the Americans and plunder their money wherever and whenever they find it. We also call on Muslim ulema, leaders, youths, and soldiers to launch the raid on Satan's U.S. troops and the devil's supporters allying with them, and to displace those who are behind them so that they may learn a lesson. . . .

Almighty God also says: "O ye who believe, what is the matter with you, that when ye are asked to go forth in the cause of God, ye cling so heavily to the earth! Do ye prefer the life of this world to the hereafter? But little is the comfort of this life, as compared with the hereafter. Unless ye go forth, He will punish you with a grievous penalty, and put others in your place; but Him ye would not harm in the least. For God hath power over all things."

Terrorists on Tape

❧INTRODUCTION: As the previous reading indicates, Osama bin Laden had three main complaints against the United States: (1) the presence of U.S. troops on the sacred land of Arabia, the home of Mecca and Medina, Mohammed's birth place; (2) the imposition of U.N. sanctions against Iraq following the Gulf War, enforced mainly by the U.S.; and (3) Israel's occupation of Palestinian land, with U.S. support, as bin Laden sees it. More broadly, bin Laden and most radical Islamists resent the economic, political, and intellectual decline of the Muslim world vis-à-vis the West, now led by the U.S.

There was a time when Islam dominated the world stage. As the dean of American Middle East scholars, Bernard Lewis, puts it, "Under the medieval caliphate, and again under the Persian and Turkish dynasties, the empire of Islam was the richest, most powerful, most creative, most enlightened region in the world, and for most of the Middle Ages Christendom was on the defensive. . . . As late as the seventeenth century, Turkish pashas still ruled in Budapest and Belgrade, Turkish armies were besieging Vienna, and Barbary corsairs were raiding lands as distant as the British Isles and, on one occasion, in 1627, even Iceland."[1]

As with all empires, however, the Islamic empire came to an end, gradually from the seventeenth to the nineteenth centuries and then finally with the fall of the Ottomans in 1918. In some ways, the Arab-Muslim world has been trying to come

[1] Bernard Lewis, "The Revolt of Islam," *The New Yorker*, November 19, 2001, p. 53.

to grips with its decline ever since. "For Osama bin Laden, 2001 marks the resumption of the war for religious dominance of the world that began in the seventh century," according to Lewis. "For him and his followers, this is a moment of opportunity. Today, America exemplifies the civilization and embodies the leadership of the House of War [ruled by infidels as opposed to the House of Islam ruled by Islamic law], and, like Rome and Byzantium, it has become degenerate and demoralized, ready to be overthrown."[2]

The Muslim fundamentalist "war" against the West began in 1979 with the overthrow of the Shah of Iran by the Ayatollah Khomeini. This was followed by a series of attacks, including among others: the assassination of President Anwar el-Sadat of Egypt in 1981; assaults on American and French troops and on the American Embassy in Beirut in 1983; the underground explosion at the World Trade Center in 1993; the bombing of U.S. troops in Saudi Arabia in 1995 and 1996; the bombing of American barracks at Khobar Towers in 1998; the bombing of U.S. embassies in Kenya and Tanzania in 1998; the attack on the USS Cole in Yemen in 2000; and most recently and disastrously the 9/11 attacks in New York and Washington.

The following selection consists of two videotape transcriptions of Osama bin Laden. The first is a message that bin Laden directed to the United States; it was broadcast on Qatar-based al-Jazeera television on October 7, 2001. At that point it was not clear what role, if any, bin Laden played in the events of 9/11.[26]

The second videotape was found by anti-Taliban forces in Afghanistan and turned over to the U.S. Central Intelligence Agency. The home-produced tape shows bin Laden laughing and boasting about the 9/11 attacks, providing strong evidence —some called it the "smoking gun" proof—that bin Laden was involved in 9/11. Initially, there was some skepticism about the authenticity of the tape, primarily in the Middle East, but under close scrutiny the tape has stood up well and is now widely accepted as being authentic.

---

[2]   *Ibid*, p. 63.

On the tape bin Laden discusses the events of 9/11 with a visiting Saudi Arabian in Kandahar, Afghanistan. Under the headline "Banality of Terror: Dreams of Holy War over a Quiet Evening," *The New York Times* described the setting for the videotape this way: "It looks so ordinary. Men are sitting in a small white room on the floor near some gray, flowered throw pillows. They are laughing, drinking, eating with their hands, adjusting their turbans. A visitor identified in the transcript as a sheik [actually a legless, 38-year-old Saudi Arabian former fighter in Afghanistan, Bosnia and Chechnya by the name of Khaled al-Harbi] sits next to Osama bin Laden. He exclaims what a nice pad Mr. bin Laden has, how clean and comfortable the guest quarters are."

This second videotape was shot on November 9 and released by the U.S. Defense Department on December 13, 2001. [27]

Smoke billows from the two towers of the World Trade Center in New York on September 11, 2001 after two airliners hijacked by terrorists flew into them. The 110-story towers collapsed shortly thereafter. (AP Photo/Gulnara Samoilova)

Tape of October 7, 2001

Here is America struck by God Almighty in one of its vital organs, so that its greatest buildings are destroyed. Grace and gratitude to God. America has been filled with horror from north to south and east to west, and thanks be to God that what America is tasting now is only a copy of what we have tasted.

Our Islamic nation has been tasting the same for more than 80 years, of humiliation and disgrace, its sons killed and their blood spilled, its sanctities desecrated.

God has blessed a group of vanguard Muslims, the forefront of Islam, to destroy America. May God bless them and allot them a supreme place in heaven, for He is the only one capable and entitled to do so. When those have stood in defense of their weak children, their brothers and sisters in Palestine and other Muslim nations, the whole world went into an uproar, the infidels followed by the hypocrites.

A million innocent children are dying at this time as we speak, killed in Iraq without any guilt. We hear no denunciation, we hear no edict from the hereditary rulers. In these days, Israeli tanks rampage across Palestine, in Ramallah, Rafah and Beit Jala and many other parts of the land of Islam, and we do not hear anyone raising his voice or reacting. But when the sword fell upon America after 80 years, hypocrisy raised its head up high bemoaning those killers who toyed with the blood, honor and sanctities of Muslims.

The least that can be said about those hypocrites is that they are apostates who followed the wrong path. They backed the butcher against the victim, the oppressor against the innocent child. I seek refuge in God against them and ask Him to let us see them in what they deserve.

I say that the matter is very clear. Every Muslim after this event [should fight for their religion], after the senior officials in the United States of America starting with the head of international infidels, [U.S. President George W.] Bush and his staff who went on a display of vanity with

their men and horses, those who turned even the countries that believe in Islam against us—the group that
resorted to God, the Almighty, the group that refuses to
be subdued in its religion.

They [America] have been telling the world falsehoods
that they are fighting terrorism. In a nation at the far
end of the world, Japan, hundreds of thousands, young
and old, were killed and [they say] this is not a world
crime. To them it is not a clear issue. A million children
[were killed] in Iraq, to them this is not a clear issue.

But when a few more than 10 were killed in Nairobi
and Dar es Salaam, Afghanistan and Iraq were bombed
and hypocrisy stood behind the head of international infidels, the modern world's symbol of paganism, America,
and its allies.

I tell them that these events have divided the world
into two camps, the camp of the faithful and the camp
of infidels. May God shield us and you from them.

Every Muslim must rise to defend his religion. The wind
of faith is blowing and the wind of change is blowing to
remove evil from the Peninsula of Mohammad, peace be
upon him.

As to America, I say to it and its people a few words:
I swear to God that America will not live in peace before
peace reigns in Palestine, and before all the army of infidels depart the land of Mohammad, peace be upon him.

God is the Greatest and glory be to Islam.

Tape of November 9, 2001

SHEIK: You have given us weapons, you have given us
hope, and we thank Allah for you. We don't want to take
much of your time, but this is the arrangement of the
brothers. People now are supporting us more, even those
ones who did not support us in the past support us more
now. . . .

BIN LADEN: [W]hen people see a strong horse and a
weak horse, by nature they will like the strong horse. This

Supporters of Osama bin Laden, in Karachi, Pakistan, burn effigies of President Bush and an American flag to protest U.S. bombing of Afghanistan. The flag is painted green and white, two colors of the Pakistani flag. (AP Photo/Athar Hussain)

is only one goal. Those who want people to worship the lord of the people, without following that doctrine, will be following the doctrine of Muhammad, peace be upon him. . . . [Bin Laden quotes several short and incomplete Hadith verses, which are the sayings and acts of Muhammad and the first Muslims]: "I was ordered to fight the people until they say there is no god but Allah and his prophet Muhammad."

"Some people may ask: Why do you want to fight us? There is an association between those people who say: I believe in one god and Muhammad is his prophet, and those who don't [inaudible] . . . Those who do not follow the true *fiqh* [Islamic jurisprudence]. The *fiqh* of Muhammad, the real *fiqh*. They are just accepting what is being said at face value."

Those youth who conducted the operations did not accept any *fiqh* in the popular terms, but they accepted the *fiqh* that the prophet Muhammad brought. Those young men [inaudible] said in deeds, in New York and Washington, speeches that overshadowed all other speeches made everywhere else in the world. The speeches are understood by both Arabs and non-Arabs—even by Chinese.

It is above all the media. Some of them said that in Holland, at one of the centers, the number of people who accepted Islam during the days that followed the operations were more than the people who accepted Islam in the last 11 years. I heard someone on Islamic radio who owns a school in America say: "We don't have time to keep up with the demands of those who are asking about Islamic books to learn about Islam." This event made people think [about true Islam], which benefited Islam greatly.

SHEIK: Hundreds of people used to doubt you, and few only would follow you until this huge event happened. Now hundreds of people are coming out to join you. . . .

BIN LADEN: [W]e calculated in advance the number of casualties from the enemy, who would be killed based on the position of the tower. We calculated that the floors that would be hit would be three or four floors. I was the most optimistic of them all . . . [inaudible] . . . [D]ue to my experience in this field, I was thinking that the fire from the gas in the plane would melt the iron structure of the building and collapse the area where the plane hit and all the floors above it only. This is all that we had hoped for. . . .

SHEIK: Allah be praised.

BIN LADEN: We were at . . . [inaudible] . . . when the event took place. We had notification since the previous Thursday that the event would take place that day. We had finished our work that day and had the radio on. It was 5:30 p.m. our time. I was sitting with Dr. Ahmad Abu-al-Khair. Immediately, we heard the news that a plane had hit the World Trade Center. We turned the radio station to the news from Washington. The news continued and no mention of the attack until the end. At the end of the newscast, they reported that a plane just hit the World Trade Center . . . .After a little while, they announced that another plane had hit the World Trade Center. The brothers who heard the news were overjoyed by it.

SHEIK: I listened to the news . . . we were not thinking about anything, and all of a sudden, Allah willing, we were talking about how come we didn't have anything, and all of a sudden the news came and everyone was overjoyed, and everyone until the next day, in the morning, was talking about what was happening, and we stayed until 4 o'clock listening to the news every time a little bit different. Everyone was very joyous and saying, "Allah is great," "Allah is great," "We are thankful to Allah," "Praise Allah. . . ."

And I was happy for the happiness of my brothers. That day the congratulations were coming on the phone nonstop. The mother was receiving phone calls continuously. Thank Allah. Allah is great, praise be to Allah.

(Quoting a verse from the Koran): "Fight them, Allah will torture them, with your hands, he will torture them. He will deceive them and he will give you victory. Allah will forgive the believers, he is knowledgeable about everything."

No doubt it is a clear victory. Allah has bestowed on us . . . honor on us . . . and he will give us blessing and more victory during this holy month of Ramadan. And this is what everyone is hoping for. Thank Allah America came out of its caves. We hit her the first hit and the next one will hit her with the hands of the believers, the good believers, the strong believers.

By Allah it is a great work. Allah prepares for you a great reward for this work. I'm sorry to speak in your presence, but it is just thoughts, just thoughts. By Allah, who there is no god but him. I live in happiness, happiness . . . I have not experienced, or felt, in a long time.

BIN LADEN: Abdallah Azzam, Allah bless his soul, told me not to record anything . . . [inaudible] . . . so

I thought that was a good omen, and Allah will bless us. . . . Abu-Al-Hasan, Al-[Masri], who appeared on al-Jazeera TV a couple of days ago and addressed the Americans saying: "If you are true men, come down here and face us. . . ."

He told me a year ago: "I saw in a dream we were playing a soccer game against the Americans. When our team showed up in the field, they were all pilots!" He said: "So I wondered if that was a soccer game or a pilot game? Our players were pilots." He [Abu-Al-Hasan] didn't know anything about the operation until he heard it on the radio. He said the game went on and we defeated them. That was a good omen for us. . . .

UNIDENTIFIED MAN OFF CAMERA: Abd Al Rahman Al-[Ghamri] said he saw a vision before the operation. A plane crashed into a tall building. He knew nothing about it.

SULAYMAN [ABU GUAITH]: I was sitting with the sheik {bin Laden] in a room. Then I left to go to another room where there was a TV set. The TV broadcast the big event. The scene was showing an Egyptian family sitting in their living room; they exploded with joy. Do you know when there is a soccer game and your team wins? It was the same expression of joy. There was a subtitle that read: "In revenge for the children of Al Aqsa, bin Laden executes an operation against America." So I went back to the sheik [bin Laden], who was sitting in a room with 50 to 60 people. I tried to tell him about what I saw, but he made a gesture with his hands, meaning: "I know, I know. . . ."

BIN LADEN: He did not know about the operation. No, everybody knew. . . . Mohammed [Atta] from the Egyptian family [the al Qaeda Egyptian group] was in charge of the group.

SHEIK: A plane crashing into a tall building was out of anyone's imagination. This was a great job. He was one of the pious men in the organization. He became a martyr. Allah bless his soul.

SHEIK: [Referring to dreams and visions]: The plane that he saw crashing into the building was seen before by more than one person. One of the good religious people has left everything and come here. He told me, "I saw a vision. I was in a huge plane, long and wide. I was carrying it on my shoulders, and I walked from the road to the desert for half a kilometer. I was dragging the plane. . . ."

Another person told me that last year he saw, but I didn't understand and I told him I don't understand. He said: "I saw people who left for jihad . . . and they found themselves in New York . . . in Washington and New York." I said, "What is this?" He told me the plane hit the building. That was last year. We haven't thought much about it. But when the incidents happened, he came to me and said, "Did you see . . . this is strange."

I have another man . . . my god . . . he said and swore by Allah that his wife had seen the incident a week earlier. She saw the plane crashing into a building . . . .That was unbelievable, my god.

BIN LADEN: The brothers, who conducted the operation, all they knew was that they have a martyrdom operation and we asked each of them to go to America, but they didn't know anything about the operation, not even one letter. But they were trained and we did not reveal the operation to them until they are there and just before they boarded the planes . . . Those who were trained to fly didn't know the others. One group of people did not know the other group . . .

[Someone in the crowd asks bin Laden to tell the sheik about the dream of Abu-Da'ud.]

BIN LADEN: We were at a camp of one of the brother's guards. This brother belonged to the majority of the group. He came close and told me that he saw, in a dream, a tall building in America, and in the same dream he saw Mukhtar teaching them how to play karate.

At that point, I was worried that maybe the secret would be revealed if everyone starts seeing it in their dream. So I closed the subject. I told him if he sees another dream, not to tell anybody, because people will be upset with him.

They were overjoyed when the first plane hit the building, so I said to them: Be patient. The difference between the first and second plane hitting the towers was 20 minutes. And the difference between the first plane and the plane that hit the Pentagon was one hour.

Reactions To 9/11

᠊᠊INTRODUCTION: While reactions to 9/11 in the United States were predictable, reactions in the Middle East were much more complicated. In the U.S., the entire nation went into shock and into a mood of determination to fight terrorism. President George W. Bush addressed the nation and vowed to pursue the terrorists wherever they were and to hold any nation who harbored them accountable. Ninety percent of the American public supported him. Within a month of 9/11, American military aircraft began bombing Afghanistan in pursuit of bin Laden and the Taliban government there that protected him. Two months later, by the middle of December, the Taliban and bin Laden's Al-Qaeda organization had been defeated by the combined forces of the Afghan resistance and American Special Forces.

Reactions to 9/11 in the Middle East, on the other hand, were decidedly mixed. All governments except Iraq condemned the attacks, and some Muslim leaders pointed out that Islam does not sanction, let alone dictate, the killing of innocent civilians, as Osama bin Laden's *fatwa* against America prescribes. But at the same time, Palestinian children danced in the streets to celebrate the attacks, and several editorial writers in prominent newspapers justified bin Laden's mission. One veteran commentator on the Arab world assessed the Middle East reaction this way: "I see public opinion in the region divided roughly into three categories. About 40 percent are with the United States and against the terrorists. Another 10 percent support bin Laden. The remaining 50 percent are what

I call the 'bin Lakin group.' Lakin means "but" in Arabic. The bin Lakin group condemns terrorism, yet uses lots of "buts" and "ifs" about the U.S. approach to Arab issues."

Whether this assessment is accurate or not is impossible to say; no broad surveys of Middle East opinion were conducted to measure public attitudes toward 9/11 and Osama bin Laden and Al-Qaeda. But the message of criticism for U.S. policy in the Middle East came through loud and clear, leaving Americans wondering, "Why do they hate us?" *Newsweek* magazine tried to answer this question in its October 15, 2001 issue. The cover of the magazine showed a young Arab boy holding a toy Kalashnikov under the headline "Why They Hate Us."

The following selection consists of a sampling of reactions to 9/11 in the Middle East and among Muslims in the U.S. [28]✺

CONDEMNING THE ATTACKS

The Becket Fund for Religious Liberty printed the following statements in the *Washington Post* under the headline, "Osama bin Laden hijacked four airplanes and a religion," and then went on to say, "Just as he must not be allowed to get away with the terrorist hijackings and cold blooded murder of September 11, Osama bin Laden must not be allowed to get away with hijacking Islam and the good name of religion generally."

- "Hijacking planes, terrorizing innocent people and shedding blood, constitute a form of injustice that cannot be tolerated by Islam, which views them as gross crimes and sinful acts."
  Shaikh Abdulazziz Al-Ashaikh
  Grand Mufti of Saudi Arabia and Chairman of the Senior Ulema
- "[the attacks] will be punished on the day of judgment."
  Sheik Mohammed Sayyed al-Tantawi
  leader of Egypt's great mosque, Al-Azhar
- "The terrorist acts . . . considered by Islam law . . . [constitute] the crime of 'hirabah' (waging war against society)."

Dr. Haytham al-Khayyat (Islamic scholar, Syria)
Fahmi Houaydi (Islamic scholar, Syria)
Sheikh Taha Jabir al-Alwani (chairman, North America High Council)

- "Neither the law of Islam nor its ethical system justify such a crime."
  Zaki Badawk
  Principal of the Muslim College, London
- "What these people stand for is completely against all the principles that Arab Muslims believe in."
  Abdullah II, King of Jordan and descendant of the Prophet Muhammad

The Institute of Islamic and Arabic Sciences in America issued the following statement, abbreviated here:

"Muslims throughout the world were deeply shocked and horrified by the terrible inhumane attacks which took place [on September 11]. To every Muslim, these regrettable attacks were vicious and cowardly. Regardless of whoever committed such acts, they constitute clear violations to the teachings of Islam (stipulated in the Glorious Quran and the authentic traditions of Prophet Muhammad, Peace be upon him and all the messengers of God the Almighty).

"Killing people is certainly evil. The Glorious Quran strongly condemns it: 'if anyone killed a person not in retaliation of murder, or (and) to spread mischief in the land—it would be as if he killed all mankind, and if anyone saved a life, it would be as if he saved the life of all mankind'" (5:32).

"The Glorious Quran states, 'Allah does not forbid you to deal justly and kindly with those who fought not against you because of your religion and did not drive you out of your homes. Verily Allah loves those who deal with equity'" (60:8). This verse, and many others, teaches Muslims to treat people justly and to avoid causing them any harm.

"Strongly believing in these Quranic teachings, the vast majority of Muslims in the world are peace-loving people. They surely disassociate themselves from these horrible crimes of terrorism. Islam and true Muslims stand for peace, harmony and justice."

On September 12, 2001, leaders of Arab-American and American Muslim groups met in Washington, D. C. and issued the following statement:

"We condemn in no uncertain terms the horrifying attacks on the World Trade Center and the Pentagon on September 11. We are shocked and angered by such brutality and share all the emotions of our fellow citizens about these attacks, which target all Americans without exception. We firmly believe that there can be no justification for such horrible acts. We join with the nation in calling for the perpetrators of this terrible crime to be brought swiftly to justice. We commend the statements of Attorney General John Ashcroft, Secretary of State Colin Powell and the numerous senators and members of Congress who have cautioned against attempts to stigmatize the Arab-American and American Muslim communities or blame them for this tragedy. We urge our fellow Americans, the government and media to follow their example and not assign any form of collective guilt against communities for the crimes of individuals."

> American-Arab Anti-Discrimination Committee
> Arab American Institute
> American Committee on Jerusalem
> American Muslim Alliance
> American Muslim Council
> Center for Policy Analysis on Palestine
> Council on American Islamic Relations
> Islamic Institute

"SUPPORTING" THE ATTACKS
The Middle East Media & Research Institute (MEMRI) issued a "Special Dispatch No. 281: Terror in America" showing columnists from the Egyptian government press

joining Egypt's opposition press in celebrating the attacks on the U.S. The following are excerpts from the Dispatch.

"Columnist Ali Al-Sayyed wrote in *Al-Ahram Al-Aarabi* weekly: 'For many long years, America made many peoples in the world cry. It was always [America] that carried out the acts; now, acts are being carried out [against] it. A cook who concocts poison must one day also taste that poison! The world has discovered that the strength of the oppressed is great when the situation becomes unbearable. The city of globalization, with its economic, political, and military symbols, has collapsed, and the theory of globalization will be buried with the establishment of the false coalition.'"

"Islamist journalist Fahmi Hueidi, writing in the leading government daily, *Al-Ahram*, criticized President Bush's policy: The catchphrase 'Either you're with us or you're with terrorism' expresses arrogance and conceit.

By permission of Mike Luckovich and Creators Syndicate, Inc.

[The U.S.] sees the world according to American interests; it sees itself as the leader of the free world, civilization, and democracy. Anyone refusing to join it is expelled from its Paradise and has no place except in Hell. The Americans have no right to classify societies in this way. Every group has the right to choose a third way, rejecting both terrorism and the Americans.'"

"Egypt's privately owned 'independent' press also celebrated the terrorist attacks against the U.S.: 'Millions across the world shouted in joy: America was hit!' wrote *Al-Maydan* (an independent weekly) columnist Dr. Nabil Farouq. 'This call expressed the sentiments of millions across the world, whom the American master had treated with tyranny, arrogance, bullying, conceit, deceit, and bad taste—like every bully whom no one has yet put in his place. True, thousands of innocents became victims, among them Egyptians who had immigrated to the U.S.

Muslims greet one another at a rally on September 27, 2001 in Peshawar, Pakistan. Many Muslims felt Islam was being blamed for 9/11 instead of the terrorists and other radical fundamentalists. (AP Photo/John McConnico)

in search of opportunity and [a better] life; but what can a person do when the neighborhood bully gets [a blow] from behind that shakes his very existence, insults his dignity, and humiliates him? Obviously [the person] is glad, even if it is wrong to rejoice.'"

"*Al-Mayden* editor Issam Al-Ghazi added, 'President Dubya Bush will continue to struggle between threatening to launch a crusader war and apologizing to the Muslims. Apparently, he doesn't want to understand that he is reaping the thorns sown by himself and all his predecessors in Palestine, Yugoslavia, Iraq, Libya, the Sudan, Afghanistan, Vietnam and Japan. Behind every act of destruction is a little American demon. America cannot see the fate that awaits it, despite everything that happened on that bloody Tuesday; America is on its way to collapse, like all the empires of oppression throughout history. If only our generation would have the chance to witness that dramatic spectacle. . . .'"

"Said Sh'eib, columnist in the Nasserist weekly *Al-Arabi*, also became enamored of bin Laden after seeing him in an interview on Al-Jazeera television. He wrote: 'I loved Osama bin Laden's face, because it inspired confidence. I was amazed by his total belief in what he says. I very much admired this man, who chose—and I am not addressing the quality of the choices he makes—to leave a life of luxury, to take up arms against [those] he considers to be the enemy, and to go down in history as a man who shook the greatest empire in history.'"

MUSLIM SELF CRITICISM

MEMRI also translated an article by a Kuwaiti professor, Ahmed al-Baghdadi, titled "Sharon Is a Terrorist—and You?" It appeared in Kuwait's Al Anbaa and Egypt's Akhbar Al Youm. Al-Baghdadi calls Sharon, Israel's Prime Minister, a terrorist, but then goes on to criticize Arab-Muslim rulers, as follows:

"Persecuting intellectuals in the courtrooms [of Arab countries], trials [of intellectuals] for heresy . . . all exist

only in the Islamic world. Is this not terrorism? . . . Iraq
alone is a never-ending story of terrorism of the state
against its own citizens and neighbors. Isn't this terrorism? . . . The Palestinian Arabs were the first to invent
airplane hijacking and the scaring of passengers. Isn't
this terrorism? Arab Muslims have no rivals in this; they
are the masters of terrorism toward their citizens, and
sometimes their terrorism also reaches the innocent people of the world, with the support of some of the clerics
. . . [Ours] is a nation whose ignorance makes the nations
of the world laugh! The Islamic world and the Arab world
are the only [places] in which intellectuals—whose only
crime was to write—rot in prison. The Arabs and Muslims claim that their religion is a religion of tolerance,
but they show no tolerance for those who oppose their
opinions . . . Now the time has come to pay the price .
. . and the account is long—longer than all the beards
of the Taliban gang together. The West's message to the
Arab and Muslim world is clear: mend your ways or else."

In another call for reform, a professor at Adrian College in Minnesota, Dr. Muqtedar Khan, issued "A Memo
to American Muslims" on October 1, 2001. Below are
excerpts from the Memo.

"In the name of Allah, the most Benevolent and the Most
Merciful. May this memo find you in the shade of Islam
enjoying the mercy, the protection and the grace of Allah."

"I am writing this memo to you all with the explicit
purpose of inviting you to lead the American Muslim community in soul searching, reflection and reassessment."

"What happened on September 11th in New York and
Washington, D. C. will forever remain a horrible scar on
the history of Islam and humanity. No matter how much
we condemn it, and point to the Quran and the Sunnah
[the practices of Muhammed] to argue that Islam forbids
the killing of innocent people, the fact remains that the
perpetrators of this crime against humanity have indicated
that their actions are sanctioned by Islamic values."

"The fact that even now several Muslim scholars and
thousands of Muslims defend the accused is indicative

that not all Muslims believe that the attacks are un-Islamic. This is truly sad. . . ."

"Muslims, including American Muslims, have been practicing hypocrisy on a grand scale. They protest against the discriminatory practices of Israel but are silent against the discriminatory practices in Muslim states. In the Gulf one can see how laws and even salaries are based on ethnic origin. This is racism, but we never hear of Muslims protesting against this at international fora."

"The Israeli occupation of Palestine is perhaps central to Muslim grievance against the West. While acknowledging that, I must remind you that Israel treats its one million Arab citizens with greater respect and dignity than most Arab nations treat their citizens. Today Palestinian refugees can settle and become citizens of the United States but in spite of all the tall rhetoric of the Arab world and Quranic injunctions (24:22) no Muslim country except Jordan extends this support to them. . . ."

"It is time that we acknowledge that the freedoms we enjoy in the U.S. are more desirable to us than superficial solidarity with the Muslim world. If you disagree then prove it by packing your bags and going to whichever Muslim country you identify with. If you do not leave and do not acknowledge that you would rather live here than anywhere else, know that you are being hypocritical."

"It is time that we faced these hypocritical practices and struggled to transcend them. It is time that American Muslim leaders fought to purify their own lot."

Fundamentalist Islam

&INTRODUCTION: One commentator sums up the goals of bin Laden and Islamic fundamentalists this way:

> Bin Laden is the most notorious advocate of a potent strain of militant Islam that has been gaining popularity in the Muslim world for 30 years. It is simultaneously theological and cultural. Its fundamental tenet is that the Muslim world is being poisoned and desecrated by infidels. These infidels include both outsiders such as the United States and Israel, and governments of Muslim states—such as Egypt and Jordan—that have committed apostasy. The infidels must be driven out of the Muslim world by a jihad, and strict Islamic rule must be established everywhere that Muslims live. These extreme "Islamists" . . . hope to re-establish the Caliphate, the golden age of Muslim domination that followed the death of Muhammad. They regard the Taliban's Afghanistan as a model for such Islamic rule.[1]

The Taliban came to power in Afghanistan in 1996 after a decade of fighting the Soviets, followed by several years of chaotic civil war. What they offered the Afghan people was social stability through the imposition of Islamic law; what they delivered was a severe form of social repression.

The Taliban forbade girls to go to school and women to work professionally, despite the fact that 70 percent of all teachers and a high percentage of doctors were women. All

[1]   David Plotz, *Slate*, September 13, 2001.

women had to wear the burka, a head-to-toe covering, when going outside the home. All men had to have beards. The list of forbidden activities included: playing music, watching television, flying kites (popular in Afghanistan), playing chess, or reading foreign magazines displaying female film stars. In fact, "merchants importing products like shampoo would find that Taliban customs officials had gouged out the eyes of the female models on the boxes. The merchants were then required to display the products with black tape over female faces, or be subject to a beating or jailing."[2]

The Taliban, who numbered about 60,000, were supported both philosophically and financially by bin Laden's Al-Qaeda organization, which numbered about 10,000 in Afghanistan. It is estimated that bin Laden contributed more than $100 million to the Taliban, who had no other outside support. Indeed, many of the Taliban were products of religious schools in Pakistan, called madrasses, which bin Laden financed generously. (The name Taliban means students; a talib is a student.)

The curriculum of the madrasses is almost entirely religious and often anti-Western. A reporter visiting a madrassa in Charikar, Afghanistan described a class this way:

> Thirteen boys gathered for afternoon lessons in a room that looked more like a cave than a classroom, dark with unfinished stone walls pockmarked with holes where hooks once held automatic rifles. Without chairs, the children sat on a dusty windowsill or on the rusty remnants of a steel bed frame. There was no blackboard as such, just a section of wall covered with dark material from the inside of batteries.

"The subject today," the teacher announced, "is jihad."

With that, he wrote on his makeshift blackboard the word that often means Islamic holy war: "jihad." Then he began writing under it: "For every Muslim, it's good. As the Prophet Muhammad said, you wage jihad against those who are against Islam."[3]

---

2 Amy Waldman, *New York Times*, November 22, 2001, p. 1-A.
3 Peter Baker, "Teaching Boys – and Girls – Another Notion of Jihad," *Washington Post*, October 2, 2001, p. A17.

Unfórtunately, this kind of education, aside from teaching conflict, does not prepare students for the modern world. Illiteracy in Afghanistan has increased and is now estimated at more than 60 percent for boys and 90 percent for girls. And in the absence of modern schools, madrassas offer the only education available for many children, and they have increased in number. In 1978 there were 3,000 madrassas in Pakistan; in 2001 there were 39,000.

The scholar Martin E. Marty has observed: "The fundamentalist . . . says there was a moment in history when a particular book, leader and original social community was perfect."[4] For Islamic fundamentalists like Osama bin Laden and the Taliban that moment took place in the 7th century. But most Muslims worldwide do not share this view. In Charikar, another teacher said, "There's a 100 percent difference from Islam and Osama bin Laden. He killed poor people, thousands of people he doesn't know. This is not a jihad. This is against Islam. They are the enemies of Islam." [5]

Yet another teacher said, "Islam is not against anything else." And referring to the Taliban, she said, "Those who are acting like barbarians, they want to bring back ancient times. We don't want that kind of Islam." [6]

The "model" Islamic state of the Taliban was never broadly supported by the Afghan people, and with the defeat of the Taliban and the ouster of Al-Qaeda, fundamentalism would seem to be in rapid decline in Afghanistan. But in other Muslim countries fundamentalism still holds sway over large minorities and claims (or extracts) the support of sitting governments. Saudi Arabia is one such country. The following selection illustrates the contest between the fundamentalists and the moderates in Saudi Arabia, a country situated at the very core of Islam and in the eye of the storm within Islam. [29]✎

---

[4]   Martin E. Marty, "Sacred Battles," *New York Times Magazine*, October 30, 2001, p. 19.
[5]   Baker, op. cit.
[6]   *Ibid.*

BURAYDAH, Saudi Arabia—Warming his bare feet before a fire in the desert air of a black, wool tent, Sheik Hamoud al-Shuaibi issued a judgment of the kind that has made him an elder statesman of the movement championed by Osama bin Laden.

"The American war against Afghanistan is the American war against Islam. Against Muslims and Islam all over the world," he said in an interview this week. "This is a jihad against the U.S.A. and its following countries."

Shuaibi, 74 and blind, occupies one half of a decades-old schism that cuts deeply through Saudi Arabian society. In a country that seeks to marry religious and political authority, sheiks such as Shuaibi are in open conflict with scholars who use religious teaching to support the legitimacy of the U.S.-backed monarchy.

The dimensions of this dispute were illustrated by Shuaibi's off-camera cameo in the videotape of bin Laden released Thursday. The video shows another Saudi sheik, Sulieman al Ghamdi, recounting for bin Laden a recent visit with Shuaibi, during which the aging scholar shared his vision of a "great hit" that inspires a massive pilgrimage of holy warriors to Afghanistan.

Such prophesies from Saudi religious figures, and reports that 15 of the 19 hijackers in the Sept. 11 attacks were Saudis, have created tension between the United States and the Saudi government and debate within the kingdom about the nature of Islamic teaching. Although Saudi officials and analysts maintain that views such as Shuaibi's are on the fringe, Saudi leaders, including Crown Prince Abdullah, have cautioned leading religious scholars to temper their rhetoric.

"We have begun to talk more about the need for moderate Islam. Tolerant Islam. We have begun to admit that we have a problem, and that is positive," said Jamal Khashoggi, a Saudi journalist who has reported extensively on bin Laden and militant movements in Afghanistan. "We have a problem with social fanaticism, and we have to address this."

That trained scholars with the same preparation vary widely in their teaching reflects a division that has per-

sisted almost since the founding of Islam. That division
continues to manifest itself from the moderate mosques
of Indonesia to the radical exhortations of bin Laden.

While one side proselytizes isolationism and an uncom-
promising vision of Islamic principles, the other, often
ensconced in government institutions that try to couple
religious values with a practical edge, advocates defer-
ence to the state on some key issues.

For example, Mohammed al-Salem, who occupies a well-
appointed office in the capital, Riyadh, has been trained
in the same sources of Islamic scholarship as Shuaibi, and
speaks with comparable authority. But he reaches an opposite conclusion about the central issue of the day, even
though he, too, feels bound by what is found in the Koran
and the Sunna, or practices, of the prophet Muhammad.

"This is not about jihad," said Salem, president of the
government-sponsored Imam Mohammed Ibn Saud
Islamic University, which produces many of the lawyers
and judges that staff Saudi Arabia's sharia law system.
"Nobody has the right to declare war. It is done through
the leadership" of the country.

The divergence in Islamic teaching—and the debate
about whether temporal, religious or some combined
authority should have credibility—arose less than three
decades after the prophet Muhammad's death in 632
A.D., when opponents of the ruling Caliph Ali concluded
that it was the obligation of a good Muslim to rebel
against society or ruler that did not follow proper
Islamic principles.

The revolt was suppressed, but the underlying views
have recurred with particular intensity during the past
30 years, becoming a precursor of bin Laden's call for
jihad.

The schism produced a strict Islamic government in
Iran. It failed to do so in Egypt and Syria, where fundamentalist movements were brutally repressed. The battle
endures in Algeria in the form of a civil conflict that has
claimed 100,000 lives over a decade.

In Saudi Arabia, where the outcome could prove critical to Western interests and future relations with the United States, the ebb and flow of the struggle has flared into internal tension.

Radicals who argued that the Saudi royal family had strayed from Islam took over the Grand Mosque in Mecca in 1979. Sheiks such as Shuaibi, in this town 250 miles northwest of Riyadh, issued lists of demands after the Persian Gulf War that led to their imprisonment. Bin Laden followers are suspected of having carried out bombings at a National Guard building in Riyadh.

Opposing these forces, Saudi leaders and others argue that the trend in Islamic history, and their own history as well, is clear: That Islam strives to coexist with the modern world and modern government.

Iran's Ayatollah Ruhollah Khomeini, before his death, outlined a doctrine of "expediency" that essentially placed the survival of the Muslim state above any particular application of Islamic doctrine. Saudi Arabia, whose royal family views itself as the protector of a faith that, for example, forbids interest, has millions of Visa card holders and a well-oiled banking industry that functions despite almost daily talk-show declarations telling people that it is illegal.

"We should not consider other communities to be our enemies and merely say there are old enmities and so we should kill," Prince Turki al-Faisal said in a television interview on the Saudi-owned Middle East Broadcasting Corp. "We are living in a world where there are several other religions. Instead of thinking about a bloody confrontation, we should prepare ourselves for coexistence and the exchange of ideas."

Given the history, however, the Saudi government remains cautious. Senior clerics were quick to condemn the Sept. 11 attacks in New York and at the Pentagon. Since the start of military action in Afghanistan, they have not gone beyond expressions of general concern for civilian lives.

Most telling, Crown Prince Abdullah, the de facto leader in place of the ailing King Fahd, called top Islamic schol-

This Buddha statue, the tallest Buddha in the world, standing almost 200 feet and dating to the 5th century, was ordered destroyed by the Taliban in March 2001, under pressure from Al-Qaeda. The Taliban said this statue and other Buddhas in Afghanistan insulted Islam, a position of intolerance of other religions held only by radical fundamentalists. (AP Photo/Amir Shah)

ars together in what seemed intended to be a clear reminder that he represented the power of the state while their role was as religious advisers.

"It is your duty to be careful," he told them, according to local press accounts of the session. "Scholars serve their religion and country and look for reasonable words that serve Islam. I advise you not to get emotional or provoked by anyone. Let there be no extremism in religion."

Writing in the English-language *Saudi Gazette* recently, Saudi writer Khaled Al-Dakheel said the meeting had only one precedent in Saudi history. That was when King Abdel Aziz was preparing in the 1920s to face down a revolt by religious conservatives upset about foreigners and telegraph lines and other innovations turning up after World War I.

Followers of clerics like Shuaibi are convinced that clerics who hold top government jobs tailor their religious views to serve state interests. It is a worldview that persists even as the targets of disdain have progressed from telegraph lines in the 1920s to television in the 1960s to the Internet in the 1990s.

With a handful of relatives and friends on an old date farm, Shuaibi recently discussed Saudi and world politics while an associate roasted coffee beans. He had just finished a short, instructional prayer service for some young relatives, who toppled playfully on one another as they bowed their heads to the ground.

There was little about the man or the setting to suggest a revolution in the making. Shuaibi issued a *fatwa*, or edict, at the start of the strikes against Afghanistan that whoever aids an infidel is an infidel—an opinion with deep import for the royal family, host to 4,000 U.S. troops at a desert airstrip south of Riyadh.

Taliban soldiers stand in front of empty shell where a Buddha statue once stood. Ignoring worldwide criticism by Muslims, Buddhists and art lovers, Taliban officials showed off their destruction of two ancient statues by taking foreigners to the Bamiyan mountainside where the relics were blasted apart.(AP Photo/Amir Shah)

While it is unknown how many of Saudi Arabia's thousands of clerics agree with the sheik's point of view, Shuaibi said he is sure the vast majority of Saudi citizens are on his side. If they are not streaming off to Afghanistan to fight, or rising up against the government, that is only because the government will not let them. Saudi officials estimate that between 200 and 1,000 Saudis are currently in Afghanistan.

"The Saudi people follow the sheiks that relay the truth and the ones that follow Koran and Sunna, not the ones that follow the political side," Shuaibi said. "Jihad is the highest form of worship. This is a very high station. So all look for this station. If the government allowed people, all the Arab Muslims would go to war."

Whither Islam— and America?

❧INTRODUCTION: All of the major Middle Eastern religions— Judaism, Christianity, and Islam—believe that God has spoken directly to man and his words are written down in the Bible and the Koran.

For those who believe they have this ultimate truth, in God's own words, it follows logically and philosophically that enemies of this truth, infidels, should be confronted and, if possible, converted. It also follows that life on earth—the social order, the state— should be run according to God's word, that is, by a theocracy. One of the main differences between Islam and Christianity is that Islam holds firm in its belief in theocracy; Christianity does not.

It should be pointed out that Christianity conducted its own wars against infidels during the Crusades, and it burned heretics at the stake during the Inquisition in the fifteenth century. But since then the power of the Church has been separated from the state: first, through a series of church-state struggles; then by a Reformation within Christianity; and finally, through the impact of the Enlightenment in the eighteenth Century, when reason replaced revelation and scholarship replaced the Bible as the basis for public discourse. Such a separation has not taken place in the Islamic world, at least not among fundamentalists.

Salman Rushdie, an Indian Muslim writer, whose novel *The Satanic Verses* sent him into hiding for several years because

of an Iranian *fatwa* calling for his death, makes the following
point about Islamic fundamentalism and Islam in general:

> The fundamentalist seeks to bring down a great deal
> more than buildings. Such people are against, to offer just
> a brief list, freedom of speech, a multi-party political sys-
> tem, universal adult suffrage, accountable government, Jews,
> homosexuals, women's rights, pluralism, secularism, short
> skirts, dancing, beardlessness, evolution theory, sex. These
> are tyrants, not Muslims.
>
> Islam is tough on suicides, who are doomed to repeat
> their deaths through all eternity. However, there needs to
> be a thorough examination, by Muslims everywhere, of why
> it is that the faith they love breeds so many violent mutant
> strains. If the West needs to understand its Unabombers
> and McVeighs, Islam needs to face up to its bin Ladens.[1]

In contrast to the absolutism of Islamic fundamentalism
stands the pluralism of Western democracies, where many religions (and atheism) live side by side, where individual
conscience guides behavior, where freedom of speech is
guarded by law, and where supposedly the French philoso-
pher Voltaire said, "I disagree with everything you say, but
will fight to the death for your right to say it."

It could be said that Islam is now at a crossroads, where it
must define itself either as an evolving religion compatible
with liberal democratic rule, or a religion that turns its back
on the modern secular state and tries to establish religious
states adhering to the most narrow and inflexible interpre-
tations of the Koran. How this struggle within Islam evolves
will have a major impact not only on Muslim nations but on
the entire world.

The following selection, an interview with American University Professor Akbar Ahmed, deals with the internal debates
within Islam, as well as the role the United States might play
in bringing about greater understanding between the West

---

[1]   Salman Rushdie, "Fighting the Forces of Invisibility," *Washington Post*, October 2, 2001, p. A23.

and the Islamic world. While the interview is not a scholarly analysis, it does shed light on these timely issues. Professor Ahmed is author of *Islam Today: A Short Introduction to the Muslim World.* [30]

Q: Speaking on *Meet the Press* recently, Prince Bandar bin Sultan, the Saudi ambassador to the United States, said Osama bin Laden "is a pariah, and anyone who supports him is a pariah." Is he right?

A: He is, in that he points out the enormity of what took place on 11 September when thousands of innocent lives were lost. People call it an American tragedy, but I would call it a world tragedy. There were so many non-Americans present in the towers, including one of my own relatives, a young man who had migrated from Pakistan. He rang his father in New Jersey just minutes before the tower collapsed. He had two little kids, and now his father has had a stroke, and the life of his family has been shattered forever. So if you asked his family what they think of Osama bin Laden, yes, they would say he's a pariah.

Yet he obviously is not just an individual acting on his own. He has a network spread across the Muslim world. Why do some people support him? In his television interview, which was relayed on American television, bin Laden clearly outlined his objectives: 1) a solution to the plight of the Palestinians; 2) a solution to the plight of the Iraqi civilians, the women and children dying there; 3) an end to the stationing of U.S. troops in the holy lands of Saudi Arabia; and 4) an end to the oppression that people in the Muslim world are suffering at the hands of their own rulers. By pointing to these four sources of discontent, he gave substance to his larger argument that there is now a clash between Islam and the West—an argument that suits him because it turns him from an isolated individual on the run to part of the 1.2 billion Muslims he would like to involve in the clash of civilizations.

The battle you're seeing is being misread in the West as a battle between Islam and the West, and Osama is trying to capitalize on that misperception. I maintain this is Islam fighting Islam—a battle for the soul and destiny of Islam. And that battle will not be decided by B-1s, B-2s, and Tomahawk missiles. It will be decided by ordinary scholars fighting within Muslim society. Upon the outcome of that battle will depend the future generations of Muslims. If scholars who believe in dialogue succeed, then we will have harmony and peace and dialogue in the future. If not, then we'll have people who believe in violence, people who declare to the world, "Our enemies are the Jews and the Christians, and you must kill them wherever you find them."

Muslim society is going through one of the most serious crises of its history. The gap between the rich and the poor is growing, as are corruption and mismanagement at most levels of society. The proportion of the young in Muslim countries is very high. Many millions of Muslims are people under 21, most of them illiterate and out of a job. The violence is coming from the young men. My hope is that Muslim women are educated and emerge as leaders. Maybe then we'd see a change in the thinking of the society. But so far that's not happening.

Q: Is the Islamic world ready to accept an expanded role for women?

A: Your readers may be startled to hear this, but Muslim civilization is far more tolerant and far more accommodating to women than any civilization in history. The first person to become a Muslim was a woman—the prophet's first and only wife, until her death—who was a successful merchant, a widow who proposed to him. I point this out because it's against the stereotype.

Yet, over time, Muslim men have corrupted Islam, and many Muslims today treat women badly. My wife is a princess of Swat; her grandfather was the ruler of the state of Swat in north Pakistan. She has been educated at the best schools. Yet the men of the family inherit the family lands, and the women are told, "You stay home and take care of the house." The uneducated women sign away half their property because their male relatives persuade them to do so, sometimes by subtle persuasion, and sometimes by crude force. Do you think they're happy about that? Do you think I'm happy as a modern, educated Muslim? I want them to fight for their rights. And these women are doing that.

Q: Jerrold Post, a psychologist who has written about both Saddam Hussein and Osama bin Laden, was recently quoted in the *New Yorker* as saying, in reference to the Gulf War and its aftermath, that "to personalize a conflict against an Arab leader is to enhance his stature." Is the current President Bush making the same mistake his father made with Saddam Hussein?

A: Yes. In an article I wrote two or three years back, I said that till the mid-'90s, Osama bin Laden was an unknown freedom fighter. And then we had the missile strikes on Sudan and Afghanistan. After that, he was on the front page of major newspapers. He was on television. And I was saying, "What are the Americans doing? By plastering him in the media, they are telling the Muslim world, 'Here you have a champion.'"

Osama used that because afterwards in my country, Pakistan, he became like a celebrity pop star. Children buy T-shirts with Osama's name on them. People name their children Osama. Now, Pakistan is generally a moderate country, so I asked, "What is going on?" Obviously, Osama has been elevated to a major world player.

Since 11 September, Osama has been on the cover of *Time* and every other major magazine, and we've seen film clips of him on television. The whole world now sees the match as America vs. Islam.

Let me give you an analogy. If I got into the ring with someone like Mike Tyson, when Tyson was in his heyday, I would not last for more than half a second. But because I got into the ring with him, people are going to say, "Oh, my God, Professor Ahmed actually went into the ring with Tyson! So if he's not a heavyweight champion, at least he's a contender." Likewise by elevating Osama

A veiled Muslim woman in a bus travels past a large billboard for the new film "Girls' Secrets" on the front of a downtown Cairo movie theater. The film catalogues the plight of a middle class Cairo family as it tries to come to terms with the pregnancy of its teenage daughter. The film received critical acclaim for capturing the prevailing mood of contemporary urban Egypt struggling to balance tradition and modernity, religion and science. (AP Photo/Amr Nabil)

bin Laden so much, America appears to be telling the Muslim world, "Here is this terrible man, this man who's shaken up America, who's made the Americans look over their shoulders, and we're going to get him and wipe him out." By doing that, you will encourage hundreds of other youngsters to say, "Hey, I want to be Osama. I want to grow up and take on the giant."

Q: How can President Bush proceed with his war against terrorism without further inflaming that kind of sentiment?

A: There are many ways. And some the administration has taken quite seriously. President Bush very sensibly went to the Islamic Center in Washington. He was shown on television with Muslim leaders receiving the Koran.

I'll give you my own example, on a very small level. Saturday, I was at Saint Aloysius Church in Washington, near Union Station. I was invited to speak on behalf of Islam. There were over a thousand people there of all religions. There were Buddhists, Hindus, rabbis, and bishops. I said to myself—my talk was very warmly received—that a very wonderful spiritual unity existed that evening that was very American, and very global.

Q: Could this sort of thing resonate if it were publicized in the Muslim world?

A: It could resonate, and in fact it does because President Bush was shown on television in the Muslim world saying that Islam is a peaceful religion, that Osama bin Laden has hijacked Islam, and the fight is not with Islam but with terrorism. And people see that, and they say, "Wait a minute. If Americans are the enemies of Islam, how come President Bush is saying these things?"

You know, there's an interesting disjunction between the image of American society here and in the Muslim world. What has attracted me about America is the libraries, the universities, the parks, the sense of freedom, the liberal openness, the people's warmth and hospitality.

If I meet an American in the street, he greets me, smiles at me, we chat about the weather. This, although I assure you that I love England, does not happen in England. There, they would look rather stiffly at you if you started to chat with a stranger. So as a new arrival in America, I ask what is happening when millions of Muslims say, "We hate America." The answer is that the true America is not being communicated abroad, so that the person in Cairo or Karachi or Kuala Lumpur has a very different idea of America than the one I have.

Why have Americans failed to project the best of their society to the rest of the world? America is a continent, a civilization in itself, so it becomes insular. America does

not need to look abroad. Take your news. When I look
at American television news, 90 percent of it is weather,
traffic jams, good shopping places, where to go for work-
outs, to lose weight, and so on. So one positive
consequence of the terrible events of 9/11 could be that
Americans will come to understand the world we're living in. Also a determined effort could be made by
immigrant Americans, including Muslims, to understand
America better and communicate our experience here.
Many Muslims in America, like me, feel we are freer to
practice our faith here, to live by the way we like within
the law as good neighbors, as good citizens, than very
often we are in our own homelands. And yet our Muslim leadership has not yet been able to communicate this
to the rest of the world.

**Q: What about the airdrops of food over Afghanistan?
Are they helping in the battle for hearts and minds?**
A: Those gestures are very important to show compas-
sion. But you've also got to think long term. You've got
to say to other governments, "We will help your regime,
but only if you make sure that there is proper democracy. We won't simply help you if it suits us because of
geopolitics." One of the most famous scholars of the Arab
world has been put in jail, in a cage, and tried and sen-
tenced in Cairo. He's an American citizen—a dual citizen
with an American wife. If that can happen to him, think
of what an ordinary scholar has to go through. Or an
ordinary citizen. If someone criticizes the local police or
the local administrator, he is arrested and may disappear.

The ordinary person in the Middle East wants security, wants to be able to live in peace and dignity, like
the average American. When law and order are collaps-
ing, he finds that difficult. Think of it: He's sitting in
his village, he has a beautiful daughter. The local land-
lord comes along and says: "Send your daughter to my
house." And he rapes her. What can that man do? He
goes to the police. The police are in the pay of the land-
lord, so they arrest the man who has complained. They
say he's stolen a cow. Now he's in jail, and his wife is
starving. What does he do? He knows, according to the

Koran, justice is the most important feature in society, and he's not getting justice.

Q: And he sees his only alternative as being Islamic fundamentalism?

A: You've got it. Along comes the religious leader who says, "Vote for me, support me, and we will have an Islamic order. And you will have justice." I'm simplifying, but at that level of society, simplistic solutions often work in the short term.

Q: So to defeat this kind of politics, America and other western countries need to strong-arm our allies of convenience so that they govern more democratically?

A: More than ever. If I told a Muslim in a bazaar that Americans are warm, open people, that this is my personal experience, he will say, "Brother, you've been brainwashed." Or "Brother, you've sold out."

Look at the range of Muslim leaders: military dictators, sons of military dictators, kings, corrupt politicians. You have a problem here. When an ordinary Muslim in the street or the bazaar looks at his leader in Cairo or Kuala Lumpur or Karachi, when he looks at his life, at the lack of electricity, at the lack of ordinary facilities to which you are used to in America, and he says, "What is going wrong in my life? Why are these corrupt rulers doing this to me? Why can't I remove them?" Many of these people are unhappy with their rulers. But who is propping them up? It is America, he believes. That is the leap in his mind. America then becomes a target of hatred.

But if he knows that America stands for freedom for everyone, for democracy for everyone as much as for Americans themselves, for good honest government for everyone, he will appreciate America. Change in American foreign policy is more urgent than ever. When demonstrations come into the streets, as is happening today, the next step is shooting and killing. The next step after that is the toppling of governments. And the next government that comes in will not be friendly at all to the United States, which means more hostages, more violence—a cycle of violence. The alternative is to send messages of dialogue and understanding to both the governments and the average Muslim. Otherwise, you're not answering Osama's questions. You're battling ideas with Tomahawk missiles.

I believe E.M. Forster's "Only Connect" lies at the heart of America's vision of the world. America can lead the world because America has the vision, the resources, and the will. If you do not lead, then you are in danger of betraying history. America can't simply say, I'm living here in Fortress America, I don't want anyone to come here. I don't want to interact. I've closed my doors. Because September 11 illustrates America is not a fortress anymore.

Sources

Part One: TRADITION AND CHANGE

1. Adapted from Yusuf Sharouni, "The Man and the Farm," in *Modern Arabic Short Stories*, selected and translated by Denys Johnson-Davis. Copyright © Oxford University Press, 1967. Reprinted by permission of publisher.

2. From Joe E. Pierce, *Life in a Turkish Village* (New York: Holt, Rinehart & Winston, 1964), pp. 22-23, 25.

3. From Hilma Granquist, *Birth and Childhood Among the Arabs* (Helsinki: Soderstrom & Company, 1950), pp. 138-39, 154–58, 165.

4. Naguib Mahfouz, *Midaq Alley* (Beirut: Khayats, 1966), pp. 4-9.

5. From Paul Bowles and Mohammed Mrabet, *The Lemon* (London and New York: Peter Owen Ltd. And McGraw-Hill, 1986). Copyright by William Morris Agency. Used with permission.

6. From Najmeh Najafi and Helen Hinckley Jones, *Persia Is My Heart*, pp. 45-51. Copyright 1953 by Najmeh Najafi and Helen Hinckley Jones. By permission of Harper & Row Publishers.

7. *Ibid.*

8. Granquist, *Birth and Childhood, op. cit.*, pp. 159-65.

9. Nuri Guntekin, *The Autobiography of a Turkish Girl* (London: George Allen & Unwin Ltd., 1949), pp. 252-54.

10. Najafe and Hinckley Jones, *Persia Is My Heart, op. cit.*, pp. 84-87.

11. *Ibid.*, pp. 87-94.

12. From Irfan Orga, *Portrait of a Turkish Family* (New York: Macmillan Publishing Company, 1950). By permission of Curtis Brown Ltd.

13. From Abdel Salam Al-Ujaili, "The Dream," in *Modern Arabic Short Stories*, selected and translated by Denys Johnson-Davis. Copyright © Oxford University Press, 1967. Reprinted by permission of publisher.

14. By Robert Pearson.

15. Mohammed Fadhel Jamali, *Letters on Islam* (London: Oxford University Press, 1965), pp. 20-21, 39-41.

16. Philip Hitti, *The Arabs* (Chicago: Gateway edition, Henry Regnery Company, 1949), pp. 47-52, 54.

17. *Malcolm X: The Autobiography of Malcolm X* (New York: Grove Press, 1964). Copyright © 1964 by Alex Haley and Malcolm X. Reprinted by permission of publisher.

18. From Adbullah Lutfiyya, *Baytin: A Jordanian Village* (Loren, Holland: Edicom, N.V., 1966). By permission of publisher.

19. Najafi and Hinckley Jones, *Persia Is My Heart, op. cit.*

20. From Daniel Lerner, *The Passing of Traditional Society* (New York: The Free Press, 1958). Copyright 1958 by The Free Press, a division of Macmillan Publishing Company. Reprinted with permission.

21. Rima Alamuddin, *Spring to Summer* (Beirut: Khayats, 1963), pp. 14-21.

22. Ayatollah Rouhollah Khomeini, "Search and Find the East," an address given on September 8, 1979, and edited here from the version which appeared in David H. Albert (ed.), *Tell the American People* (Philadelphia: Movement for a New Society, 1980), pp. 204-10. Copyright © 1980 by Movement for a New Society; reprinted by permission.

Part Two: PAST GLORIES, FUTURE HOPES

1. Robert Merle, *Ahmed Ben Bella* (New York: Walker & Company, 1967), pp. 39-46, 52-53, 68-73, 77. Copyright © 1965 by Editions Gallimard (Paris); reprinted by permission.

2. By Robert Pearson.

3. Adapted from Richard Hakluyt, *The Principal Navigations, Voyages, Discoveries of the English Nation* (London, 1589), Vols. V and VIII, as quoted in Bernard Lewis, *Istanbul and the Civilization of the Ottoman Empire* (Norman: University of Oklahoma Press, 1963), pp. 62-64. Copyright 1963 by the University of Oklahoma Press.

4. From Evliya Chelebi, *Narrative of Travels in Europe, Asia and Africa,* J. von Hammer, trans. (London: 1834), as quoted in Lewis, *op. cit.*, pp. 112-15.

5. From Ahmed Emin Yalman, *Turkey in My Time* (Norman: University of Oklahoma Press, 1956), pp. 170, 172-81. Copyright © 1956 by publisher.

6. Gamal Abdel Nasser, *Egypt's Liberation: The Philosophy of the Revolution* (Washington, D.C.: Public Affairs Press, 1955), pp. 105-14.

7. Merle, *Ahmed Ben Bella, op. cit.*, pp. 142-45, 149-58.

8. Adapted from Hakon Mielche, *Lands of Aladdin* (London: W. Hodge, 1965), pp. 90-100.

9. By Leon Clark.

10. From *In Search of Islamic Feminism* by Elizabeth Warnock Fernea, copyright © 1998 by Elizabeth Warnock Fernea, pp.80-88, 111-113. Used by permission of Doubleday, a division of Random House, Inc.

11. By Robert Pearson and Leon Clark.

12. Joseph Baratz, *A Village by the Jordan* (London: Harvill Press, 1954), pp. 1-10.

13. *Ibid.*, pp. 11-19, 26-27, 31-33, 40-45, 47-52.

14. *Ibid.*, pp.65-70, 74-75, 122-24, 126-28, 150-53, 157-59.

15. By Leon Clark.

16. Jackson Diehl, "For Israel, Wave of Soviet Immigration Brings Promise and Problems," *Washington Post*, January 21, 1990.

17. *Ibid.*

18. Dov Friedlander and Calvin Goldscheider, "Israel's Population: The Challenge of Pluralism," *Population Bulletin*, Vol. 39, No. 2 (Population Reference Bureau: Washington, D.C., 1984); and Leon Clark.

19. Adapted from Penny Rosenwasser, *Voices from a Promised Land* (Willimantic, CT: Curbstone Press, 1992), pp. 37-46, 116-28. Copyright 1992 by Penny Rosenwasser. Distributed by InBook. Reprinted with permission of Curbstone Press.

20. By Leon Clark and Robert Pearson.

21. Khalil Hindi, "Common Thread," *New Internationalist*, September 1991, pp. 8-9. Reprinted by permission.

22. John M. Goshko, "Roots of the Dispute," *Washington Post*, September 30, 1991. © 1991 *Washington Post*. Reprinted by permission.

23. By Robert Pearson.

24. Tom Segev, "A Retreat to the Familiar Ground of Zionism," *New York Times*, August 12, 2001. © *New York Times*, 2001. Reprinted by permission.

25. "Declaration of the World Islamic Front for Jihad Against the Jews and the Crusaders," Al-Quds al-Arabi, London, February 23, 1998.

26. Transcript of a videotape translated and released by al-Jazeera televison, Qatar, on October 7, 2001.

27. Transcript of a videotape released by the U.S. Department of Defense on December 13, 2001.

28. The Becket Fund for Religious Liberty, "Osama bin Laden Hijacked Four Airplanes and a Religion," *Washington Post*, October 17, 2001; The Institute of Islamic and Arabic Sciences in America, "A Statement About the Horrible Attacks that Occurred in New York and Washington, D.C. on Tuesday, September 11th, 2001," undated; American-Arab Anti-Discrimination Committee, et al., Joint Arab-American, Muslim-American Statement, September 12, 2001; The Middle East Media & Research Institute, "Special Dispatch No 281: Terror in America," October 1, 2001; M.A. Muqtedar Khan, "A Memo to American Muslims," October 1, 2001.

29. Howard Schneider, "Saudi Arabia Wrestles With 2 Views of Islam," *Washington Post*, December 15, 2001.

30. David Reich and Linda McHugh, "Root Causes of Terrorism and Anti-U.S. Sentiment in Islam," *American Magazine*, Fall 2001, pp. 31-33.

Index

In this index the use of *f* indicates a figure in the text and the use of *n* indicates a note.